Heaven's Kitchen

HEAVEN'S KITCHEN

Living Religion at God's Love We Deliver

Courtney Bender

THE UNIVERSITY OF CHICAGO PRESS
Chicago and London

COURTNEY BENDER is assistant professor
of religion and sociology at Columbia University.

The University of Chicago Press, Chicago 60637
The University of Chicago Press, Ltd., London
© 2003 by The University of Chicago
All rights reserved. Published 2003
Printed in the United States of America

12 11 10 09 08 07 06 05 04 03   1 2 3 4 5

ISBN: 0-226-04281-2 (cloth)
ISBN: 0-226-04282-0 (paper)

Library of Congress Cataloging-in-Publication Data

Bender, Courtney.
Heaven's kitchen : living religion at God's Love We Deliver / Courtney Bender.
      p.   cm.— (Morality and society)
   Includes bibliographical references and index.
   ISBN 0-226-04281-2 (alk. paper)—ISBN 0-226-04282-0 (paper : alk.
paper)
   1. God's Love We Deliver (Organization)—Case studies.   2. New York
(N.Y.)—Religious life and customs—Case studies.   3. Volunteer workers in
social service—Religious life—New York (State)—New York—Case studies.
I. Title.   II. Series.
BL2527.N7 B46   2003
306.6'09747'1—dc21   2002073563

⊗The paper used in this publication meets
the minimum requirements of the American National Standard
for Information Sciences—Permanence of Paper for Printed
Library Materials, ANSI Z39.48-1992.

CONTENTS

PREFACE

How does religion in modern American life happen, day to day? How do people who consider themselves religious talk about religion, and how do they practice it in their daily lives? *Do* they do so? We are used to hearing that religion is "personal" and "private." When we are with acquaintances, neighbors, and coworkers, there are certainly enough other things to talk about (movies, television, sports—even politics) to make religion a relatively minor subject. Given the glut of conversational topics and Americans' legendary sensitivity about broaching personal or private matters, it's not much of a stretch to imagine that we engage in little religious talk, and perhaps not much religious action, outside religious collectivities (churches, voluntary organizations) and the home. *Heaven's Kitchen* shows that this is true—but only to a point. In the nonreligious nonprofit organization where I cooked meals and talked with fellow volunteers for fifteen months, I didn't hear much religious talk. But religion was far from absent or missing from what volunteers did or what they talked about together. *Heaven's Kitchen* analyzes how, and when, religious talk happens in daily life and explains why it matters that it does. Its stories present an argument for why those concerned about the place of religion in modern America need to pay close attention to the full scope of daily action and talk—in particular to the often overlooked talk and action that occur in nonreligious settings.

I have written *Heaven's Kitchen* with three story lines in mind. First I tell the story of the kitchen volunteers at God's Love We Deliver, a nonreligious nonprofit organization in New York City that cooks and delivers meals to homebound people with AIDS. (Despite its name, GLWD is not a religious organization, an issue I address fully in chapter 2.) I was a participant observer in GLWD's kitchen from September 1994 through December 1995, and I recount the hard physical and emotional work that went into cooking meals from scratch for hundreds of New Yorkers each weekday.

Second, I use this story to investigate how religion happened in this nonreligious space. Sociologists know remarkably little about how people practice religion in their daily activities, including work, volunteering, and other interactions with acquaintances and friends. Whether this is because scholars presume there is little to study or think such talk does not matter in the larger scheme of things, we have little insight into the structures of daily religious talk and action. I thus analyze how volunteers understand religion, and how they practice it in the kitchen, by focusing on the way daily talk and actions shape their lived experience of the sacred. The kitchen volunteers at GLWD did not share the same religious background or worldview, nor did most assume they did. Volunteers went to the kitchen to make meals, not to build a shared religious culture. But some of them nevertheless practiced religion there, and they sometimes talked about it with each other. Their talk was often indirect, drawing on and creatively molding topics of everyday conversations to develop arguments about things that mattered to them. Likewise, the actions that volunteers called, or understood to be, religious worked out in mundane tasks that were consciously invested with meaning and symbolic force. These daily conversations and practices demonstrate, on a very basic level, how individuals navigate religious identities in worlds that are religiously plural, perhaps antagonistic toward such identities, and by no means "naturally" enlivened by the sacred.

The third story is embedded in a dialogue between the endnotes and the main text. I urge sociologists of culture and religion to embrace the consequences of the maxim that sociological writing often overemphasizes (and often "writes in") shared cultures. In general, we are much more aware of the limits of shared culture in our daily lives than when we conduct sociological studies and write about our findings. We tend to make sense of others' worlds (and our own) by positing cultures shared and by focusing on shared symbols and actions. Even recent studies that are more attuned to conflicts in social settings begin by assuming that the power or force of certain symbols is not contested (even if their meaning is). This sociological work of describing (and in describing, also constructing) shared cultures is an explanatory project that can tell us much—yet it also leaves much unexplained. I have taken seriously the fact that symbols and actions are multivalent. Symbols and actions "mean" many things, often simultaneously. What is shared is produced in particular social interactions, and as such it is always being put to new uses and always being revised. In studying a tertiary cultural issue (religion) in an organization devoted primarily to other things (cooking, caring for people with AIDS), I have been made conscious, in ways that ethnographers studying a group's "primary" themes are not, of the very limited degree to which culture is shared. I found that volunteers shared little not only when it came to religion, but when it came to cooking. Despite this lack of shared culture (in fact, I argue, because of it), volunteers worked to communicate with each other across perceived differences. As such, this book suggests, at least provisionally, a number of practices and strategies for communication that lie between "shared meaning" and mutual incomprehension. At the very least, I hope this story line will serve as a renewed invitation to the painstaking and rewarding study of how the social world is created out of the muddle and mayhem of daily life.

Since much of the theoretical discussion appears in the book's endnotes, a few further words about my perspective on religion are in order here. I view religion as practice (a view I discuss in detail in the first chapter). I have studiously avoided asking the commonly posed question of *how religious* the volunteers were. This question, which has often been asked of me, suggests that "religion" or "religiousness" is a stable quality or characteristic that individuals carry and translate in the same way into various social settings. It implies that religion is a set of values, presumably learned in a religious community or through self-guided seeking and then carried by individual egos into their daily surroundings. This view presents analytical difficulties once we begin to analyze religion "outside" religious institutions. How, for instance, does one apply this measure of "religiousness" if an individual is very expressive religiously in one setting but not in another? What can we say about the religiousness of people who cannot clearly articulate what "religion" means from setting to setting? As we know, it is almost impossible to learn what is in people's heads, to gauge how thought translates into action, or to establish the stability of worldviews over time. Using such a measure of individual religiousness begs the questions we need to answer, including where and how religion is learned, expressed, and recognized as such throughout social life. In short, it closes off the path to understanding how people interpret, understand, and enact religion in social settings.

Most sociologists recognize the limitations of such questions about "religiousness," at least in theory. *Heaven's Kitchen* demonstrates what we can gain if we set them aside in practice. Once we replace them with a more culturally specific, discursive, practical, or institutionally mediated understanding of religion we can, for instance, begin to ask how ordinary events influence religious practices and how religious practices influence nonreligious actions and spaces. We can, in short, think more clearly about how the very categories of the religious are defined and made understandable over a range of social and cultural institutions. Shifting toward a view of religion as practice thus allows us to branch out from the two dominant models maintained by sociologists of religion: the story of religious groups (where we study how religion is generated and shared and sometimes contested within the community itself) and the story of religion's forays into nonreligious public spaces (where it is more or less successfully defended from encroachers). Once set loose from the concepts and boundaries that support these stories, we can engage in the creative study of religious action as it is lived by modern Americans.

Having set aside the question of how religious individual volunteers are, I asked *how religion is practiced* by various volunteers in the kitchen at God's Love We Deliver. I have sought to understand how volunteers in daily encounters with others mold religious ideas, practice, and identity and how people discern who is and who is not religious. I have described how nonreligious practices (in this case cooking, daily small talk, and doing something for people with AIDS) contribute in specific ways to volunteers' understanding of their own religious and spiritual lives.

At the outset, this study required a field site that was not religious and where people talked and interacted informally but regularly. Investigating these issues in a single case study has provided the time and focus necessary to attend to the subtle and easily overlooked actions that make up daily life. Without question, the story I tell here is unique: the combination of time, setting, and participants developed in a singular matrix of practices and social realities. I would not have encountered the same array in a bingo hall in Lancaster, Pennsylvania, or a community center in Cambridge, Massachusetts. Indeed, I doubt I would encounter an equivalent complex if I returned to GLWD now and conducted my research again. In any of these settings, particular individuals, time-bound concerns, and available social practices would influence how religious practice would sound and look and be made possible.

God's Love We Deliver and its volunteers are thus in no way incidental to the story I tell here. I hope that whatever else the book is, it will remain a document of the ways some people made sense of suffering as they experienced it in the mid-1990s. The questions engaged, however— how religion is practiced, and how it is practiced in nonreligious settings— can and should be extended to other situations. Consciously engaging in evaluations of how we make ourselves known to each other, how we make moral arguments, and how we enliven the routine with ritual when we consciously do not share "meaning" or language with those around us will ultimately broaden our collective evaluation of religion's changing meaning and location in American culture.

———

This book would not be possible without the support of volunteers and staff at God's Love We Deliver, most of whom I cannot thank by name. These wonderful people cheerfully accepted my presence, taught me how to use a knife properly, and constantly asked what I was finding. Now, with several years between the fieldwork and the book, I continue to be inspired by their dedication to laughter and to "getting the meals out" no matter what, and by their fearlessness in the face of gallon cans of tuna fish. I hope some will come upon this book and recognize themselves in its pages. Of those I can thank by name, Monica Kaiser and Bernhard Blythe in particular made the way easier while I was at GLWD. Many, many thanks also go to Diane Groman for her generous gifts of shelter, friendship, and wit.

Heaven's Kitchen was first inspired by independent conversations with Robert Wuthnow and Paul DiMaggio in reading courses on American religion, cultural analysis, and the sociology of culture. Both challenged me to search out interesting ways to turn my theoretical concerns into empirical research; I could not have learned from more able masters of the craft. Bob Wuthnow deserves many thanks for having faith that my initial ideas would flower into a substantial contribution to the field and for providing the rich intellectual environment in which that could happen. His deep and broad knowledge continues to inspire and challenge me. His ability to distill the main points of my argument (sometimes before I could articulate them myself) never let me doubt that I was working on interesting stuff. His support in the later stages of dissertation writing, in the form of funds from a grant from the Lilly Endowment for research on devotional practices, allowed its speedy completion. One could not hope for a better mentor.

Paul DiMaggio demonstrated his near legendary talents as a critical commentator in his ongoing questions and challenging marginalia in the many chapter drafts I presented to him. Paul's engagement, despite his disclaimer that he knew very little about religion, encouraged me to develop arguments I would not otherwise have had the temerity to pursue. He saw what the book could offer to a broader range of readers and encouraged me to expand my arguments' reach throughout. Lynn Davidman's support at the dissertation stage was essential. Lynn's skill and experience in conducting and teaching qualitative methods and, more particularly, in the qualitative study of American religion are nearly unparalleled. I learned much from her. Many thanks to the brilliant Caryl Emerson, who consented to guide several eager graduate students in the social sciences through Bakhtin's translated works in spring 1993.

Bethany Bryson, Tim Dowd, John Evans, Jeff Hass, Kieran Healy, Jason Kaufman, Erin Kelly, Matthew Lawson, Michael Moody, John Schmalzbauer, and Hiromi Taniguchi each contributed feedback, criticism, and questions on various chapters of my dissertation and in general made graduate school a stimulating intellectual enterprise. The outstanding community of scholars at Princeton's Center for the Study of American Religion between 1991 and 1997 grounded my investigation and expanded my scholarly horizons. Diane Winston, R. Marie Griffith, John Giggie, Ann Braude, Brad Verter, Cynthia Eller, Leigh Schmidt, and Nancy Ammerman asked hard questions and provided great suggestions. Michael McNally and Rebecca Kneale Gould, compatriots in the study of lived religions, read and commented on various chapters, as did Priscilla Ferguson, Susan Chambré, Herb Gans, Jeff Olick, and Nina Eliasoph. Fred Kniss, David Hall, Joy Charlton, Craig Dykstra, and Randy Balmer invited me to speak about this project in various seminars and lectures.

I received a generous dissertation fellowship from the Louisville Institute for Protestantism in American Life, directed by James Lewis and overseen by a dynamic board, and I benefited greatly from several lively discussions that took place on the Institute's beautiful grounds. The Program on Non-Profit Organizations at Yale University, directed first by Peter Dobkin Hall and then by Lisa Berlinger, likewise supported this research, both financially (with a John D. Rockefeller III Summer Research Grant and a grant from the Kellogg Foundation) and intellectually. The Center for the Study of American Religion at Princeton, directed by John Wilson and Robert Wuthnow and expertly administered by Anita Kline, provided additional research support through my years at Princeton.

As this project moved from dissertation to book, Kieran Healy, Pamela Klassen, and Jody Shapiro took on the task or reading the manuscript once more, commenting on the arc of my logic and ferreting out grammatical errors. I am delighted beyond measure that Alan Wolfe (as series editor), Douglas Mitchell, and Robert Devens at the University of Chicago Press picked up this book—and with such enthusiasm and goodwill. Thanks also to Alice Bennett for her attention to detail and commitment to clarity.

This book is much stronger for the advice and criticism that all these people have generously offered. It has undoubtedly suffered where I have failed to thoroughly address their comments: no one is responsible for this but me.

My parents Jon Scott and Nancy Bender, my sisters Madeline Bender and Sena Bender, and my in-laws Barry and Susan Dworkin proved ceaseless supporters and superior conversational partners about the issues in this book. Solomon Ezra Dworkin has been the best one-, two-, and three-year-old any mother could hope for and has lightened every step of the revisions with laughter and good-humored acceptance of his parents' crazy lives.

My husband Jonathan Dworkin has lived this book with me. He has thought all these thoughts and in ways both small and large has made time and space for this book to happen. He has done all this while pursuing his own research and teaching me some general points of chromosome positioning effects in *Bacillus subtilis*. Most important, he has presented a constant example of how to integrate our commitments to the life of the mind with the mysteries and pleasures of daily life. Jonathan, this book is for you.

CHAPTER ONE

Decorating Holiday Bags at the Friends Seminary, Making Dinner in the Kitchen

In the week before Christmas 1994, I rode downtown with Jackie and Hannah,[1] the development and volunteer directors at God's Love We Deliver (GLWD). We were on our way to a private school, the Friends Seminary, where students (and their parents and nannies) were decorating large white grocery bags for the agency's "Holiday Feast." Later that week volunteers back at GLWD's main offices would pack half of the decorated bags with warm socks, body lotion, CDs, novels, candy, and other gifts. On Christmas morning other volunteers would fill the rest of the bags with containers of piping hot prime rib and Yorkshire pudding, fresh green peas with pearl onions, winter squash soup, cranberry and Waldorf salads, two kinds of pie, and fruitcake. More volunteers would deliver the meals and the gifts to eight hundred of New York City's homebound people with AIDS.

Going to the Friends Seminary was an unusual field trip for me. I was in the middle of fieldwork in God's Love We Deliver's kitchen, where volunteers and a few trained chefs prepared the Yorkshire pudding and roast beef for Christmas and the more quotidian meals delivered throughout the year. As I helped to cook meals in the basement kitchen, I was also studying how volunteers practiced religion in the course of their everyday lives, researching how and when religious topics came up in conversation and how volunteers gave meaning to their work, individually and collectively. I accepted Hannah's invitation to go to the Friends Seminary with some reluctance, since it meant I would miss an afternoon in the kitchen. But I had heard so much from her about this event that I agreed to go.

In retrospect, my two visits to the school allowed me to think clearly about several juxtapositions between GLWD's daily kitchen ritual and the ceremonies at the Friends Seminary, and between my ongoing research in the kitchen and much other recent work on how religious life happens in American culture. Entering the school after three months of steady concentration on the kitchen's daily conversation and events, I found the students' actions saturated with symbolic meaning, much of it intended, planned, and plotted. Kitchen volunteers, by contrast, focused on vegetables and tin containers, and on getting the meals out. The kitchen's tiny, crowded spaces provided little time or room to step back and reflect on the work we did. It sometimes seemed to me that the volunteers were working as hard to deflect any attempt to interpret their work symbolically as the kids at the school were working to invest theirs with meaning.

That said, the sorts of "daily" activities of acquaintances and friends that I took part in at the GLWD kitchen were precisely what I wanted to study, to gain a better idea of how religion happens in our contemporary society. Religious life is lived in great festivals, yearly holidays, public commemorations, and public speeches. It is also lived (at least if we believe those who tell us about their religious worlds) in daily rituals and fleeting interactions. We know much more about the former than the latter, and we have even less understanding of daily experience of religion outside religious institutions and the home. I wanted to study how, and when, the prosaic and sacred combined in the warp and woof of ordinary people's daily public lives. As my two trips to the Friends Seminary reminded me, my decision to study religion in a nonreligious space had the immediate consequence of making my subject of inquiry very elusive—more than in most studies. That elusiveness is part of the texture of this book. *Heaven's Kitchen,* however, is a chronicle of my examination of the ways people make religion within their daily routine. As such, it is a first attempt at theorizing the processes by which religion happens within the myriad contexts we call everyday life.[2]

———

My impulse to study religion in daily life began with a dissatisfaction with recent debates about the character of religious life in modern America. Now that age-old expectations of increasing "secularization" have fallen into disfavor, the discussion turns to the various locations of religion: Is it more or less private? More or less institutionally bounded? Are its language and symbols becoming more restricted (and limited) or more broad (and meaningless)? The answers to all these questions, of course, depend on exactly what we mean when we say "religion" and where we decide to look for data. In recent years both sides of the debates on the qualitative decline (or rise) of religious discourse in the United States have backed up their claims with surveys and interviews that focus on individuals' reports about how they talk about religion and when. While the value of these surveys and interview studies is not to be discounted, they do not provide much firsthand knowledge of how people talk about and practice religion in daily settings. [3]

In venturing to GLWD, then, I wanted to observe how people in our time practice and talk about religion. This journey was not intended to definitively ascertain whether religion is declining or reviving. Given the limited existing data on religious practice and the intrinsic boundaries of any particular study, such questions will remain open for debate and refinement. My aim was to use my observations to generate some reflections on the ways religion and spiritual things are made manifest daily in public statements and action. Given that we know very little about this aspect of Americans' engagement with religion, I believed that illuminating these practices and activities in situ would bring new insight into the debates about how Americans are religious.

God's Love We Deliver is not a "typical" setting—I do not know what such a setting would be. Yet several of its peculiarities bear mentioning at the outset. Some friends and colleagues questioned whether anything religious would happen in a nonreligious AIDS organization on the liberal Upper West Side of Manhattan. [4] Some of their concerns stemmed from conceptions about the shrinking place of religion in American urban life. Cities, and New York in particular, are often thought of as singularly lacking in religious fervor. In addition, the Upper West Side's notoriety as a liberal outpost and GLWD's focus on AIDS suggested that its volunteers would be even more reluctant to bring religion into their work (or might actively oppose it). [5] Others suggested that the sheer fact of diversity in New York would prove a stumbling block for those who wished to draw on particularistic languages in talking with one another. The former concerns were easier to address. New Yorkers on the whole are no less religious than their suburban or rural counterparts. [6] The volunteers, who were gay and straight, male and female, liberal, moderate, and politically uninvolved, did not fit neatly into secularized pigeonholes.

The concern posed about the changing quality of religious talk was less easy to tackle, since it is embedded in several ongoing theoretical discussions about the quality of religion in American life. Few sociologists now argue that religious language and practice have evaporated from public life, [7] yet many suggest that what we see and hear has been significantly altered (for the worse) over the past forty years. In particular, scholars have argued that religious diversity—or rather the recognition of religious diversity and pluralism—limits the salience of particularistic religious language. (Hence a bland civil religion of the "Abrahamic faiths" surpasses appeals to any one religious tradition.) Particularistic religious language may persist in private conversations and community gatherings, but it is not often heard in casual conversations among passing acquaintances and coworkers or from the presidential podium. A shift to a "general" spiritual language is bolstered, sociologists argue, by the late twentieth-century growth of religious seeking and the extensive free market in religious and spiritual options.[8] Pluralism and the "spiritual marketplace" combine to foster a public feel-good "spirituality" with little particularity or moral force, where all religions are equally good and all true religions produce good neighbors and citizens.[9] Given the limited opportunities to make strong moral arguments using religious language and the bland and unspecific characteristics of the "spiritual" in public discourse, sociologists predict that people will forget that such moral discourse is even possible within regular conversation.

The argument about fuzzy spiritual talk displacing specific religious talk makes an interesting complement to recent studies of the changing role of religious institutions in fostering public religious discourse. The past half century has witnessed the exponential growth of religious special interest groups and social movements committed to public debates about specific social and moral issues.[10] Yet recent entries into the field tend not to depend on broad and active membership bases, and they cultivate few individuals in the rank and file who actively learn or use the organization's rhetoric or language. This work is left to professionals (often lawyers and lobbyists) who speak for such institutions—but not always to the benefit of religiously motivated actors.[11] Religious language remains an important element of national public discourse but, such scholars suggest, is also shifting its location. We are witnessing a change from the previous century, where local, regional, and national political and civic forums gave individuals a range of opportunities to speak publicly using a variety of specific languages learned in local communities.[12]

Such negative descriptions of religion's place and quality in modern America, focusing on individual "shoppers," the rise of professional religious speakers, or the decline of civic religious organizations, nevertheless strike many people as off the mark. Not everyone finds it difficult to talk about religion in every public setting, not everyone shops around or abandons firm religious ideas for "empty" spirituality. How then should we address the concerns that changes in institutional structures and growing religious pluralism lead to Americans' taking (or having) fewer opportunities to talk about religion? We need to begin, I believe, with a closer look at daily interactions where religion becomes a possible, or impossible, topic of conversation. We need to extend our view to the ways individuals in public settings analyze and interpret *how* they speak about religion and at what such talk and practice sound and look like. We need to pay particular attention, at this point, to those settings that are "outside" the obviously religious ones and those to which such great attention has been paid. While I do not dispute the necessity of continuing to study religion in religious communities, we also, as Nina Eliasoph argues in her book on political participation, need a "way of listening that makes us notice how people create contexts for . . . conversation."[13] I analyze how people make contexts for talk about religion and how, in the process, they create shared expectations for what the religious is and what its public manifestations should be. A few words thus are in order on sociological understandings of shared meaning in social spaces and of cultural and social practices.

First, given that volunteers did not share religious ideas, backgrounds, or principles, it became necessary to think about ways to analyze how people talk about things that they consciously do *not* share with others. Typically, ethnographers study the main components of a group and what they share and adhere to—in other words, those things that make them a group or a "culture." Assemblies of people who meet over time develop their own languages and ways of going about their daily business. Their "rules of the game" and the consequences of not playing correctly are fairly apparent in daily interactions. Thus we say that organizations have core values or "cultures" of particular kinds and that people in communities or groups share meaning and language, or at the very least an assumption that they share language, symbols, or "culture." Sociologists spend a good deal of time talking or thinking about social life as space where shared meaning, language, and artifacts make communication possible. Without these shared things, we posit, it would be impossible to talk with each other.[14] Some social theorists have extended this assumption, arguing that heterogeneous (or "multicultural") societies like our own find it harder and harder to talk about the common good because we do not share a language or other ways of communicating.[15]

These interpretations nevertheless fail to acknowledge how far individuals are aware of the "limits" of shared culture and meaning within everyday interactions.[16] We are much more conscious of the limits of shared meaning in our everyday lives than we are when we write sociology.[17] Although living and writing are different tasks, our writing often fails to reflect the work we do in settings where we clearly and consciously do not share meaning with others. Learning how people deal with difference is

increasingly necessary for our society's common life; understanding the
variety of ways we engage difference in daily encounters is even more so.[18]
Studying religious talk and practice at God's Love We Deliver brought the
limits of the shared cultures perspective into relief. Volunteers did not
share religious identities, sentiments, or traditions, nor did they create a
new religious culture of their own. This did not keep them from talking
about religion, however, nor did it appear to keep them from practicing it.
In contrast, those things that volunteers assumed they shared, including
commitment to particular methods of cooking and to caring for people
with AIDS, became sites of struggle and danger. Beginning the study by
looking at what was not shared led in the end to a broader reflection on
the tenuous nature of those things that we say hold social groups together
and on how frequently those very things fail to do so.

Since I did not study religion in a religious organization, I could not
count on the usual research procedures. I could not assume that the volunteers had a corporate religious culture or gesture toward shared religious symbols or rituals. Religion was brought to the kitchen, and made
real there, by individual volunteers who had differing religious backgrounds and understandings of how (and whether) they could practice
religion there. These religious acts, talk, and associations, I assumed, were
at least in part built through engagement with a variety of religious institutions—including childhood and adult experiences with religious groups,
literature, and rituals. To make sense of the ways volunteers carried out religion, I drew on the language, theory, and metaphor of "practice." Practice has as many definitions as it has interpreters, and as a "key symbol" in
the social sciences it arguably carries more symbolic resonance than actual
analytic punch. It is useful for my study, however, given that "practice"
points to the ways structures are reproduced by living, breathing people
who have some kind of agency to create their worlds and who embody
various actions and use them in different ways to communicate and get
things done.

Practices, we know, do not merely reproduce social structures. Since
they are embodied in actors who live in particular social settings and who
use those practices to build unique perspectives on the world, they are
always subject to creative change and reinterpretation. Individuals both
reproduce structures and change them.[19]

Religious practices have received great attention in recent years under
the rubric "lived religion." This idiom marks a shift in attention from
the binary distinctions between popular and official, public and private,
institutional and individual religion to closer analysis of the interactions
between them.[20] Historians and sociologists have emphasized how indi-

viduals craft daily religious practices within given religious structures and how, in doing so, they reframe "official" symbols and structures to make something new (here, social change happens daily). Such lived practices challenge (and sometimes subvert) the conventional interpretations of established routines and rituals by creatively reordering their content and meaning. [21] These insights are substantial: scholars now focus on the negotiations of actually creating and enacting religion in daily life and are less likely to promote artificial (and often inadequate) oppositions between popular and official pieties. In other words, looking at religious practice as lived religion pays attention both to the meanings that individuals and groups make, and invest, in particular settings and to the "structures" of history and institution that shape those lives and meanings.

The way individuals' practices reproduce institutions and structures becomes of great importance when we analyze religious practices as they occur outside religious institutions. At God's Love We Deliver, volunteers brought practices to the kitchen individually, enacting them either consciously or habitually. In doing so, they drew structures and expectations of social relations from other settings into the kitchen. These practices enlivened volunteers' work and helped make it important and real. They also had the potential to disrupt the ongoing work by calling into question the unarticulated (yet established) cluster of practices that "everyone" knew. This centrifugal tug of religious and other meanings, interpretations, and evaluations embedded in these very practices forced volunteers to confront just how much less there was uniting them than they sometimes imagined.

Employing "practice," furthermore, provides a way to speak of the overlap and occasional provisionality of the adjectives we use to describe social actions. Sociologists write, for instance, about *urban* practices, *social* practices, *civic* practices, *political* practice, *gendered* practices as those activities that correspond loosely or directly to institutions of urbanity, civic life, or gender. [22] In this regard we might think of religious practices as including acts such as praying, singing religious songs, and reading Scripture, as well as others that are easily understood "as such" by any reasonable person. At the same time, such taxonomies are never complete or clearly bounded, and they always include actions and practices that belong to other institutions as well. Some acts reproduce several structures simultaneously (for example, the rite of marriage, a religious "practice," also reproduces family, economic, and political structures). [23] And we also complicate the simplicity of practices by assigning our actions new, complex, and alternative meanings. When volunteers told me they thought peeling carrots was "meditative," or that delivering a meal to a sick person was a political act, they extended the boundaries of both institutions, at least for a time. Such acts were (and are) everywhere, as practices, transposed to new settings, and took on new provisional meanings that, once having taken hold, further complicated the task of assigning meaning to an act.

Thinking like this about religion draws us well away from the notion that the world is divided into sacred and mundane spheres. Such a view, rooted in classical social theory, has often led sociologists studying "modern" society to operate on the assumption that religion happens in church, business happens at work, "family life" happens at home, and so on.[24] The compartmentalizing of institutions is sometimes extended to include mental orientations.[25] People thus understand and use many cultures but jump from one to another: these many languages do not speak to each other in any meaningful way. Such a view is questionable: to begin with, it leaves those of us who are interested in religious action in daily life without much room to move. If institutions and cognitive states are so distinct, or if a setting becomes religious merely by an actor's evoking the religious within it, then there is little point or logic to studying religion in everyday life. As recent work in cognitive and cultural sociology demonstrates, however, viewing space and mental sites as compartmentalized obscures as much as it illuminates.[26] Once we move, mercifully, away from the notion that "switching" between nonreligious and religious practices is always complete (logically whole), predictable (corresponding to particular institutional contexts), or distinct (nonoverlapping), we can learn more about their "unfinished" and overlapping qualities and their internal variegations.[27] Focusing on practice allows us to see how habitual, personal, or lexical meanings of religious practice or language are always acted out in relation to other meanings, languages, and practices within specific contexts. Religious practice is not bracketed or given special status but rather is part of a dialogue among other practices in particular situations. We are thus poised to learn more about the creative, subtle, and wholly social ways that people talk about religion and practice it through daily experience and the ways they assess what it is possible to say and do.

I stepped out of Jackie's car at the Friends Seminary and followed Hannah past the school band practice and a bake sale. We descended into the cacophonous basement cafeteria, which had been temporarily converted from a place to cook and eat to a place to paint, cut, glue, and paste. Several hundred people were bent over their work of decorating large white paper bags as toddlers ran around the tables. Yards of yarn and ribbon, pipe cleaners, and Mylar scraps (all donations from a neighborhood notions shop) were piled up at one end of the room, where John held forth above the fray. We pushed forward, watching as kids fluttered around him. Many weeks before, Hannah had told me how they devised the bag decorating project one afternoon four years ago over tea at the Stanhope Hotel. John, now retired from teaching art at the Friends Seminary, had also been a delivery volunteer at God's Love We Deliver and wanted to involve his students in AIDS education in some way. The bag decorating party had become a big event, and it became even bigger after John told the school community he was HIV positive. This was the first decorating party since John's health-imposed retirement.

Jackie set to work with her camera, and John greeted Hannah and me in a marked Australian accent. "Make yourself at home! Do you want to make one too?"[28] A ten-year-old tugging at his hand distracted John from my murmured decline; he turned to admire Charlie's bag. "This is beautiful, isn't it, Hannah?" John pronounced, holding up a bag that said "No Fear, No Hate, Just Love." "Charlie's uncle died last year," John told us, squeezing Charlie's shoulder before pinning the bag up on the wall to dry. I had started to meander off toward the tables in the adjacent room when John thrust a stack of papers at me, "When you walk around, make sure that everyone's read this, will you?" I nodded.

I looked over the photocopied guidelines in my hand. They included instructions on how to attach pipe cleaners and thick cloth ribbing so they wouldn't fall off the bags. There was a reminder not to use glitter, even though there was none to be found on John's table of supplies. (Later Christopher, the volunteer outreach coordinator at GLWD, told me that glitter rubs off bags and cards and sometimes gets in the food.) Another line detailed appropriate and inappropriate themes: there should be no references to illness, or sickness, or getting well soon. As Christopher explained later, "Children learn about people with AIDS and then they make these cards, and they say things like 'I'm So Sorry' or 'Get Well Soon.' [But the recipients are] not going to get well, and they know that—it can be kind of cruel to see 'Get Well Soon,' even if it's meant from the heart. We like happy themes."

Following this, the sheet noted that not all of GLWD's recipients celebrated Christmas and that sectarian themes might not be appropriate. Unlike the command to avoid "get well soon," however, this appeared to be only a suggestion. This was one of the many peculiar features of the agency I was studying, which began with its name and went on to touch much of its daily work. God's Love We Deliver made a special point of celebrating any

day possible, including clients' birthdays (delivering personalized decorated cakes) and holidays both religious and secular. In some respects,
and like many other nonprofits, GLWD drew on the language of giving
at Christmastime to bolster its volunteer numbers and year-end donations.[29] Yet GLWD's staff also tried to mitigate the sectarian themes of
Christmas by calling the Christmas delivery a "Holiday Feast."

As I walked around the room I noted that many of the parents were
decorating bags with Santa Claus, Christmas trees, wreaths, wrapped pack-
ages, and stars. The children, in contrast, concentrated on snow scenes
and abstract designs (a few young boys drew Power Rangers). I also noticed
several clusters of junior high girls who were intently pasting red ribbons
and other AIDS symbols to their bags.

The instructions in my hand had an emphatic command in bold capital
letters: "NO BAG SHOULD INCLUDE ANYTHING THAT WOULD IDENTIFY THE
RECIPIENT AS A PERSON WITH AIDS." As I knew from experience, GLWD's
delivery volunteers could not wear GLWD baseball hats, AIDS ribbons,
or AIDS Walk T-shirts when they took hot meals to recipients' homes. We
could do nothing that might give away our clients' health status; we had
to avoid bringing on any stigma or harassment from neighbors or land-
lords. On nonholidays, volunteers delivered meals in nondescript brown
paper bags and gained entry to buildings by announcing "meal delivery"
into intercoms or to doormen. Likewise, GLWD delivery vans displayed
no outward identification.

The confidentiality and accompanying air of secrecy that God's Love We
Deliver ensured for its recipients and that John asked the bag decorators to
respect stood in contrast to the work the students and parents were doing
as they glued AIDS ribbons to their bags. The junior high kids were not
decorating these bags for clients receiving the meals in the South Bronx
or Kips Bay, where disclosing one's illness could lead to discrimination or
worse. They were decorating them for John, just as Charlie had decorated
a bag that said "No Fear, No Hate, Just Love" for his uncle. And John,
I saw, accepted their gifts with love and thanks, without comment about
the rules. Later, when the bags were in GLWD's hands, two members of
the volunteer office took out those with AIDS symbols. They did not go to
waste: Christopher pinned the best ones to the walls of the volunteer and
development offices.

Dodging a father staring bleakly at the tempera spilled down the front
of his blue oxford shirt, I walked back through the crowd toward John.
A shortcut led to the relative quiet of the cafeteria food line, where some
of the finished bags lay drying. I stopped to look and soon found myself
trying to make room for a deluge of incoming children: John had run
out of space in the main room and was directing the children to lay their

finished bags out to dry on the counter. A preschooler gave me a heavy bag, plastered with as much Elmer's glue as thick chartreuse satin ribbon. "This will never dry," I thought to myself, as he ran to find his mother. He pulled her over, pointing and declaring, "I want to take it with me!"

"You can't, sweetheart," she replied, "all these bags are going to people for their Christmas, people who are not going to have any other presents."

"I want to take it to Grandma!" he insisted. "I'll tell you what," she said, hefting him onto her hip, "I'll call Grandma, and we'll tell her all about it."

I was a bit put off by this mother's suggestion that the gifts and food were going to people who would not receive any other presents. Some of GLWD's clients were wealthy and lived in well-appointed apartments, surrounded by nurses and caring family members. I thought of telling her about the shady streets of Brooklyn Heights where I delivered meals one day, and about the judge who was going blind in his spacious, art-filled brownstone. The agency provided hot meals to homebound people with AIDS regardless of their ability to pay, with the idea that sick people need love and care and delicious food. GLWD's food was not charity, I wanted to say.

This was not the first time I heard someone equate the problems faced by people with AIDS with those of the poor, nor had the brute facts escaped my attention. I also regularly delivered meals to clients who lived in the roach-infested single room occupancy hotels on upper Broadway. More and more of GLWD's clients depended on the agency for all their sustenance, and the agency struggled to shift its five-day delivery program to include weekend meals. I watched helplessly as Barb, the client services director, sobbed at her desk after calling to tell a desperately poor immigrant grandmother (who spoke no English and had no job) that her grandchildren would no longer receive GLWD meals now that their mother had died. The grandmother had wailed into the phone, "What am I going to do, what am I going to do?" Barb had no answer. My negative reaction to the young mother's explanation stemmed from my ongoing work in the kitchen, where discussions of these realities were few and far between. Right or wrong, kitchen volunteers thought of the clients as similar to the people they knew who had died of AIDS. We worked with the notion that our clients were "like us," with excellent palates and exacting standards. We thus cooked to our tastes as much as theirs.

In this respect kitchen volunteers often acted like the junior high students who ignored John's instructions and rational reasoning to pursue their own agendas. Volunteers cooked for the people they loved and demonstrated that love in the smell and taste of things they cooked. The tensions between desire (to do something for someone) and necessity (to cook for many others) rarely were openly articulated, but volunteers' practices constantly drew such potential conflicts close to the surface of our work. These comparisons, important to the ways I would eventually come to understand volunteers' cooking practices, were nevertheless far from my thoughts as I rode home from the Friends Seminary, weighing John's invitation to return to the bag dedication ceremony later that week.

———

A few days after my first trip to the Friends school, I found myself in the chilly antechamber of the historic Friends Meetinghouse, which doubled as the school auditorium, watching John direct several high school students who were stretching a clothesline hung with decorated bags across the hall's circular balcony. As if watching John interact with students in the cafeteria hadn't been enough, Hannah warned me that it was a profoundly moving experience to stand under a canopy of decorated bags and sing carols. Kathy Spahn, GLWD's executive director, arrived and echoed Hannah's sentiment: "Breathtaking," she sighed.

John beckoned to us, and we stepped into the meeting room. He pointed out his favorite bag, showing two boys hugging, with AIDS ribbons on their shirts. I looked for the bag with chartreuse ribbon and smiled to myself when I found it. "How many?" Kathy asked. "One thousand sixty-eight, at least two hundred more than last year," John reported with pride. Added to the decorated bags made by students at another private school, there were close to seventeen hundred ready to go.

As children began to spill into the hall, Kathy, John, and I settled on the front row of benches and watched as they pointed to the bags hanging above them. When they all had made their way in, the room became still. We waited for a few minutes in Quakerly silence. Then the headmaster picked up his guitar. Someone had placed Christmas carol books on the benches, and we found the appropriate pages to sing along with the headmaster and a small group of teachers. We sang "Silent Night" and "Jolly Old Saint Nicholas," "We Three Kings of Orient Are," "The First Noel," and the "Dreidl Song." The music teacher sang a solo, "O Holy Night," and the junior class came to the front to sing a parody of "The Twelve Days of Christmas" directed at the senior class.

As Hannah predicted, I found it hard not to be moved by our singing. I spent a moment trying to anticipate the clients' reactions to receiving these bags, and I imagined how touched I might be to receive such a gift. As I looked around the room, I realized I had expected my feelings to be mine alone, but now I was not so sure. As we sang the line "they looked up and saw a star," I heard a faint rustle and watched others turn their heads to look up at the bags. The signs of Christmas were all around us—in our hands, in our mouths, hanging above us. This was indeed a religious service.

Nevertheless, the Christian story of "God's gift" shared unequal space with Hanukkah songs, secular Christmas songs, and the children's excitement about the four weeks of winter recess that lay just minutes ahead. I wondered what, if anything, John and Kathy would say about this mixture of religious and secular symbols and activities when they rose to speak.

John was nervous. As the kids were filing in he had leaned over and whispered that he'd lost his notes on the way from chemotherapy earlier that morning and didn't know if he could remember what he'd planned to say. I was sobered by this large, charismatic man's flustered worry that his mind would fail him, and by the importance he gave to his short speech. As he stood up to talk, however, and the kids started to applaud, his nervousness seemed to disappear. Opening his arms as if to embrace the bags and the children all at once, he said in a booming voice, "Thank you for this gift." The children screamed and yelled as he began to speak in earnest.

"What you have done here, this is not the end, this is just the beginning. What you have accomplished here is not going to stop here—*unless you let it.* I want to give you an assignment to do over your holiday break," he continued with missionary zeal. "If you tell one person, *if you tell just one person* what you have done here, then we will keep hope alive. Remember, remember to keep hope alive!" The cheers and clapping masked his breaking voice. He regained his composure and, banishing all sentimentality, introduced Kathy as the "fine woman in charge of the organization that makes all this possible."

Kathy stood next. She thanked the school on behalf of the agency and, like John, motioned toward the bags overhead. Then she began to tell the students about the people who would receive the bags on Christmas morning. She told them what kind of toys and socks and sweaters GLWD volunteers would deliver, mentioning several times that many of the recipients would be "children just like you." As she spoke, an unsettled hush fell over the audience. Kathy's statistics continued to tumble into the room: she noted the number of children on the GLWD recipient roster, those who were HIV positive and those whose parents had AIDS. Kathy then thanked the children again and told them, "You can be very proud of what you have accomplished here." As she sat down the headmaster picked up his guitar, and we sang two verses of "Hark the Herald Angels Sing." With that the program ended and the students' winter break began.

Our last carol restored the earlier mirth, but I was left uneasy by the counterpoint that Kathy's statistics gave to John's missionary call. Kathy was a master of the crisis's many forms. She knew how to shape her comments to her audience, but in this case her attempt to explain, or frame, the students' efforts seemed misplaced. Their visceral reaction to her remarks brought home how resistant they were to locating AIDS in relation to their own experience. They associated AIDS with John, political slogans, and red ribbons, not with their own presents under the family Christmas tree. Each time Kathy invoked the name of the disease, I realized that John had not given it a name at all. In what would later become an issue in my work with the volunteers, I realized how many times talk about "it" stood in for talk about "AIDS."

As it was, however, the varied and somewhat unsettling commentaries about AIDS were contained within a familiar and orderly ritual form. It explained our participation (both as bag decorators and as carol singers) and gave explicit meaning to both. As silence gave way to singing, then "sermons," and then a closing song, ritual, symbol, and action built a sacred story for the decorated bags. Their mission now was not just containing food but also saying something to the people who would receive them. As the words John and Kathy spoke moved through the room, they stuck fast to the bags and communicated new things back to their makers.

It occurred to me, as I sat there, how lovely all this symbolic work was, and how comparably devoid of collective symbolism were the meals I helped cook. When the hot Christmas meals were placed in the bags these children had made, no one would gather to pray over them or call the cooks together to reflect on what they might mean. This did not mean that individual volunteers did not give meaning to the meals, of course. But it did mean that such meanings were located in different parts of the work and discussed, if at all, in less communal fashion. Work in the kitchen was more akin to work in the Friends Seminary's cafeteria, where different bag decorators variably ignored and followed the rules, expressed meaning and relations to people with AIDS, and struggled to place their mark and remembrances on the objects in front of them.

Kitchen volunteers used potatoes and carrots to work out their responses to AIDS. As I had learned long before the Christmas season, potatoes and carrots do not lend themselves so obviously to communicating purposes or ideas about AIDS, or about religion for that matter. Neither the raw material of kitchen work nor the exigencies of kitchen time provided much space for reflective talk about the meaning of what we were doing.

Volunteers often thought hard about what they did, reproducing rela-

tionships between themselves and dying people as they worked. Nevertheless, we rarely discussed what it "meant" to chop and dice. In fact, talk in
the kitchen was marked by a lack of commentary on what it was all about.
There was no space, no time, and (many felt) no reason to "step back"
and talk about why we were feeding people with AIDS. As I learned after
asking a few innocent but out of place questions, some volunteers chose
to work in the kitchen precisely because they would *not* have to talk about
meaning or purpose while they were there. It was relatively easy to sit in the
Friends Meetinghouse and imagine the different meanings of the gifts and
the pathos and hope that the children and the singing teachers brought to
the occasion. It was much more of a challenge to develop such reflection
while hunched over a low sink full of cold water scrubbing hundreds of
pounds of potatoes. At first I wondered if it would be possible to glean
anything more from that experience than cold hands and calluses. But I
had taken on that particular task to see what I could learn about religious
talk in just such a setting.

My first trip to the basement kitchen at God's Love We Deliver was disori-
enting and rather disheartening. Hannah led me down the stairs, talking
nonstop as we navigated the course through a heavy fire door on the first
floor, down a flight of dingy steps, through a labyrinth of hallways, into
an empty "cafeteria," and around through the pantry and down a ramp
to the kitchen. "It'll be an interesting group in the kitchen today because
you'll have some people who are pretty diverse—we have a group coming in
who are learning disabled, for instance. How does that sound? Any questions?" There was no time for questions, however, since at that moment
we rounded a corner and entered the kitchen.

Hannah walked up to a young Asian man decked out in a white chef's
smock and houndstooth check pants. He wore sneakers rather than the
more typical chef's clogs. "Hi, Lee. This is Courtney. She's going to be
with us for a while. I want you to show her around today; she's going to be
in the kitchen." He wiped his hands on the towel tied to his apron strings
and shook my hand. He nodded and looked around the small room as if
deciding where to begin. My eyes followed his gaze.

There were ten people in the kitchen: six paid chefs, dressed like Lee,
and four volunteers who wore T-shirts and jeans. I had come at a transi-
tional hour, after the early morning volunteers who packed out the day's
hot meal had left and before things got humming again in the afternoon.

I would later learn to judge the time of day by the number of volunteers in the kitchen and the jobs left on the bulletin board (this was a useful skill, since my watch was usually in my pocket). The smallish rectangular room with a sagging ceiling and walls painted industrial yellow felt more cramped than cozy. Convection ovens and steamers, a large stockpot, and a professional range lined one of the long walls; warming ovens, an industrial-sized mixer, sinks, and counters lined the other. I smelled garlic roasting and caught a whiff from a simmering stockpot.

Volunteers were chopping vegetables at a long stainless steel counter in the middle of the room. A porter stood scrubbing oblong metal "hotel pans" at a three-sink dishwashing area. Behind those sinks stood more counters and one of the two walk-in refrigerators. In the space between the coatracks and the refrigerator, the "specials chefs" had carved out an area no larger than a small closet where they made meals for clients with dietary restrictions. A small compact disc player sat on a shelf above the counter in the middle of the room, flanked by at least a hundred CDs. They were volunteer donations and mirrored the diverse tastes of the group. At the moment, the radio was turned to a rock station.

Hannah left abruptly, and Lee took me back to the coatrack to find an apron, a hat, and latex gloves. "Since you didn't bring a baseball hat—most people do—you can wear one of these paper ones," he said, presenting me with a flimsy white paper hat. "You probably want the medium-sized gloves," he noted, pulling two out of a box. I saw that he didn't wear gloves. ("He's allergic to latex," a volunteer later explained.) He handed me a clean apron and then introduced me to Charles, a volunteer wearing a neon "Provincetown" cap and old jeans. "Charles will show you around. I have to make lemonade for the board meeting. I completely forgot!"

Lee dashed off as Charles made a name tag for me and stuck it on my apron. "We'll get you a real one," he said, pointing to his computer-generated plastic name tag. Many of the regulars on the shifts had reusable name tags, setting them apart from the new volunteers. Charles showed me how to adjust my hat and spun me around to a mirror to inspect it. "You might want to bring your own hat—but frankly, that one looks very good on you. Oh, but honey, those gloves are too big. Here, try the small ones."

Once I was appropriately attired in the required safety garb, Charles turned me toward the main kitchen and showed me the drawer where they kept the large chef's knives and plastic cutting boards. "Always walk with a knife to your side, point down. Never hold it on top of your board, OK?" I nodded. I was responsible for washing my knife and board with soap and hot water, Charles told me, as we walked over to the preparation area where two and a half cases of romaine lettuce sat on the counter.

Lee came over to demonstrate how to cut the lettuce into inch-square pieces, and I followed his directions dutifully. When Lee turned back to his lemonade, however, Charles showed me an easier way. We pulled off the dirty, yellowish outer leaves, then cut each head in half. We made one-inch slits along the length of each half, then cut crosswise to make pieces, throwing the hearts and the limp leaves into large trash cans. We dumped the cut, unwashed lettuce into a huge white plastic tub of cold water in the sink beside us. Before long a volunteer wearing an AIDS ribbon cap came over to rinse the romaine in two tubs of cold water and spin it dry in a twenty-five-gallon salad spinner. He transferred the cut, washed, and dried lettuce to clean white tubs and stacked them on an empty counter.

Lee came back to our area to help and to talk about the Emmys. "Can you believe that *Picket Fences* won and not *NYPD Blue?*" he asked incredulously.

"I kind of like *Picket Fences*," said a volunteer in an AIDS ribbon cap.

"I never watched *NYPD Blue*," Charles said. "And that awful stupid guy from Seinfeld, what's his name—he won for best actor."

"Well, I'm glad that they didn't give it to David Caruso," I added, relieved to be able to participate in the conversation, even if it was only about television.

"*Gypsy* didn't win either," Charles pointed out.

"Well, frankly, I don't think it deserved it. Really. I mean Bette Midler was great, but I didn't really like it that much. But she opened the show and then didn't get the award."

"She opened the show? What did she sing?"

" 'Rose's Way' from *Gypsy*—it was very good."

"And did anybody win anything for *And the Band Played On?*"

"No—but there were nominations for that—yeah, I think Ian McKellan was nominated for some category."

Our conversation broke up as Sharon, a slight woman with salt-and-pepper hair, arrived at our worktable and gave Charles a hug. She wasn't wearing a hat, so Lee brought her a paper one. She grudgingly put it on, rolling her eyes as she fished two bobby pins out of her jeans pocket to secure it. "Schmutzig!" she shouted theatrically, picking up a dirty head of lettuce. Charles had apparently been waiting for such an announcement and picked up a worm he'd been saving with the tip of his knife.

"Ewwwh, gross! Look at this!" Charles said, and started singing the children's song, "Nobody likes me, everybody hates me, I'm gonna eat a worm." Sharon looked on in feigned disgust. "Didn't you ever sing that song?"

"No!" Sharon retorted.

Charles turned to me, "Oh, no, I'd better watch out—you're not going to put that in your paper are you, Courtney?"

I chuckled and nodded as Charles explained to Sharon that I was a sociologist doing a study on volunteers. "Weren't you here a few weeks ago? I think there's someone who's interviewing people. I think that she only came once, though," she asked me.

I shook my head emphatically. Sharon smiled and changed the subject, asking Charles about an airplane crash near Pittsburgh the week before.

"Spooky, isn't it?" Sharon asked. "They haven't found anything, have they?"

I began to offer my version of what happened but stopped when Charles shook his head knowledgeably. "No, no, that's not what happened. Believe me, that kind of thing doesn't happen with a plane that big. I'm an airline steward, I know. But yeah, it was weird," he said, turning again to Sharon. "I was just leaning back—on my way to Munich when the news came over the radio . . ." He grew quiet as Lee came back to the table to ask Sharon whether she was following the U.S. Open.

———

Kitchen work was repetitive and kitchen talk often superficial. This was a boon to the new volunteer. Very few conversational barriers kept workers like me from speaking on our first days in the kitchen. Volunteers assumed that people who came to the kitchen all shared a desire to cook and some experience with people with AIDS. Other than that, they relished difference and the "diversity" of their coworkers. If a "city is a place of talk," as M. A. K. Halliday put it, where heterogeneous speech communities intersect, are maintained, and are consciously noticed by its varied participants, the kitchen was exemplary urban space.[30] To a researcher looking to study how people make meaning and talk about religion, however, the drudgery of kitchen work and the first-blush superficiality of the talk were somewhat overwhelming. As it turned out, however, first impressions were deceiving.

The apparent absence of conversation about meaning allowed volunteers to practice cooking in ways that often continued, or reinterpreted, work they had done for others in other times and places. Often, though not always, this was directly related to memories of cooking for someone who had died of AIDS. The silent spaces around what cooking meant (and the arguments that flared up when silence would no longer work) were critical points in the structure of kitchen life. Small talk was more than idle chatter. Walking into the kitchen meant entering conversations that continued from week from week and that built on stories remembered and replayed. After a few months I realized that even the most apparently offhand comment could resonate with layers of meaning and association far removed from the topic at hand.

In this respect, volunteers' conversational work coupled a desire to keep the conversation light and open with a desire to comment on things that mattered. This banter took effort and sometimes drew attention away from the potatoes and beans in front of us—to the consternation of the chefs. "This is not a social club," said Perry, the tall, gaunt executive chef, as he peered out of his small office into the kitchen one day. I nodded half-heartedly, watching the other volunteers laughing, talking about the latest episodes of *Melrose Place* and *Absolutely Fabulous* and discussing Goldie Hawn's latest hairstyle. He was right to complain; it was a social club of sorts, one often marked by a self-consciously campy and ironic aesthetic popularized in New York's gay communities.

On his better days, Perry admitted that his frustrations were overblown. All volunteers agreed that our first task was to get the meals out. Most cared very much about the work they did and took it seriously. In arguments with chefs and other volunteers, they attempted to stake out and preserve the conditions that made it possible to get out the meals. This most important goal, and volunteers' commitment to it, united them in the midst of silences around things they shared and their curiosity about things they did not. I learned just how important volunteers thought this goal was on that first morning in the kitchen after the learning disabled adults arrived.

Shortly after Sharon appeared, the group of learning disabled volunteers that Hannah mentioned found their way to the doorway of the kitchen and moved shyly around its perimeter, much as I had done only an hour before. Lee put John, Michael, Florence, Kimberly, and their leader Marsha to work on the other side of the kitchen scrubbing sweet potatoes. The kitchen was small enough, though, that we could all see that they were struggling with the large and unwieldy potatoes. They worked hard, splattering water and dirt over the countertops and floor as they scrubbed and scrubbed with vegetable brushes. Florence announced loudly, "I'm sweating so much I got sweat in my mouth," causing Sharon and Charles to share a look that was half amused, half disgusted.

When the group entered, the joking and casual banter virtually stopped.

I shifted uncomfortably from foot to foot, trying to think of a topic that would start up the laughter again, and feeling at a loss. Within fifteen minutes, all the volunteers except Sharon and me got ready to leave, washing off their boards and knives and moving toward the coatracks at the back of the kitchen. "Can't you stay a little bit longer? I hardly had a chance to say two words to you," Sharon asked Charles, but he shook his head. He was on his way to see his chiropractor. I was sure this volunteer exodus was not what Hannah had in mind when she spoke so energetically about the wonderful diversity in the kitchen.

Not all kinds of diversity were equal, apparently, even though volunteers generally spoke proudly of their differences (in age, sexual orientation, gender, background, and life experience). Almost every each kitchen shift had several volunteers who lived in Brooklyn or Queens, and a number of Asian, African American, and Latino volunteers reflected some of the city's racial and ethnic diversity. Accountants, housewives, people "between jobs," film editors, and schoolteachers chopped vegetables side by side. Some were not completely "voluntary" participants, entering the kitchen through rehabilitation or job-training programs. Nevertheless, most kitchen volunteers knew someone who had died of AIDS, most were either gay men or straight (mostly married) women,[31] most lived in Manhattan, and most appeared to be comfortably within the city's middle class.

I had not yet made these distinctions on that first morning. Someone handed me some disinfectant spray and a dry cotton cloth to clean the counters; I wiped up while the other chefs prepared the special meals and Charles and Sharon stood talking near the coffee machine. I decided to go join them, but as I approached, Charles put his backpack on his shoulder and kissed Sharon on the cheek, giving me the distinct impression that they had been talking about something private.

"Bye, Courtney, it was nice to meet you—Watch out, Sharon, she's writing about us and she'll remember what she hears! Don't tell our secrets!" He turned and chuckled to me, "We don't have many secrets around here, honey . . ." But Lee stopped him with an impatient gesture.

"Here, guys, we need to set up. Sharon, will you show Courtney where to get the small salad containers?"

We lifted a case of a thousand aluminum salad containers off a pantry shelf in the back of the kitchen and put a tub of washed romaine lettuce on the counter. Lee and one of the porters placed a heavy tub of egg salad next to the lettuce. Then Lee called the group of learning disabled volunteers over to join us.

Lee explained the job of packing out egg salad. Sharon put a handful of lettuce into each tin, then Marsha and I put in a scoop of egg salad.

Kimberly and Florence placed plastic lids on the containers, and John and Michael sealed them with the onomatopoetically named "kachunga," a heavy metal device that sealed the tin lip down over the edges of the plastic lid.

The job went slowly, primarily because the "lidders" were asked to push the sides of each container's sealing edge inward so it would be properly sealed by the kachunga. This required a deft touch—too much, apparently, for the impatient Florence. She wanted to "kachunga" and persuaded Michael to change places with her. To pass the time Sharon began to ask me about my research, but then Julie, a short older woman with bobbed graying hair, arrived. Sharon asked Julie to take her place and escaped for a bathroom break.

Julie surveyed the gloomy pack-out line, the aluminum containers filled with egg salad piling up to the left and Kimberly and Michael struggling with the lidding technique. Julie called over to Lee, "This is taking *way* too long!" Lee, shrugging, told Julie to do whatever she could—we were low on volunteers, but now that we were in the middle of the job, we had to finish it.

Julie moved from the lettuce end and took charge, positioning herself in Kimberly's spot and showing Michael how to push in on the containers without deforming them. Florence, envious of the attention Michael was receiving, berated him loudly, but Julie continued to encourage him. Nevertheless, I could feel Julie's frustration was mounting. She turned to me every so often and shook her head. It felt strange to receive knowing looks from a total stranger. After all, I was a new volunteer too.

Sharon returned to our uneasiness, and with her help we quickly finished filling 625 containers with "regular" egg salad and 27 with "special" egg salad. Compared with the hour of efficient romaine cutting and laughing conversation, the two hours spent scooping egg salad stretched out with long patches of silence.

Nothing on my first day encouraged me to think I had chosen a site where I could find out anything about how people practiced religion or spirituality. There were no hymns, songs, or sermons. Aside from Sharon's announcement at the end of the morning that she was off to choir practice, I heard not one reference to religion.

A few of us did, however, talk about the learning disabled group after they left to get their lunch. ("We're gonna have pizza and I'm gonna have pepperoni!" Florence shouted as she walked out the door.) Julie pinned the blame on Hannah, noting that the "disaster" could have been averted if she would recognize that not everyone was suited for the task. She added that she didn't want any of us to think she believed those people were incompetent in general. But Hannah's commitment to volunteer education was getting in the way of making the meals.

Julie's feelings were further complicated when Sharon got ready to leave and discovered her sunglasses were missing. No one had seen them, and no one could find them. "Are you sure you brought them in?" Julie asked, and Sharon snapped, "*Of course* I'm sure." Tom, one of the porters, decided to search the learning disabled group's bags, and he found them. He told Sharon, and Sharon told Marsha, the group leader. She was so offended that she and the group left immediately. Sharon and Julie both went to Kathy Spahn's office to defend Tom, then returned to the kitchen to tell the story. "It's probably better for all of us," Sharon remarked, half smiling as she told Charles about it the following week. Julie, however, remained troubled: "It was just too complicated a place for them, I think. It wasn't appropriate, and it wasn't fair."

After months of working with Julie, I returned to study the notes I'd made from this first day of fieldwork, and I heard and saw different things than I had that first day. By then I had learned that Julie's sense of "fairness" and appropriateness was fitted into a broader sense of duty and commitment, one that she linked to her Jewish identity and practice. As I continued to work in the kitchen, I likewise learned that offhand comments like Sharon's reference to choir practice helped others make inferences about their fellow volunteers' actions and beliefs and then take steps toward further conversations. Fragmentary ways of becoming known in such conversation assisted volunteers in their varied attempts to make their work rewarding and to communicate those meanings to others.

———

Religion was part of what happened at God's Love We Deliver, but it was not the only thing: the organization of this book reflects and reminds us of this "reality" of my field research. Religion happened, when it did, in the midst of other important goings-on. To come close to understanding how religion looks in this setting, we first have to situate it within its broader context and, for a time, displace it from the center of inquiry. By decentering religion (focusing on other aspects of the agency in the next two chapters), I have sought give a specific description of religion as it happened at GLWD, that is, within the course of other things including, most important, making hundreds of meals by hand.

Chapter 2 presents the "big picture" story of God's Love We Deliver's growth as an institution between 1986 and 1994, when I began field research; chapter 3 focuses on cooking practices and the daily life of the kitchen. These chapters also explain how kitchen volunteers and kitchen staff viewed the relationship between GLWD's mission and their work, and how both kitchen staff and volunteers used the agency's explicit goals with winks and laughter to bend the rules and create provisional space for making their work meaningful to them. The kitchen's tight space and the staff's concerns about food contamination and injury also required specific rules about kitchen procedures, and some conflicted with volunteers' cooking skills, practices, and memories developed in their home kitchens. Volunteers' cooking practices were expressed in action rather than in clearly articulated statements and were intimately connected to their underlying memories of cooking for people who had been sick. In this respect they differed from the chefs' practices in that they were not fully articulated, detailed, and logically formed through education or formal training. When chefs suggested they do things differently, the volunteers were sometimes surprisingly hurt or offended and often unable to respond. Volunteers had little equivalent language to explain or defend their ways of cooking (hence, at times, their use of the various GLWD missions to justify their actions). This did not make their practices any less important or deeply felt, of course. The kitchen's loosely connected culture and, more important, the way it was constantly imperiled by undercurrents of individually expressed practices, memories, and commitments led to a further investigation of such practices.

Chapter 4 investigates volunteers' practices and interpretations of their work. I focus on conversations with four volunteers who felt their work was in some ways religious or spiritual. I use both interviews and observations to tease out some of the links between practice and action in religious or spiritual activity. In doing so, I often heard a lay distinction between religion and spirituality that has been discussed in recent studies of American spiritual life. Others have noted the apparent tension (often unresolved) between individual and institutional, or nonofficial and official, descriptions of religion that come to the fore in this rhetoric. In this case, however, we see that the distinctions between religion and spirituality are somewhat differently aligned. Volunteers' distinctions, in speaking of their work at God's Love We Deliver, do not clearly reflect tension so much as they evoke their understandings that religious activity looks different, and is different, in various contexts.

It was not easy to practice "religion" in the kitchen: volunteers' descriptions evoke a complex relation between religious practices and the various settings where they are enacted. In chapter 5 I focus more closely on the ways religion was made possible (or not) through daily conversations about religion and related matters. Volunteers talked about all kinds of things as they chopped and diced; most of the conversation concerned what was immediately present in our lives. At certain times of the week and year, conversation was more likely to turn to things having to do with religion. Talk about religion most often began in one of three typical ways: talk about going to church, talk about holiday preparations, and talk about (and parodies of) particular conservative Christian groups. These kinds of talk were recognizable to most volunteers, and for the most part they were not risky to discuss. However, the limits of this kind of talk, enforced within the context of conversations between volunteers, also suggested (and occasionally demonstrated) less safe ways to talk about, and practice, religion and spirituality. In addition, volunteers built on the apparent ephemera of random, freewheeling talk about religion to construct more extensive, though more allusive and elusive, conversations about religion. I describe these partially hidden, "double-voiced" ways of talk that volunteers used to give ballast to work they saw as religious.

Chapter 6 extends this discussion of the ways daily conversational topics and genres structure expressions of meaning. Though all the volunteers were in the kitchen to "do something" about AIDS, talk about AIDS was almost always absent. My evaluation of these apparent silences changed through my time GLWD, and it gradually prompted me to think more clearly about how volunteers' expectations of shared culture structured their work and conversation. The portrait that emerges from these chapters is much more complicated than I imagined at the outset.

In the conclusion I return to address some of the nascent and explicit themes in this book. These include the place and promise of religious practice in daily life, the role of interacting speech genres and cultural practices in articulating such practice, and the methodological promise of such study.

CHAPTER TWO

The Meals Are the Message:

God's Love We Deliver, 1985 to 1994

"Bread and wine have their own truth."   —MIKHAIL BAKHTIN

"The meals are the message," volunteers and staff at God's Love We Deliver told me again and again. Feeding sick people was "so basic" a principle that it was unnecessary to elaborate or to defend it. Who indeed would dispute that carefully prepared hot meals carry an unmistakable message of good-will? I too was at first quite taken with GLWD's noble and unmistakably important purpose. Nevertheless, after just a few days of working in the kitchen and the offices, I saw that I would have to take a closer look at the ways it elaborated this message and how the meals were meant to convey it.

On closer inspection, "The meals are the message" was an agreeable, if not very specific, comment. It suggested the meals *had* a message, but it left that message up to the eyes and ears of the beholder. The phrase made room for a number of meanings, which would become important as GLWD expanded its missions and purposes. Saying it made it easier for people to pass over the contradictions in three distinct, competing meanings that the agency presented in its official literature.

In this chapter I chronicle GLWD's cultural and physical expansion from its origins until I began field research in 1994. Over this time its original pithy mission statement, "food is love" was joined by two other phrases: "food is therapy" and "food is charity." GLWD's growing number of missions helped the agency develop connections across a wide range of organizations. I conceive of these different missions, purposes, or inter-pretations as its official cultural repertoires. Repertoires grow and mutate in particular contexts. They attract (or repel) various communities and networks and can be important strategic resources for nonprofit organi-zations in search of funds or backers. Repertoires are nevertheless more than ideology or strategic advertising. They also express ways of enacting relationships, allocating resources, and making daily decisions.[1]

GLWD developed its official repertoires to respond to particular situations and constraints, within particular social circumstances. For this reason it did not drop its original repertoires as it added new ones. "Food is love" continued to attract donors, capture the imagination of volunteers, and influence the ways GLWD conducted its affairs, even after "food is therapy" became an important interpretive repertoire. Although this is in part due to its continued attraction for certain sets of donors, "food is love" also remained potent because it was embedded within particular relationships with other groups and organizations and within its own practices and rituals.

The presence of three official repertoires led to an interesting situation in the kitchen, which I discuss in the next chapter. To foreground that discussion, it is important to know that the missions were almost entirely the province of the staff in the offices "upstairs." They only occasionally lent heft to conversations "downstairs" in the kitchen.[2] When kitchen volunteers used the missions, they often did so in ways that signaled their collective distaste for the "ideology" or their individual desire to preserve alternative evaluations of good cooking.[3] Their uses of the missions were in this sense ironic, strategic, and often more "mischievous than righteous."[4] Before I explore these various expressions, it is important to lay out the development of GLWD's formal cultural expressions during its rapid growth from 1985 to 1994.

EXPANDING MEANINGS

In May of 1985, a hospice volunteer named Ganga Stone delivered a donated bag of groceries to the apartment of a man with AIDS. The man, Richard, had not eaten in two days. He was covered with sores and too weak to get out of bed. There was no food in the house, and no money to buy food.

Richard went through the uncooked groceries only to find that there was nothing there of immediate use to him. "I need a meal!" he pleaded.

Ganga responded by purchasing a prepared meal for him with her own money. Upon returning home, she made her own determined pledge: Richard and other homebound people with AIDS must not go hungry. Nine miraculous years and over three quarters of a million hot meals later, not one eligible client within our reach has been turned away.[5]

This is the basic story of GLWD's origin, told over and over throughout the agency, with shifts in emphasis depending on the context. Sometimes listeners learn that Stone bought a meal for Richard only after discovering that "no one" in his address book would, or could, help him (many were dead or were sick themselves). Sometimes Richard is angry rather than pleading. Often we hear how poor Stone herself was, and what a commitment it was for her to buy a single meal for Richard.

Details notwithstanding, the story's basic contours remain. A hungry, helpless, and dying man admonishes Stone. Thus chided, she discovers another blessing she can grant and sets out to deliver it to Richard and everyone else in similar straits. In this and every other telling, God's Love We Deliver begins with a selfless act by one individual who pledges that "people with AIDS must not go hungry." The "miracle" of GLWD develops from this simple pledge.

GLWD's purpose, as articulated in the origin story, is firmly intertwined with Stone's personal history. It grows out of her singular, almost numinous confrontation of self and purpose, embodied in Richard's rebuke. This call is without question framed in religious terms. While the story conceals much of the real work that made GLWD a reality, its details and specificity succeeded in confronting others (donors, volunteers, and sympathizers) with an unquestioned need.[6]

Stone told this story to everyone who would listen. It framed care for people with AIDS as a necessary and urgent task. The story worked: she quickly amassed a core of friends and supporters to deliver meals in Manhattan, and in 1986 GLWD incorporated as a nonprofit entity. It soon applied for a state grant for "hunger relief," and in 1987 it received its first large grant. This allowed GLWD to begin cooking meals itself. It rented the kitchen in the West Park Presbyterian Church on West Eighty-sixth Street, hired chefs and a van driver, and shuttled meals to distribution points throughout Manhattan. At the church, GLWD could cook meals for fifty people, and for the first time the agency started to actively recruit clients. No one, Stone said, would be turned away. In 1988 GLWD started delivering meals outside Manhattan, and by 1989 it delivered meals in all five boroughs. The church space was far from adequate, however; the kitchen was too small, and staff had to store their files each Friday to make room for Sunday school.

In 1991 God's Love We Deliver found a new home at the American Youth Hostel on West 103d Street, at the edge of Morningside Heights. Chefs projected that the new kitchen was large enough to make daily meals for 750 clients. For the first time, GLWD had enough office space for its entire staff. Client numbers rose (it delivered close to 900 daily meals in late 1995), and so did staff—from twenty part-time and full-time workers in 1991 to fifty-five full-time and part-time delivery van drivers, grant writers, secretaries, dispatchers, chefs, nutritionists, computer specialists, and volunteer coordinators in 1994. Its active volunteer base likewise expanded from two hundred to over a thousand. In 1994 its budget came in at just over $5.5 million. The year 1994 also marked Stone's exit from the agency.[7]

In late 1995, God's Love We Deliver moved to the SoHo building it had purchased in 1993. The "David Geffen Building" (so named to honor the $1 million donation that allowed GLWD to finish renovations) sits on the corner of Spring Street and Sixth Avenue. The move was viewed ruefully by some observers, who noted that GLWD was literally moving away from its clients, who increasingly lived in the poorer neighborhoods in northern Manhattan and the Bronx. On the other hand, the new building had multiple loading docks for vans, had a sumptuous, extensive kitchen large enough to produce two thousand meals a day, and was close to three subway lines.

GLWD's transformation in these nine years was no "miracle," regardless of its phenomenal growth from grassroots community to multilayered service organization. Stone and her friends and employees worked hard to attract state, federal, and corporate grants and to expand its donor base. The agency took advantage of existing community networks and created new ones, and it increasingly juggled a variety of interpretations of its message as it navigated these networks and funding streams. God's Love We Deliver's mission of delivering food expanded outward from Richard's "call" to Ganga Stone, eventually developing into three competing articulations.

Food Is Love

Although "love" eventually took on a variety of meanings and purposes among a variety of donors and audiences,[8] Stone meant it initially as *God's* love. "Many of the people whom we serve have come to feel that God no longer loves them. Our presence in their lives is proof that they have not been forsaken."[9]

Ganga Stone was a deeply spiritual woman for whom feeding the sick became a spiritual task. She came to this understanding through a long journey. After an early adult life full of twists and turns, Ingrid Stone found herself on an ashram in India. She became a devotee of Swami Muktananda Paramhansa, who renamed her Ganga and gave her a charge to minister to the dying.[10] She returned to New York when the AIDS epi-

demic started to rage and became a hospice volunteer. As her confrontation with Richard demonstrates, her mission was, as she saw it, to share
with the dying the continuation of life after death. As she told the *New Yorker*
in 1991, "My sense of my own role in life was to share with people what I
know about the deathless nature of the human self, but you can't comfort
people who have not eaten, so it seemed to me that my earnest money for
God was my willingness to take on a really very time-consuming, labor
intensive, expensive mission, which was feeding whoever asked."[11]

With her mission thus transformed and her "earnest money" dedicated
to feeding the sick, Stone started to think about a name for the organization. As she told the story (often in conjunction with the story about
Richard), the name came to her when "a voice" whispered in her ear,
"God's love—God's love—we deliver." She had been brushing her teeth,
and when she heard the voice she "started laughing because 'We Deliver' is
on the marquee of every West Side restaurant. But it's the perfect thing—
it's so nonsectarian it's impossible to misunderstand."[12] Although "God's
Love We Deliver" now runs as one phrase, it is an awkward one that cannot
help evoking Stone's original reading of the agency's name: "God's Love
(We Deliver)." In fact the first business cards Stone had printed up on
salmon-colored stock attested to this: "God's Love" stood front and center, and "We Deliver" and Stone's home phone number were in small type
in the lower corner.

God's Love We Deliver thus marked a transformation of love from spoken assurances to embodied demonstrations that God cares for those who
are dying. The food she delivered could *itself* embody love. In this respect,
the meals themselves *were* the message. Furthermore, it "spoke for itself."
Stone early on stipulated that delivery volunteers were to let the meals
speak and not offer clients anything "but the food and a smile." Expressly
downplaying the connections between God, food, and love and focusing
on their "interchangeability" made the place of God, and the sacred, more
ambiguous. Addressing this issue in 1990, Stone stated: "For folks who
don't have a sense of God or care for the word, we just say love is love,
or your mother's love is love. . . . The food is the love. And we deliver."[13]
Stone, and the organization, stopped well short of providing an explicitly
religious definition of "God" or "love."[14] Yet it was clear that Stone's original impetus, and some aspects of the agency, were spiritually oriented.[15]

We see here the beginnings of a dance around the appropriate uses of
sacred language in an agency and a situation where God, religion, and
spirituality were not entirely accepted—and indeed were in some instances
radically rejected—by its clients and constituents. The argument embedded in GLWD's name that God loved people with AIDS created a niche for

spiritually motivated action within the AIDS community at a time when many mainstream religious groups were slow (at best) to respond to people with AIDS.[16] The phrase "God's Love" was both rebuke and refuge. This powerful and effective argument, however, also kept others at arm's length. And not all volunteers, or all donors who believed in the meals—and certainly not all clients—believed in God or were open to the notion that gifts of food were from, or evocative of, God.

As the organization grew and circumstances in the world of AIDS funding changed, the spiritual meanings of GLWD became increasingly lodged in Stone's personal story or cast in the words of particular clients or volunteers. GLWD's grants and public relations writers, in other words, situated this language in identifiable, individual voices. One 1993 fundraising letter, for instance, inserts a remarkable level of religion by quoting from a client's letter. "I couldn't believe what I saw, smelled and tasted," the letter read. "Every day, when eating seemed like the most impossible but crucial task in the world, your food was not just food. It was a message: 'This is love. Take it in. It will heal you.'" The overt reference, linking the food to a liturgical, eucharistic meal, resonated strongly in this letter, but at the same time it placed religious language outside the organization's central purpose.[17]

This becomes clearer when we see how staff actively worked to provide alternative, nonsupernatural definitions of love. Parents' love, love for humanity, love for others all had their turn in GLWD publications. A 1993 advertisement published simultaneously with the letter quoted above states that the agency's name "combined the idea of universal love *like that of a parent for a sick child* and New York practicality."[18] As we will see, the gloss from God's love to a parent's love also fit well within the developing understanding of the therapeutic aspects of the meals.

Love was represented with more than words, however: it also became apparent in the meals' aesthetic qualities. Since volunteers were not supposed to talk to clients about God (although some surely did, as many early delivery volunteers and clients became friends), the meals themselves literally had to evoke love.

GLWD initially drew the symbols of loving food from the realm of gourmet, restaurant-quality meals. This makes sense when we consider that Stone had bought Richard's first meal from a nearby restaurant and that many of its early meals were purchased from restaurants. In GLWD's early days, Stone and her friends sometimes cooked meals for their clients. Since funds were scarce and Stone was admittedly a lackluster cook, however, she was prompted to ask restaurants to help. She asked chefs at several select Manhattan restaurants to prepare first-quality meals from their menus for her clients, on order and free of charge. According to one restaurant owner, Stone "dictated the terms on which she would accept them: hot, fresh, nothing left over from yesterday."[19] Impressed, many chefs agreed to help. Coordinating this effort of ordering, dispatching, and delivering meals from multiple sites around the city required a good deal of organization and limited the number of new clients the group could take. Although this system did not stay in place for more than a few months, this early association with "quality, gourmet" food influenced the ways GLWD understood its own kitchen production of meals.

GLWD's first chef created elaborate menus with expensive ingredients and oversaw volunteers who prepared everything by hand, modeling restaurant kitchen work. One 1988 Monday menu, not notably more elaborate than any other that week, began with "creamy carrot bisque and Caesar salad" and continued with "prime rib, scalloped potatoes, asparagus tips." Diners finished off the meal with "white chocolate mousse with raspberries." The meals were typically rounded out with bread and brownies delivered fresh from some of the city's fanciest bakeries. Florists provided table arrangements weekly for each client. On Christmas and Thanksgiving, clients "reserved a table" for themselves and as many guests as they wanted to join them. Volunteers delivered elaborate holiday meals replete with chocolate truffles and cognac.[20] The practices of restaurant cooking were likewise manifest in GLWD's hiring decisions. Its chefs boasted experience in two-star restaurants or degrees from first-tier cooking schools. Emphasis on cooking and professional work in the kitchen attracted volunteers who were experienced or interested in skilled cooking.

The connection between restaurant-quality meals and love was emblematic of several aspects of GLWD's purpose and its relation to its clients. GLWD delivered "gourmet" food to neighbors and friends with equal, if not exalted, status in relation to the giver. This was not "charity" delivered to strangers and others: GLWD served "clients" who ordered and received (rather than passively accepted) meals.

In retrospect, presenting meals of this quality evoked a tinge of pathos. In the 1980s most clients remained on the program only for several weeks; long-term clients were so rare that staff from the agency made a piece for the AIDS Memorial Quilt for its first long-term client.[21] Staff meetings began with a roll call of clients who had died since the last meeting. Volunteers and staff attended countless funerals and memorial services. Given that all the clients were dying, they got whatever they desired. "Ganga's deal was, if they want to eat bonbons, let them eat bonbons," one grant writer quipped when I remarked on the agency's profligate and delicious-sounding menus. Delivering more courses and more food than people

with AIDS could possibly eat placed great emphasis on the symbolic nature of the meals. They suggested, above all, that life was a feast, that it was
worth celebrating, and that it would continue to the next meal. In this
atmosphere, excessive and elaborate meals embodied beauty and hope,
two concepts that were not only in short supply but in some respects inexpressible. [22]

"Food is love" also provided a magical phrase in the realm of private
donors in New York, both inside the "AIDS community" and outside. [23]
While many, if not most, of GLWD's earliest supporters and volunteers
were from Manhattan's gay and lesbian communities or were close family
members of persons who had AIDS or who had died of it, its language and
purpose allowed the agency to build bridges to many other communities
as well. "Love" marked GLWD as an AIDS organization with a definite
benevolent purpose. As such, it was uniquely suited among AIDS organizations to capture the attention of New York's mainstream social and cultural elites. Where organizations such as ACT UP and Gay Men's Health
Crisis were situated within an increasingly vocal, and charged, politicized
struggle over AIDS funding and research, GLWD was fundamentally a
charity with an "unquestionably" basic mission. It thus presented a way for
New York's elite to get involved in AIDS work without the risk of taking an
overtly political stand on issues of government intervention, funding, or
the like. [24]

GLWD's ability to take advantage of these networks became clear in the
early 1990s. In 1990, GLWD raised $400,000 in a single night at a ben-
efit auction at Sotheby's attended by sports, entertainment, and media
celebrities. [25] Stone was interviewed in a number of major media outlets,
and GLWD's kitchen appeared in *Vogue*, with socialites Blaine Trump (a
board member and a tireless backer of GLWD) and Carolyn Roehm chopping zucchini in cocktail dresses. Thanksgiving Day delivery became an
annual mayoral photo opportunity in 1990, when David Dinkins's visit to
a client in an single room occupancy hotel was covered by every local television station. Rudolph Giuliani and his family continued the tradition.

Although the heady, celebrity-filled days of the 1990s were still to
come, the late 1980s proved a challenging time for AIDS-related organizations seeking funding of any kind. Limited opportunities existed.
New York's private and public funding agencies did little to assist AIDS-
focused groups in the 1980s, since most large private charities and trusts
had charters or traditions that barred them from giving to "single disease"
concerns. [26] Likewise, very few government agencies funded AIDS service
organizations, and what money was available was allocated to patients' total
care and to prevention and education. [27] These realities fostered GLWD's

initial dependence on private individual giving and also pushed it to couch its purpose in terms of "hunger relief," which gave access to state-level nutritional and poor-relief funds. GLWD garnered its first large grant (close to $750,000) from New York's Supplemental Nutrition Assistance Program (SNAP) in 1987.

Billing itself as a hunger relief agency proved a critical moment for GLWD and paved the way for the therapeutic mission that was to come. "Food is love" soon began to share space with "food is therapy." This therapeutic interpretation added another layer of meaning to the meals' "unmistakable" message. Therapeutic goals did not fit easily with loving ones, and they added a new, and somewhat different, set of relationships between the clients and the agency. [28]

Food Is Therapy

GLWD staff members and volunteers devoted their efforts and energies to providing a last service to the sickest of the sick. Yet some members of the staff started to think more concretely about the meals' therapeutic and nutritional value. Neglected, sick people were certainly receiving intangible love with the meals—but they were also receiving physical sustenance. It was not such a stretch, particularly since "love" was associated with a mother's chicken soup, to reason that proper nutrition might improve clients' quality of life. These ideas gained even more ground as HIV positive individuals started to refer to themselves as people living with AIDS or, more simply, people with AIDS (rather than AIDS victims or AIDS patients).

Observations of clients' health status, changes in funding opportunities, and the growing emphasis on living with AIDS contributed to the development of "food is therapy," the second cultural repertoire at God's Love We Deliver. Eventually this repertoire was incorporated into the story about Ganga and Richard. A version printed in 1993 editorializes that in the early days of the organization, "Ms. Stone purchased whatever the patients wanted even if it was some snack food, because in those days, she didn't know that AIDS patients need more than 2,200 calories a day and a high protein diet." [29]

GLWD's first focus on AIDS nutrition was simple. The agency concentrated on food safety and on getting sick people to eat. The emphasis on food aesthetics fit within this framework: the beautiful meals were supposed to entice those with small appetites to "take a few bites," as one staff member related. GLWD also emphasized the importance of correct storage and handling of foods when spoilage could prove fatal to clients whose immune systems were damaged or destroyed. As one early analysis of clients' nutritional needs put it, to ensure that its meals were "free from microbes," GLWD needed to maintain both a high quality of ingredients and strict attention to preparation and delivery.[30] Delivery became a serious point of concern: delivery volunteers were instructed *never* to leave a meal at a door where no one answered.[31]

GLWD began to pay explicit attention to a medical notion of nutrition after a site visit by New York City Health Commissioner Stephen Joseph in 1988. GLWD reported to donors that "in cooperation with the Board of Health, God's Love We Deliver is compiling data which will determine the impact of good nutrition on people with AIDS." This emphasis gave GLWD a goal beyond its desire to succor the dying and helped carve out a national niche for the organization. Staff members testified before the President's Commission on the HIV Epidemic about nutrition's role in keeping people out of hospital beds.[32] Over the next several years, staff members would attend and lead national workshops on AIDS nutrition programs.[33]

The growing promise of the meals' nutritional worth presented a practical hope to GLWD's staff, volunteers, and clients. In short, it meant that the food might actually help clients feel better and perhaps even extend their lives. In 1989 the agency hired a certified nutritionist to work with the chefs to develop appropriate meals. They designed high-calorie, high-protein menus to stave off the wasting syndrome that accompanies a final spiral of declining health.[34] Over time, the nutritionists successfully curtailed many of the "gourmet" flourishes in the menus. GLWD stopped delivering bread, since many people with AIDS develop mouth sores that make it painful to eat yeast-raised baked goods. Likewise, chefs discontinued cooking with alcohol after nutritionists provided statistics on the high percentage of people with AIDS who have substance abuse problems. In 1990 the holiday meal gift basket included sparkling apple juice instead of cognac. The nutritionist and chefs also instituted modified meal programs for clients with substantial dietary and health restrictions. Making special meals for clients who were on different restricted diets required an expansion in the kitchen staff. The agency reported to SNAP in 1990 that "twenty-five percent of God's Love We Deliver clients are on special diets."

Therapeutic interpretations and the growing specialization of meals did not radically change kitchen practices, however. Volunteers and chefs continued to cook the meals from scratch and to chop vegetables and meat by hand. Chefs continued to favor hiring colleagues with restaurant experience. Variety and high aesthetic quality were seen as important aspects of the meals' therapeutic content. The 1990 SNAP summary report claimed that "in addition to meeting nutritional requirements the meals are also designed to be attractive and tempting to eat. Persons with AIDS often experience lack of appetite due to the effects of prescribed medications or the course of the disease itself. . . . Clients receive a different meal each day over a four-week period before any menu is repeated."[35]

Chicken soup rather than creamy carrot bisque was now the order of the day. These changes to the menus at GLWD had an obvious effect on the way "food is love" was understood. Clients were expected to find in the meals (not only) an overwhelming cosmic and sacred care, but also (or instead) nutrients that would help them "get better." Stone's original project of giving people with AIDS something to eat had focused on the palliative and symbolic meaning of food (bonbons included). Everyone admitted that the meals GLWD delivered in the 1990s became more nourishing, even if they were at some symbolic level less exciting than those from earlier days.

The effects of the changes in the kitchen radiated throughout the organization. To create a modified special meal program for clients, GLWD needed to know more about each client's medical condition (and keep updates). GLWD's client "intake" information rapidly expanded from name, address, and emergency contact to three full pages of questions. The "simple phone call" initially required to get on the program became a full-length interview. Clients were expected to answer questions about allergies, infections, and medications. Social workers and caregivers became more involved in helping put clients "on the program," and clients' "simple petitions for help" were increasingly mediated through third parties. The rapid expansion of the client base, from under one hundred to over five hundred (without a proportional increase in client services staff) diminished the one-on-one contact GLWD prided itself on providing.

In this changed atmosphere, clients no longer "ordered" meals but were prescribed food as one more form of therapy that might help them "get better." The reality of the death of clients, so present in the daily world of GLWD in its early years, became a distant rumble. The language of living with AIDS became dominant in New York's most affected communities, and GLWD established itself as an important part of that transformation. Clients went off the program when they "got better," even if they came back on in later months.

In this milieu, the language of succor and service at the center of GLWD's early years took a backseat, especially after a new, activist client services director came on board in the early 1990s. Faced with a limited staff and an overwhelming client base, she described a new understanding of GLWD's client relationship in 1994: "To remain as effective as possible, the Client Services Department has shifted its approach over the past nine months. We have become partners with our clients and our clients' support networks. We have developed a working relationship with our clients whereby we both have responsibilities. No one is a victim and we all work together."[36]

GLWD clients found themselves in an increasingly normalized social service relationship when they called God's Love We Deliver. This relationship was meant to give clients more active agency and control over their lives. Yet since it came into force at the same time as GLWD's client base shifted to a nonwhite majority, it ironically played a role in the agency's third developing mission.

Food Is Charity

One of GLWD's early distinguishing features was that it would deliver meals to anyone with full-blown AIDS who asked, regardless of financial resources. Simply put, meals were delivered to the sick. Since GLWD did not conceive of its meals as mere sustenance, it did not restrict them to those who could not afford to order out from the local diner or Chinese restaurant. Likewise, its meals did not conform to common expectations about charity food. This confused some commentators. One society news editor asked, "Why are you giving your clients such good food?" Stone was dumbstruck at the question. "Excuse me, I'm not sure I understand you—you're saying that our food is *too good* for our clients? Can I quote you?"[37]

GLWD's view that food was a gift of love stood in contrast to the more common perception of charity food, where meals meant to alleviate poverty nevertheless symbolically reinforce its meaning (for instance, the breadline, government surplus cheese, and other "charity foods" and practices have their own symbolic persistence).[38] The contrast between charity and "love" became less clear at GLWD as it started to cook for hundreds each day, as the "gourmet" aspects of the meals became less apparent, and as its client population shifted to include many individuals and families living in New York's poorest neighborhoods. A client survey conducted by the nutrition department in 1993 revealed that close to one-third of its clients had no other source of food. GLWD started to send "double meals" on Fridays and later began to supply "emergency food" that could be kept on hand. Its large portions, which initially signified abundant and profligate love, likewise took on additional meaning in this context.

Where "love" appealed to New York's social elite and the "therapeutic"

repertoire gave GLWD access to government funding, the "charity" repertoire gained value in the agency when its service expanded to clients in
the outer boroughs—outside its original Manhattan-based, white gay networks. In 1988 GLWD opened a kitchen in the Bronx and started serving
clients in Brooklyn from its Manhattan kitchen.[39] Although it planned
to raise money to open a third kitchen in Brooklyn, fiscal issues led the
agency to close the Bronx kitchen and centralize its offices and kitchen
in Manhattan. It bought vans and hired drivers to ferry meals from the
Upper West Side kitchen to neighborhood meal distribution centers in
the outer boroughs.

This expansion of service increased the agency's reach in minority
neighborhoods and poorer areas of the city. Its client base grew to include
a sizable percentage of women and children. This estimable growth posed
some new issues for the agency, including how it would recruit reliable
cadres of delivery volunteers far from its organizational center. Until this
point, GLWD had not actively recruited volunteers, relying instead on active members of its own "AIDS community" to step forward and help or on
serendipitous encounters with key individuals. Expansion meant stepping
outside these taken-for-granted networks, however, and in 1991 GLWD
hired a volunteer coordinator with previous experience in Catholic social
services to develop neighborhood connections.

Over the next three years the volunteer coordinator organized a large
number of neighborhood distribution sites in the outer boroughs, primarily in churches and religious organizations. Other social service agencies and businesses also served as distribution centers, but the coordinator found that churches were the most reliable. Responding to reports that
some church groups resisted acknowledging the presence of AIDS in their
communities, she framed her pitch along the lines of a traditional religious call to feed the hungry. She talked about the importance of "taking
care of those close to you" and "feeding the poor" and, as she put it to me,
"brought AIDS in through the back door." She also revived the "God" in
"God's Love We Deliver. (A furious church secretary from Queens once
called Hannah to complain about a van driver who had cursed in her presence; she asked if the "God" in "God's Love We Deliver" meant nothing
to "that young man." The driver, a longtime GLWD employee who usually
drove in Manhattan, shrugged when confronted. "I had no idea they took
it so literally," he said.) The volunteer coordinator trained ladies' missionary clubs in Bedford-Stuyvesant (Brooklyn), French Catholic nuns
in Spanish Harlem, and Italian Catholic high school boys in the North
Bronx to deliver meals. Her work drew new populations of people with
AIDS into GLWD's universe.

The charity repertoire introduced changes to clients' menus, just as therapy had done earlier. In 1992 GLWD hired two bilingual nutritionists and developed "culturally appropriate" menus and food guides for clients and people with HIV/AIDS, including charts with foods native to African American, Latino, and Caribbean cultures. For kitchen volunteers, most of whom still hailed from Manhattan, the modifications suggested that the people they cooked for were different from themselves. Volunteers encountered unfamiliar vegetables (not the ones found in haute cuisine restaurants) that nutritionists insisted were "comfort foods" for many of GLWD's immigrant, poor, and non-English-speaking clients.

The changing perception that AIDS was a poor person's disease and that AIDS service organizations provided traditional charity was felt throughout the entire field of AIDS service organizations in this period. AIDS was increasingly integrated into other social service provisions and providers: the client services department was increasingly likely to hear from a client's caseworker rather than directly from the client. In 1994 GLWD's Strategic Plan complimented itself on being able to maintain its public perception as both a hunger agency and an AIDS service organization. Nevertheless, just as adding a "nutritional" component influenced the organization's understanding of its role and its relation to its clients, this shift in the client and volunteer bases had consequences far beyond the agency's new ability to bill itself as a "hunger relief organization."

In 1994 the meals were indeed the message; perhaps more to the point, however, they were the messages. GLWD continued to manage the three meanings it gave to its meals, largely through developing specialized tasks and divisions in the offices. The nutrition department, for example, was devoted to a mission of therapy. Its members attended workshops and classes at local universities to stay up to date on the growing understanding of AIDS nutrition, and they hosted nutrition interns who wanted firsthand experience. Nutritionists were also fluent in the love and charity repertoires, but they were not responsible for them. In contrast, the volunteer department's staff and volunteers recruited using the languages of love and charity. Its volunteer speakers used Stone's original story, and its spiritual connections, to great effect when telling about their involvement, whether they were speaking at a leather bar in Chelsea or the Concord Baptist Church. Client services, most acutely aware of the clients' multiple needs, struggled to balance "therapy" and "charity" notions in its decision making. Grant writers, in contrast, juggled these repertoires and combined them, when possible, tailoring their explication of the program to its various potential and actual donors.

A mother's love, the love of a stranger, and the love of God all were brought to bear on Stone's original notion, and they played out in the ways the volunteer director, the nutritionists, and others talked. Similarly, the therapeutic notion of providing food as medicine called to mind the psychological healing of caring words and actions. [40] The multiple explications of why GLWD served its clients, who the clients were, and even what was served had a noticeable effect on the organization's daily life and also on the kitchen's operations. This effect, however, played out differently than I expected when I first plunged into fieldwork.

COOKING UP THE MISSIONS

Volunteers and staff who cooked meals were ultimately responsible for demonstrating these meanings at work. GLWD performed its three formal repertoires through its food, and it used the kitchen as the main stage in displaying commitment to its goals. [41] Donors and members of the press regularly were given tours of the kitchen, and staff tour guides pointed out just how love, charity, and therapy entered into kitchen work. These demonstrations had the opposite effect on volunteers listening to these recitations, who quickly realized that the missions were tangential to our "real" work. This bred a certain amount of cynicism, and camaraderie as well, as we chortled at the stories and the presentations we heard Jackie give visitors while we sweated through our chores.

Almost weekly, Kathy or Jackie appeared in the kitchen doorway with well-dressed individuals who beamed nervously at us as they picked their way through narrow passages. Volunteers waved and said hello but then went back to their work. Visitors rarely talked to volunteers, and Bill, the head chef, or Perry, the executive chef, usually kept them at the kitchen's perimeter. After all, the rest of us were trying to get work done. (At times, however, this was not possible. Magazines set up photo shoots in the midst of our work; visiting celebrity volunteers like Rikki Lake and Tyra Banks had to be shown the ropes. When Monique, the evening chef, told us that "MTV is bringing a camera crew later this evening, and I want something colorful for those volunteers to work on," the afternoon shift knew there would be no hope of chopping red peppers.)

Bill and Perry told the visitors that they ran the kitchen with more attention to details than Manhattan's best chefs. Bill rattled off the credentials and job history of each of the chefs as they met the donors. "Lindsay was first in her class at the French Culinary Institute," he would say. Bill talked about how all the food was prepared "by hand" and "from scratch" using fresh ingredients.

Tours progressed from the main cooking and chopping area to the alcove where two chefs prepared the modified meals. Bill told donors that one-third of GLWD clients received meals tailored to their particular nutritional needs. Locating these special meals in one area of the kitchen where they came under the management of two trained chefs emphasized both therapy and love. The specials chefs stressed the attention they paid to the clients by pointing to their shelf of cookbooks, which included nutritional guidelines and fancy vegetarian cookbooks. The chefs rarely mentioned that a large proportion of the special meals were small portions sent to children on the program, nor did they mention that special meals included modifications based on clients' personal tastes and preferences, including vegetarian meals and "no chocolate."[42]

"Charity" was not lacking in the kitchen during the tours, but it was not something the chefs stressed. Jackie and the other upstairs staff understood that the chefs bristled under the rubric of charity, since it distanced their work from restaurant work, so Jackie prompted them to tell visitors about GLWD's policy against accepting food donations.[43] Nevertheless, since many donors were interested in how GLWD responded to shifts in the population of people with AIDS, Jackie also emphasized our ethnically sensitive menus. She always pointed to the crates of tin boxes lining the walls and the industrial-sized ovens, and she talked about the "double meals" the kitchen made for the Friday delivery—sometimes as many as 1,200 entrée portions.

After such a kitchen tour, some visitors ate lunch with the executive director in the tree-lined courtyard behind the youth hostel. Lunch al fresco on a beautiful summer day was a wonderful way for Kathy to demonstrate "what the kitchen can put out." These meals were almost always specially prepared by Perry, even though they were also touted as what "the clients eat." It went without saying that the guests would not eat out of the tin containers that were sent to clients. The kitchen kept a set of china on a high shelf for these occasions.

Perry was dubious whether these special presentations did their job, and he often talked with the volunteers about how irritating it was to make them in the crowded and frenetic kitchen. He was more interested in the sideline catering he occasionally did for board members. Although I was never privy to the exact nature of the arrangements, Perry sometimes devoted an afternoon to steaming lobsters and roasting duck breasts for a board member's private party. One evening I bumped into him on a downtown train. He carefully pulled back the aluminum foil from the large wicker basket he was carrying to reveal the most elaborate crudité arrangement I have ever seen. He was delivering it to an extremely wealthy and well-connected volunteer who was holding a cocktail party.

Such performances, impossible to ignore, gave kitchen volunteers a crash course in the agency's repertoires. We made room for MTV cameras, learned statistics and nutritional tidbits, and ladled out huge portions of food for sick people. We helped put together "emergency meals" for new clients who could not wait until the next day to get something to eat. We produced elaborate Thanksgiving and Christmas feasts, watched Bill or Sean decorate birthday cakes, and helped dye Easter eggs. We took instruction from Charlie on how to chop yucca and batata root for the Puerto Rican beef stew. But we also knew that clients were not getting roast duck. We knew these performances did not tell our real story. This bred a cynical stance in us. [44]

While the kitchen was a staging ground where potential and current donors, board members, and the press looked for demonstrations of love, therapy, and charity, it was also the same space where the meals had to get made. The real time requirements, judgments, and arguments that arose during the press of preparing meals for eight hundred people each day made it clear that the notions of food, love, and charity had little to do with the kitchen's daily tasks. The discrepancies between formal presentations of the missions and this unending labor were hard to miss. Kitchen volunteers and staff focused on other aspects of work.

CHAPTER THREE

Getting the Meals Out: The Daily Life of the Kitchen

Volunteers said that "getting the meals out" was our main task, and they called the ways we went about doing it "what we know to do." We spent comparably little effort articulating the reasons we cooked meals for people with AIDS. "Isn't it obvious?" Emily responded, when I asked her why she cooked meals. While the "upstairs" staff who worked at GLWD focused on how the meals embodied food, love, and charity, "downstairs" staff and volunteers proceeded to cook them without much commentary. Dicing onions left plenty of time to talk, but little of this conversation focused on the reasons for our work or our reasons for volunteering.

"Getting the meals out" allowed volunteers some room to preserve their ideas and memories about what was important in cooking for people with AIDS. For this reason it is important to see kitchen culture "in action," in order to grasp how and when volunteers talked about, and practiced, religion there. To a large degree, volunteers and chefs focused on what was necessary to make and package meals for eight hundred people, and most interpretations of kitchen work—whether aesthetic, political, or spiritual— remained hidden. Volunteers worked hard to keep the kitchen free of what they understood to be ideological incursions, such as when a new chef tried to redefine kitchen work around the notion of "love." Volunteers' cynical and knowing interpretations of the organization's three repertoires helped create a space that was largely free of specific corporate meaning making. That said, the practical routine of "getting the meals out" contained its own culture, its own assumptions, and its own practices, which often broke down in translation from staff to volunteers. The arguments and confusion that ensued about "what we know to do" offered me some early flickers of volunteers' personal readings of their work at GLWD.

Halfway through my time at the agency, the kitchen experienced some turnover in staff, and Bill hired a new chef, Sheldon. Sheldon was a friendly young man with a wife at the Columbia University journalism school. His previous job, he told me on his first day, had been at "the ashram kitchen," referring to the Siddha Yoga Dham Association (SYDA) ashram in South Fallsburg, New York. Bill hired him over other candidates because he was used to working with volunteers and handling large quantities of food.

On his first morning in the kitchen, Bill asked Sheldon to demonstrate how to dice onions. The Tuesday morning group all gathered round, even though we all knew how to cut onions. The chore of dicing onions always began with a chef's demonstration. We were unprepared for Sheldon's, however. He hastily grabbed a whole onion, raised his knife theatrically into the air, and brought it down with a loud smack. Oblivious to us as we cringed and looked at each other in surprise, Sheldon cut off the ends and peeled the halves, wielding his seven-inch chef's knife as if it were a paring knife. He chopped up the onion and tossed the pieces into a white tub. "Easy," he said, adding, "Go to it!" I could tell that the others—Julie, Barbara, and Alexis among them—were not happy about this demonstration.

Sheldon's "sloppy" and "lackadaisical" manner became a large concern for volunteers like Alexis, a twenty-year-old whom I met a few days later for coffee. When I mentioned Sheldon, she said,

I think Sheldon seems very nice, very sweet, but I just think he is a little **much**. I wish I knew the words but—we've been there a long time, you know? You know there are new people, there are people who've been there for five years—but we know what we're doing.

There's a difference between having Sheldon come over and telling you how to cut onions and Bill coming over to tell you how to cut onions. It's—we know if you do the lettuce, it's gotta go a certain way, and if you're on the [pack-out] line that you have to push in the sides of the containers in a certain way.

Alexis was not alone in thinking that Sheldon should listen to volunteers who knew what to do. One day Barbara used her knife to scrape the carrots she had been dicing into the large white communal tub. Sheldon suggested "Hey, folks, why don't we scrape off our boards with the knife blade up instead of down?" When Sean, another chef, asked him why he made this suggestion, he said that it "kept the knife blade from dulling." Barbara did not listen to him, however, and she made sure he noticed that she continued to scrape her board blade down. "That supercilious punk!" she laughed to me later; "using the royal 'we'!" She commented on how she had said nothing when he made the suggestion but had continued to scrape her board "with the blade down," and how Sheldon turned bright red as she did.

The next week Barbara shook her head when Sean showed us the cut he had received when a volunteer, following Sheldon's "blade up" advice, cut him across the knuckles. "Yeah, we had to throw a whole bunch of carrots away because we were worried the blood got in the big tub," he said as I wrinkled my nose. Sean showed us again how to scrape the cut onions into the tub without using a knife. "Don't do it like Sheldon tells you," Sean added.

Coincidence or not, volunteers could not help discussing Sheldon's accidents in relation to his vegetarianism. Sheldon's job as the new evening chef required him to cook meat in large quantities. He never started the job without groaning and grimacing. While complaining, he told us about his previous job at "Ganga's" ashram, where he cooked vegetarian meals for a thousand people. He often described in great detail the meatless recipes he cooked at the side of Japanese and Indian monks. He told us about soy sauce reductions with shitake mushrooms, nasturtiums, and brown rice to persuade us that vegetarian food could be just as delicious as meals with meat.

Sheldon believed—and tried to tell us—that his techniques were based on love and care for food and people. Volunteers did not see it that way, however. Sheldon's frequent kitchen accidents and unrelenting desire to make the kitchen vegetarian frustrated volunteers. He found few allies in his quest to make food more loving: even vegetarian volunteers shook their heads when he pushed them. "C'mon, Tanya, you're a vegetarian," he cried as she wrinkled her nose while dicing turkey breast for the next day's soup. "I am, yes, but I'm not *sick*," she answered, continuing to dice. She argued that it was important to give the clients "what *they* need," separating her own diet from the diets of those she cooked for. In deploying the language of therapy, she provided a mild rebuke to Sheldon's interpretation of "loving" food.

Sheldon's actions also gave more credence to volunteers' underlying commitments to the various logics of home cooking. On hearing Sheldon suggest that the kitchen would be calmer and more peaceful if we used less meat, Julie sniffed, "Well, of course it would be, for Sheldon. . . . But I would never feed anyone something I wouldn't feed my own grandchildren." And as Roger put it, "We call them clients because we're working for *them*." Julie in particular associated this with the judgments she made when she fed her family. They suggested that their methods were more loving, since they gave clients "enticing and familiar" food, not foreign and alienating soy sauce reductions. Julie's and Roger's arguments situated them within the same circle as the clients.

The self-conscious irony with which volunteers drew on the formal repertoires to gain authority became most obvious to me one day shortly before Sheldon quit, only four weeks into his tenure. Sheldon showed us a bad burn, telling us hot fat had splashed on him the day before when he dropped a pan of pork tenderloins. Pointing to the six-inch red welt, he commented with exasperation, "I rubbed aloe on it right away, and it still looks like this." He went on, "I wish we didn't use meat. After you stop eating it, you never notice it. Especially when you have other good recipes."

Not getting any response, he continued. "If the food is *delicious*, they'd like it. And if we didn't cook with meat, then I wouldn't have this burn."

"Oh, you can burn yourself on anything," Monique said dryly.

"Yeah, Sandra burned herself on tea, just the other day!" Judy offered.

"And it was herbal tea, at that!" Sandra laughed, showing Sheldon a small red blotch on her hand.

Sheldon waved them off. "But you know, you can get all the protein you need in other sources. I just can't stand eating meat!"

"Well," I said, trying to soften everyone's growing irritation, "I think moderation is important. Everything in moderation."

"Except *love*," Monique said, smiling and batting her eyelashes. We all started to laugh—even Sheldon.

Sandra's comment about herbal tea suggested a certain sympathy toward vegetarianism, but it also made the point that she thought the differences in practice between nonvegetarian and vegetarian cooking were minimal. Her jokes (and Monique's) demonstrated that we all knew "food was love," but that we didn't take it seriously. That is, we didn't "believe" that food was love in any one particular way. Sheldon did not last much longer: he left without fanfare, and no one (it seemed) mourned his departure. I bumped into him several months later in Balducci's, a fancy downtown food shop. He winced when he saw me, as if reliving a bad moment. I felt bad, smiled weakly, and turned into the produce section.

Even though the volunteers "knew what to do" and actively argued against those who, like Sheldon, attempted to put a specific ideological spin on our joint efforts, our shared practical culture of getting the meals out was not as purely practical or as "obvious" as volunteers suggested. "What everybody knew" loosely followed the structures of professional cooking as practiced in city restaurants and large catering firms.[1] Since most volunteers learned to cook in home kitchens, and did most of their cooking there, what we "knew to do" was not as obvious or straightforward as they suggested. These practices, including kitchen rhythms, spatial arrangements, modes of efficient work, and rules about cleanliness, had to be learned. Such learning happened piecemeal at GLWD, and there was little articulation of the differences between home cooking and GLWD kitchen cooking (in part because differences were not always wholly opposed, in theory or practice). As a result, even though everyone "knew what to do," not everyone did what we knew. Volunteers constantly broke the rules, exposing the meanings and expectations that accompanied their practices.

WHAT WE KNOW TO DO: IMAGINING KITCHEN TIME AND SPACE

The kitchen's shared culture focused on getting the meals out. The mantra "as long as the meals get out" soothed flaring tempers and aching backs: it provided a potent goal that smoothed over all sorts of differences in personality. In the crush of the daily workload and the cramped space, all hands and all minds focused on organizing time, space, and bodies and avoiding accidents. In this way the kitchen's daily routine constituted a world where expectations were fairly obvious, where methods and rules were fairly precise, and where, as volunteers would explain to me, everyone knew what to do.

Getting the Meals Out

Although the kitchen probably seemed spacious when GLWD served only 250 clients each day, it was barely large enough to contain the raw ingredients, equipment, and human bodies required to prepare meals for 800. The two walk-in refrigerators were stacked to the top with white tubs filled with celery, diced potatoes, cooling bulgur for tabouli, onions, carrots, lettuce, and countless other things. (Mort, an engineer, joked that prospective chefs had to take a special test in spatial relations before they were hired.) The evening chef spent an hour each afternoon rearranging tubs and crates so we could get to what we needed.

The kitchen day started when the baker arrived at 11:00 P.M. He worked alone, making pies and cakes from scratch until 5:00 A.M., when two volunteers came to help him "pack out" the desserts. The music switched from show tunes to Top 40 when two day chefs and one specials chef also arrived at 5:00 to assemble the day's entrée and vegetables and to mix and heat the soup.

The next volunteers arrived at 7:00 to ladle the soup into plastic pint containers. Van drivers, shaking off sleep, carried the hot soup to the pack-out room and allocated the containers according to their routes. While the kitchen volunteers and chefs set up the assembly line to pack out the entrées, the drivers opened the walk-in refrigerator and pulled out salads packed the night before.

At 8:15 volunteers and chefs collected to pack out the hot entrées, vegetables, sauce, and side dishes. The tins' contents were piping hot: volunteers passed the containers along quickly to keep from burning their fingers. Right behind the line at the dishwashing sink, a porter and a volunteer furiously tried to keep up with the empty dishes and hotel pans.

The drivers packed the hot entrées in insulated tubs and waited their turns to load their vans and leave. By 10:00 the meals were on their way through the city. Most would be dropped at neighborhood distribution centers and picked up later by delivery volunteers; the drivers and their assistants would deliver the rest. Back in the kitchen, the volunteers were wiping down the counters and sweeping the floors. The porters finished the dishes while the volunteers stood by the coatrack drinking coffee and eating fresh coffeecake. Most who had come in for the pack out were getting ready to leave. They said their good-byes (and marked on the schedule when they would next return) as the chefs listed the day's tasks on the large chalkboard in the corner.

Between 10:00 and noon, vegetable, meat, and dairy deliveries appeared. Porters packed the new ingredients into the recently emptied refrigerators. Fresh volunteers started to arrive to stand, chop, and talk for a three-hour shift. These smaller groups, usually between five and ten assembled at any time during the day, switched the music to classical (over the porters' objections). By 3:00 the fresh chicken or beef stock, bubbling since late morning, needed to be strained. The client services director called down with the following day's final meal count. Just before 6:00, volunteers for the largest shift started to assemble, many changing from their work clothes into jeans in the basement bathrooms. The first volunteers to arrive claimed the sharpest and newest knives and the best spots at the long table. With counter space at a premium, they placed custom-fitted wooden boards over the sinks so everyone would have room to work. Later they mopped the floors, washed the remaining dishes, and took out the trash. On a good night, the last volunteers would leave between 9:00 and 10:00 for a meal at a diner two blocks down on Broadway. The kitchen would be dark for two hours. At 11:00 the baker arrived again.

This stylized portrait suggests the kitchen's daily pace, but it gives little sense of what happened on any given day. In reality, a spilled pan of lasagna or too few volunteers pushed back the schedule, a late delivery forced the chefs to rethink the next day's menu, or the baker went on vacation. Like chefs in most restaurant kitchens, GLWD chefs mounted an ongoing battle against too little space and too little time. Yet they also faced what appeared to be a relentless increase in clients and directed a workforce with varied skills and concerns about safe and efficient cooking. These realities made this portrait of the kitchen's daily work more fiction than fact. Yet when asked, volunteers and chefs alike would tell me a story something like the one I just presented. The daily schedule was the first part of what everyone knew, and it told a tale where efficient corporate activity focused on getting out the meals.

The Way "We" Do Things Here:
Being Efficient, and Guarding against Contagion and Contamination

When I asked Emily, a forty-three-year-old Episcopalian volunteer what she liked most about working in the kitchen, she said without missing a beat: "I come in and I open up a can of tuna fish and I drain it and mash it up. I know exactly what to do. And I like that." Emily was not alone, most volunteers who worked for more than two or three weeks learned the routine. Onions were always cut in the same fashion. Emily knew how to find room to drain tuna. There were not many surprises in what we were supposed to do. These expectations focused on the most efficient ways to get the work done rather than on working toward affective goals such as love or therapy.[2] "Everybody gets dirty here," Emily noted; "there's no sense of one-upmanship. Everyone's doing their best to be helpful."

Volunteers like Emily focused on what they did together, not on ide-ologies, beliefs, or politics. "You meet so many different people here," volunteers said to me again and again when I asked how they saw their re-lations with other volunteers. Volunteers' sense that they could be unified around a concrete task despite their "diversity" provided room for them to talk together about things they might not have broached had they assumed they shared them. At the same time, the assumption that volunteers did not have much in common except a willingness to get dirty and do the work placed a burden on them to demonstrate that they did know what they were supposed to do, even when those rules were not clear.

GLWD's practices had to be learned, given that the kitchen operated very differently from home kitchens. This was obvious to all who took note of its industrial-sized ovens, mixers, and cookers. A few volunteers who followed GLWD in the move from the West Park Presbyterian Church to the youth hostel stopped coming after their first encounters with the "giant and unsanitary soup vats" in the new kitchen. GLWD needed the industrial-sized equipment to make hundreds of meals, but the equipment also underscored that the agency's definition of "home cooking" did not mean chintz curtains and enjoying a lazy cup of tea while the pie baked.

Even though the main time pressure here came early in the morning rather than at the dinner hour, GLWD's kitchen operated like many restaurant kitchens. All the chefs I worked with during my field research had experience in restaurants, and they ran the kitchen with expectations learned in those institutions. Their responsibilities mirrored those they would have had in restaurant kitchens: the executive chef set the menu and ordered supplies from the same distributors that delivered to other New York restaurants. Board of Health inspectors made the rounds at GLWD just as they did in other restaurant kitchens, so the agency retained a kitchen consultant to conduct unannounced checks on kitchen cleanliness. We occasionally saw her poking around with a flashlight, looking for roaches and rodent droppings and pointing out the stray bottle of cough syrup on the pantry shelf.

Most new volunteers realized (if they had not already assumed) that the chefs tried to make decisions that balanced the need for speed with the need for quality preparation. Thrown into the work on my first day, I quickly learned that "we" cut whole heads of romaine lettuce *before* we washed them. This took less time than breaking down the heads leaf by leaf, washing and spinning them dry, and then cutting them into pieces. When I inquired why we cut rather than tore the lettuce, others pointed out that even though cutting bruises the leaves more than tearing, tearing up four cases of romaine took too much time and caused too much waste. In the days that followed I learned much about how we did things. Without anyone's spelling it out, I learned how to set up a pack-out assembly line, found that volunteers working with meat stood at the smaller counter to avoid contamination, and discovered that clean kitchen cloths were sometimes hidden behind the extra hats on the coatrack.

Everybody knew we had to guard against contamination. Most volunteers were familiar with the problems caused by salmonella and other bacteria found in raw and undercooked meat. Others educated me in the pathogens sometimes found in other sources, including New York City's tap water. While all kitchens confront contamination and invest in symbolic and practical methods to combat it, [3] God's Love We Deliver felt heightened concern about contamination's potentially deadly effects. In a word, spoiled, old, or improperly cooked meals could "kill a client."[4]

This worry (and potential) required certain actions. Any food that fell on the floor stayed there. We washed our knives and our boards after we finished each job, then cleaned the counters with antibacterial spray. The chefs tried to keep meat and dairy products in one refrigerator and vegetables in the other. This, they said, cut down on the chance that raw meat or eggs (which might contain bacteria but would be cooked) might contaminate vegetables (which might remain raw). Everyone wore a clean cotton apron supplied by GLWD, a baseball cap (we brought these ourselves), and latex gloves. This clothing ensured that contaminating hands and hair did not come in contact with food. Wearing disposable gloves and washable aprons made cleaning up between jobs rather easy. We changed gloves before beginning a new job or after sticking our hands in dishwater, and after sneezing. We also changed gloves—and aprons—after working with raw meat.

Although dirty vegetables and raw meat posed real problems for clients, human blood was the most troublesome contaminant in the kitchen. Some volunteers and chefs were HIV positive, we knew from gossip, but we rarely talked about AIDS. AIDS entered the kitchen in our work and our actions more than in our discussions. Work came to a halt whenever anyone got cut or even nicked. A chef inspected the wound and dressed it with bandages from the first aid kit (or someone called an ambulance). Back at the counter, someone else would clean up the site, dumping all food on the board into the trash and washing the wounded volunteer's knife and board with bleach. The rest of us milled around during the cleanup, telling stories about cuts others had received and listening to the inevitable chef's lecture to be more careful. The veritable Superfund site duly cleaned, we would get back to work.

"It feels so weird to cut yourself here in this kitchen!" muttered Amy, a sixty-year-old matron with manicured nails, after an eggshell pierced her latex gloves and cut her finger. She did not elaborate but came back to our work area wearing a Band-Aid and two layers of latex gloves. She laughed when Sean joked that she was wearing "double protection." Amy did not signal whether she caught on to Sean's allusion, but the rest of us chuckled uneasily to have the association of latex gloves with latex condoms put forward in such a way. Blood's potential for contamination and its symbolic purchase on this AIDS organization nevertheless hovered over all of our work with knives (which was most of our work). It undoubtedly led those of us without professional experience to cut more tentatively than the chefs would have liked.

SUBVERTING THE KNOWN:
HOME AND PROFESSIONAL COOKING PRACTICES

Volunteers constantly contradicted, subverted, and ignored what "we knew" to do. For the most part they knew what the rules were, so breaking them did not signal ignorance. They wanted to do the right thing. Nevertheless, they often forgot (or disregarded) the rules, requiring the chefs or other volunteers to decide whether to correct or ignore the infraction.

One way to think about why volunteers broke the rules is to focus on the habitual elements of culture. We perform many acts without thinking about them or, as Bourdieu suggests, without the idea that they should even be thought of.[5] There is indeed a large habitual dimension to cooking. The way I hold a knife is not something I think about consciously. I just pick it up and chop. I learned my technique, I imagine, first by watching my mother and grandmother, later by watching Julia Child and Jacques Pepin on PBS, and most of all, through much practice. I do not think about what I am doing, nor do I (regularly) think about my mother or grandmother or Julia while I am chopping onions for dinner. I imagine this is an obvious point for anyone who does much regular chopping. We hold a knife the way that "feels" right or natural, even though at some point we had to learn what was natural.

Just because I do not think about my mother or grandmother while I cook does not mean they are not part of the practice, however. Practices are not merely habits; they are freighted with culture, memory, and experience. While chopping or cutting might be habitual or rote, it is hardly mindless. It reproduces various experiences, notions of worth and authority, and relationships. It also produces a result: those who chop onions well can tell the difference (in texture, appearance, and even taste) between an onion chopped with a knife and one chopped in a food processor. It is not surprising, then, that volunteers who went to GLWD to do something for people with AIDS, to help the sick, to care for the needy, and to make delicious food for others used the methods they genuinely thought were best. Nor is it surprising that their ideas and practices were not always easy to explain to others.

Of course, what feels right when I chop an onion for dinner in my own house might feel terrible after I've diced a hundred onions at GLWD. I for one learned that my home cooking practices did not play out comfortably in GLWD's kitchen. In my first few weeks I went home exhausted, with tired feet and an aching back. I developed a callus on my right hand where the chef's knife rubbed. I most obviously did not possess the techniques that would minimize my calluses and my aches.

I was not the only one who failed to master the professional kitchen methods while volunteering. The chefs had little time to offer individual tutorials, except for the cursory demonstrations they gave at the beginning of each task. But I had things to do besides learning new tricks. I listened to other people, told jokes and stories, and thought about the people I was cooking for. The other volunteers also had other things to do in the kitchen. When Perry fumed that "volunteers talk too much" or that they thwarted his attempts to create order, I found myself siding with them. Getting the meals out was the most important thing we did, but making that work meaningful and important was also necessary.

Navigating Authority: Home Cooks and Professional Chefs

In most restaurant kitchens, the line of authority between chefs and porters is settled within a fairly narrow range of tasks and expectations. This was also true of staff relationships at God's Love We Deliver: the porters took orders from the chefs and attended to various scheduled routines. Since they worked in the kitchen forty hours or more every week, they knew when to mop the floors, skim the stock, wash the dishes, and take out the trash without being reminded. Chefs were accountable within a hierarchy established by seniority and position, but they often shared jobs.

Several aspects of our work kept such established lines of authority from applying directly to volunteers. Volunteers, most obviously, were not paid employees, and their obligations were moral rather than contractual. They were supposed to do what chefs asked, but they could come and go as they wished. Likewise, most came for only three or four hours each week. Their limited shifts provided little time to apprentice in particular positions or receive systematic training. Things might have been different had volunteers worked more hours or had there been different social cues to establish the chefs' authority. As it was, volunteers' priorities and privileges allowed them room to define kitchen expertise in ways that diverged from the chefs'.

Older women volunteers, for instance, had authority and expertise by virtue of their age and gender. Old enough to be mothers to the (mostly) younger gay male chefs, Barbara, Julie, and the others often offered unsolicited advice to Lee, Sean, and even Bill. A few of us joked that Sean was "looking for a mother," given that he often ended up at their sides. Some of these older volunteers had lost sons to AIDS, and the attraction and love between them and the chefs appeared to be mutual. Mothers are known for cooking for the sick, and their expertise was hard to trump in the course of daily kitchen events. Mothers, one might expect, are also hard to correct, especially when it comes to cooking. When Sean took Barbara and Julie's advice on matters such as looking for an apartment or a roommate, it became harder for him not to take their advice on cooking.

In a related vein, chefs sometimes relied on volunteers ("mothers" and nonmothers) to make their own judgments about how to cook. When Sean asked Nancy, a new volunteer, to help pick through two cases of cherry tomatoes and throw out the rotten or soft ones, she asked Sean's opinion in every borderline case. After assessing several, Sean told her to "just do whatever you'd do at home." This puzzled her, since she did not consider herself a knowledgeable cook. Never in her life had she seen so many cherry tomatoes, she muttered. Sean's comment did not surprise me, however. I had heard it many times before and recognized the chefs' expectation that volunteers were competent enough to translate their practices into this space. While some were happy with this autonomy and authority, those with shaky cooking skills found little comfort in it.

When things ran smoothly, shifts in authority from chefs to volunteers could go unnoticed. In most cases volunteers deferred to the chefs' authority and looked to them for hints, help, and honest criticism. Likewise, chefs tried to keep in mind individual volunteers' abilities and limitations, as in giving feebler ones the chore of destemming parsley and asking more skilled workers to oversee roasting chicken breasts. Nevertheless, when chefs criticized volunteers, or when volunteers challenged chefs' authority, the differences in our practices became much more apparent. Such arguments over authority or breaking the rules also exposed how limited our shared practices were.

Cooking for Many or Cooking for One: Efficiency Undone

Several months before my field research started, Bill asked the last volunteer shift to trim and cut up several hundred pounds of raw beef for the next day's stir-fry. This was an arduous task in any circumstances. When several volunteers asked for another job, apparently citing their revulsion to working with raw beef, he told them he didn't have anything else for them to do. He had decided earlier in the day to save this one large job for the evening, expecting that there would be enough people on hand to make light work. An argument broke out, and fifteen volunteers took off, leaving and Bill and three remaining volunteers to work on the beef. They stayed on the job until after midnight.

Bill was both indignant and mortified, he told Ganga and Hannah the next day. He thought he was doing everyone a favor by leaving this one large, unpleasant task for the largest volunteer group. Leaving it until all the vegetables and salads were put away was likewise a very sanitary decision. Ganga and Hannah drafted a letter asking those who walked out to take some time to reconsider their commitment. Stone wrote, "The gift of your time is best utilized by us when it is given unencumbered and without reservation" and reminded them that they could not choose tasks or refuse to work with meat.

Of the fifteen who walked out that evening, twelve did not return. Several wrote letters explaining why, castigating Bill's behavior and Stone's interpretation of the event. Said one in protest, "I was confident that, as only a few volunteers on our shift really felt strongly about not cutting meat, some sort of solution would be found." "This vegetarian issue totally ignores the problem," another argued. Bill had not been sensitive to their desires and had failed to balance them against the necessity of getting the meals out. Another wrote angrily that Bill had no "sympathy to those of us who needed to rest from time to time because of back strain from performing the same task for hours at a time." A fourth stated hotly that Bill "has not once thanked the group for their time, and has repeatedly chastised us for minor 'infractions' (such as not cutting the onions small enough) and large ones (such as not caring about the clients)."[6]

Although this controversy was unusual in scope (and documentation), it highlights some of the differences in the ways volunteers and chefs perceived kitchen work. The chefs focused on orchestrating the entire day's meal, culminating in the early morning pack out. Most volunteers, in contrast, focused on the work completed within the three hours they volunteered. From their perspective, lengthy and repetitive tasks made it difficult for volunteers to find fulfillment in their work.

Barbara talked with me about this one morning as we stood side by side cutting onions. She rolled up her silk shirtsleeves, dropped her gold bracelets into her pants pocket, and started in on the task. The three other volunteers present had excused themselves from the job (Tamar was allergic to onions, and the other two opted to wash dishes rather than chop). Given the huge pile before us, we calculated that we would be cutting onions for the rest of the morning. After an hour or so, Barbara turned to Sean as he walked past our table.

"Did you know that we're doing this job now two weeks in a row?" she asked.

"I'm sorry, I didn't realize it—no—but we have to get these things done for soup, you know."

"My wrist is about to give out on me," Barbara said. Following Sean with her eyes, she called out, "We're not professionals. I've trained cooks in cooking school, but I'm not a *professional.*" She paused, then turned to me. "Let me tell you, it used to be different around here."

"How so?" I asked.

"Many, many things were different," she said. "Mostly, it was a lot more fun. We *never* spent three hours doing just one thing. This is kind of boring; two weeks in a row we do onions for three hours. Now, it's hard to feel that you're really helping someone. You don't see as much of the process. You just see one thing. Like these onions. And you know, there just wasn't so much emphasis on standards." she added.

We worked in silence for a few more minutes. Barbara spoke up again, adding, "Not that I mind standards. I think the quality of the food has gone up recently, to tell you the truth."

Barbara did not mind what she saw as an increasing emphasis on standards, but she wanted to stress to me that she did not like her role in the way these standards were carried out. She felt less connection to the food she cooked when she did the same thing for three hours. Barbara calculated her role in terms of what she completed. She thought of cooking as a process in which she could identify her individual part. She recognized that as client numbers grew it would be harder to assess her role in the day's meal, and she saw no easy answer to this conundrum.

As the angry letters about Bill's "insensitivity" demonstrate, many volunteers thought that attention to particular standards such as cutting onions correctly was a minor point that was unconnected to whether volunteers cared about the clients. Chefs like Bill (and volunteers like Barbara), on the other hand, saw adherence to standards and care for clients as part of a whole. If some onions were cut small and others large, then some would be raw while others turned to mush. In the end, the meals would not taste as good. Dicing onions to the same size ensured quality and demonstrated a corporate and individual concern for clients that went beyond individual prerogative. Volunteers like Barbara understood their contribution to the agency's work from an individual perspective and focused on the specific tasks they completed each week.

In doing this, volunteers recreated intimacy within the kitchen's chaos and momentum. Sandra similarly thought of her work as intimate, individual, and important. As she put it, every day that she worked at GLWD she "put a spoonful of food" in someone's mouth. This is exactly what she had done for her brother in the months before he died. Sandra told me that in cooking at God's Love We Deliver "I felt like I was still feeding my brother. Especially when I started doing prep work in the kitchen and I was cutting, I was ever mindful of the ways he liked things cooked." Sandra kept thinking about what she prepared and how the clients would find the meals, and she imagined they would be people like her brother.

When another friend of Sandra's became a client, he confirmed her notions about cooking meals for particular individuals. As she told me,

I remember we were making meatloaf and we were putting green peppers in the meatloaf, which I felt personally were difficult to digest. Meatloaf as it is can be quite rich. And I remember thinking, "Peppers?"

And then my friend called me the next day and said, "You might tell some of those people there at work that putting green peppers in the meatloaf is a little hard to digest!"

*And I said, "You must have just gotten the meal that I cooked!" It was a full circle. I remember thinking, "Gee, maybe he was eating the **actual** dish that I cooked. And I remember we packed it, and sealed the containers, and I thought, "Who knows? Maybe he got **my meal**."*

This exchange solidified Sandra's self-understanding that her practices worked in the clients' best interests. It also demonstrates just how specific she believed her role to be. Sandra remembered not only cutting the peppers but packing the finished meatloaf in a tin and sealing it. Given that Sandra volunteered in the afternoons, her hand in the meatloaf meal had been only to cut up the peppers and perhaps mix the meat—certainly not to cook it or pack it out. These tasks were completed the next day. Despite all this, Sandra could still say, "Who knows? Maybe he got *my meal.*"

Barbara and Sandra located the power of their work within individual acts and meals well made, not within the efficient production of food in quantity, guided by "professionals." Such power resided in the actions as much as in the words volunteers used to describe them. When Bill criticized Sandra's method of cutting onions, explaining why we needed to cut them as uniformly as possible, she angrily left, mystifying the chefs and most of the volunteers as well. Chefs' unsolicited suggestions were sometimes interpreted as criticism. Nevertheless, as even Barbara acknowledged, volunteers' more intimate notions of kitchen work could disrupt the routine.

Clean Kitchens: Drawing the Line against Contamination

As authority was defined differently within "home" or "professional" cooking practices, so were notions of guarding against contamination and contagion. This was evident in myriad daily events. When Judy and Melinda dropped a potato on the floor, they picked it up and washed it off rather than throwing it away or leaving it on the floor as they were instructed. Judy (and countless others) casually and constantly snacked on the raw vegetables we chopped. A few volunteers worked without gloves, citing latex allergies, and others with long hair only symbolically tucked their locks under their baseball caps. We sneezed into our arms rather than our hands so we would not have to change our gloves. When (as usual) there were no clean kitchen cloths to be found, we used cloths fished from the laundry hamper to wipe up our areas. We dipped our dirty knives in dishwater and let them drip dry rather than finding a scrubber to do the job.

I often wondered how we could ignore these rules as frequently as we did, especially when the consequences were so serious. Contamination was a potentially deadly problem for clients: they were not anonymous, faceless restaurant patrons who would blithely eat a spicy vegetable stew made with half-rotten tomatoes. To be sure, limited time and space made it impossible to undo every contaminating act and begin again from scratch.[7] When a coworker and I fished out five compact discs we had accidentally knocked into the chicken stock, we whispered to each other that the broth would be brought to a simmer the following morning when the chefs assembled the soup. Heating it up would (we reasoned) probably kill any germs lingering on the discs. Besides, no one had seen us do it, and no one had time to make more stock. The kitchen's "backstage" properties, and its distance from the clients, made such infractions easier to gloss over.[8] Yet these considerations did not adequately explain why volunteers did the things they did.

Their cooking practices were learned in home kitchens, where standards of cleanliness and contamination were built on the assumption that the kitchen was more clean than dirty.[9] Guarding against contamination and contagion suggested, in contrast, that the kitchen and its workers were dirty unless defined otherwise. The gloves and other attire we wore marked us as dirty beings who had to be kept away from the food. Rules about not picking food up off the floor and not snacking on the vegetables we chopped reinforced the assumption that whatever was not food was dirty.

Finessing the professionally based distinctions between clean and dirty in the cramped kitchen required skill. For instance, Monique drew a centimeter-wide boundary between raw and cooked chicken by placing hot pans of roasted chicken breasts directly *above* pans of raw chicken waiting for their turn in the oven. Kitty asked Monique how she could do something so "unsanitary." Monique pointed out that the cooked chicken was above the raw chicken, so it was unlikely that the raw would touch or drip on the cooked.

Bill offended Libby, an older volunteer who was Judy's and Sandra's friend, when he chastised her for washing a pineapple in the dishwashing and pot-scrubbing sink. She saw no difference between sinks devoted to scrubbing dirty pans and sinks devoted to scrubbing vegetables (after all, most home kitchens only have one sink). Given that she did not understand the boundary she had transgressed, she interpreted Bill's criticism as an arbitrary and mean-spirited personal attack. Bill's attempt to maintain this boundary led to an ongoing argument that eventually disrupted the long-standing camaraderie of the Wednesday afternoon volunteer group.

Volunteers' assumptions about the kitchen as a clean site similarly influenced the ways they understood contagion. One day Libby became vexed to distraction when the man slicing jalapeño peppers next to her told her that he "had AIDS." She marched over to one of the chefs and asked him in a carrying voice, "Did you know that guy has AIDS? Is that all right, for him to be working in here?" She was astonished that GLWD chefs let a "sick person" work there. Allowing sick people into the kitchen was not in keeping with safe cooking. Libby drew the boundary between clean and dirty, sick and healthy, at the doorway of the kitchen rather than on the body (with gloves and aprons) or the food. Challenging the policies about the presence of PWAs and, by extension, the boundaries of safe cooking put the chefs on alert. In the end, their ongoing questioning of the appropriateness of Libby's behavior would lead to her departure.

PRESERVING "WHAT WE KNOW TO DO":
DRAWING ON THE MISSIONS

Although on most days "what we know to do" helped preserve some space for the volunteers to continue cooking with the intimacy of home kitchens in mind, at times chefs' practices and priorities challenged or infringed on them. Chefs turned to mechanical ways of finishing products and used shortcuts that, while foreign in homes, are rather usual in large-scale kitchens. Some of these processes and procedures, particularly ones that took away volunteers' hand work, became points of tension. Volunteers then argued with the chefs, often by drawing on the language in GLWD's missions. Just as volunteers and staff winked knowingly at the overly ideological ways Sheldon approached "love," volunteers consciously drew on the authority of the missions of love (and at times therapy and charity) to preserve the standards they had come to observe in the kitchen. I conclude with one such example, in which the Tuesday morning volunteers argued with Sean to preserve a tedious "handmade" method of making egg salad.

I arrived few minutes after ten, finding Sean in charge and already running behind schedule. Bill, Sean told us, was in Miami staging a runway show for a designer friend. While Sean helped us quarter several hundred pounds of new red potatoes, he asked Charlie, a new chef, to make the egg salad in the industrial-sized mixer.

Usually we made egg salad by pressing shelled hard-boiled eggs through large metal sieves into white plastic tubs. Then we mixed in mayonnaise, celery, minced red onion, relish, mustard, salt, and pepper by hand. This time Charlie did not ask us to help him press the eggs through the sieves. Instead, he dumped half the eggs and their seasonings into the mixer and turned it on. Eyebrows rose around the mounds of red potatoes. I waited for someone to say something.

Sean, oblivious to the looks darting around the table, tossed the potatoes with olive oil and rosemary and began to tell us how wonderful it was to have Bill out of the kitchen. "My blood pressure goes down every time he leaves—he wants everything done perfectly. But he doesn't realize how long it takes. Like, the other day, he told a volunteer to squeeze the extra water from the parsley after we chopped it so Chris could use the juice to make an infusion. Do you have any idea how long that took?" We laughed with him at the absurdity of the task.

Sean continued, nodding his head in Charlie's direction. "Take that job of making egg salad. Charlie's doing it in about fifteen minutes when usually it takes, like, an hour at least to push them through the grate."

Charlie called out from over the noise of the mixer, "Yeah, this is how we did it at the Sheraton. We cooked for lots more people than this."

Barbara cleared her throat and said, in a challenging way, "Why does it matter if it takes a little longer?"

"It's much more sanitary this way," Charlie answered, calling again over the hum of the mixer.

Sean nodded, adding, "Because you can have bacteria growing pretty fast, especially on eggs, and salmonella. This way we can get it back into the refrigerator quickly. That is just the kind of thing that Bill never thinks about."

Roger then asked, "Don't you think the texture is different that way, in the mixer?"

"Yeah, isn't it all mushy when he puts it in the mixer?" Barbara chimed in—"I hate egg salad that has no texture. It gets like paste."

Sean, startled by the volunteers' tone, shook his head adamantly. "No, no it isn't—it's the same. It tastes the same." He put down his knife and walked over to Charlie. He took a taste, and the two conferred. Charlie shrugged his shoulders and Sean came back over to our table to toss potatoes without a word. Charlie finished the second batch of egg salad in the mixer before we had finished with the potatoes. When Bill returned the next week we went back to mashing and mixing the egg salad by hand.

Making egg salad in the mixer was both more efficient and more sanitary than doing it by hand. Sean assumed that these were the most important aspects of making food in large quantities for people with AIDS, especially when he was running behind schedule. Roger and Barbara thought otherwise: moments after laughing with Sean about Bill's crazy, time consuming tasks, they argued against a shortcut. Like Sean, they based their argument on the expectation that clients' needs came first; but they started with the idea that aesthetics was first among those needs. "Food is love" overcame practical kitchen issues, including efficiency and food safety. It was not enough to just get the meals out. GLWD was not the Sheraton, and preserving the texture of egg salad was just as important, if not more so, since it also preserved volunteers' practices and by extension their authority, meaning, and imaginative work.

Appealing to the missions justified cooking practices in terms that everyone acknowledged as legitimate and that at the same time allowed volunteers to preserve practices that stood apart from the standards of what "we know to do." Of course, given that the volunteers and chefs all "knew" the missions had more symbolic than practical importance, using them also risked further cynical comments. As such, when volunteers' used the mission repertoires they drew to the surface a question about what "really" propelled their interests and arguments: in other words, they called to mind other important, though unspoken, reasons for cooking for people with AIDS.

THE NOT SO SECRET LIFE OF VOLUNTEERING:
DISCLOSING PERSONAL PRACTICES

Despite—or perhaps because of—our shared practical knowledge and common goal of "getting the meals out," volunteers put divergent practices, meanings, and metaphors to work, often unwittingly but sometimes quite consciously. This work went on largely under the surface of the flow of kitchen work. As long as everyone participated, volunteers did not question others' actions or motivations. Whenever a circumstance arose that might have required disclosing such personal motivations, a surplus of institutional repertoires allowed volunteers to argue for continuity (or change) without directly articulating the idea.

Even though most of our individual differences were ignored in the course of our daily work, our shared culture was constantly being challenged and chipped away by the tug of personal motivations and practices. Our culture of knowing "what to do" therefore often served less as an overarching template of meaning than as a bumpy grid on which we piled all manner of metaphors, actions, and meanings that came to define our work. Volunteers' own home-based cooking practices changed as they (however incompletely) learned professional ones. They navigated a variety of justifications for their work and coupled these notions with their own private, preconstructed, and ongoing ways of cooking and caring for others.[10] Their "own" practices changed as they came to life in the kitchen.[11]

As a result, then, even though we did not explicitly hash out the reasons or purposes of our work, they were not completely hidden. They bubbled to the surface during arguments. We alluded to them in the course of daily conversations about other topics. We talked about movies, gossip, tennis, and restaurants, but we also talked about things that mattered to us, sometimes obliquely, other times using hints and guesses. In the midst of the clatter and focus on the work at hand and "getting the meals out," conversation about values happened. As we will see in the chapters that follow, translating personal motivations, notions of responsibility, and the like into action and conversations required other kinds of work.

CHAPTER FOUR

Religious Practice in the Kitchen

Volunteers gave kitchen work all kinds of meanings, from the intimately biographical to the grandly political.[1] In this chapter I focus specifically on the ways they assigned religious and spiritual meanings to what they did.[2] As I explained in the previous chapter, volunteers did not talk about such things in the course of their kitchen work. Yet almost all had a story (or several) about why they worked in the kitchen and about how the work mattered. Volunteers who showed up week after week were committed to their work, and I turned to interviews and informal conversation to learn more about their reasons. Here I examine those stories and discussions to see what it meant to act and live religion at GLWD.[3]

Interviews were useful windows into volunteers' personal, civic, political, and religious commitments. The stories volunteers told were meaningful to them and to me insofar as they were relevant to their own experiences and insofar as they related to my questions.[4] Like windows, interviews provided only partial views of the range of ways they could speak of what they did.[5] Interviews by nature demonstrate our limited ability to ascertain "meaning," even though they can provide some sense of the associations and connections individuals draw on to explain their actions.

Given the symbolic weight of food, cooking, and eating and the value many religious traditions place on feeding both spiritual and physical hunger, I wanted to investigate how, and whether, volunteers who found their work to include a religious element would relate it to the carrots and the potatoes we scrubbed.[6] Many did indeed make such connections. For instance, Cynthia stated, "Whatever work I do here, even if it's counting containers, it's as though I'm praying." Lydia, another volunteer, once piped up in the middle of an uncharacteristically quiet afternoon to ask, "Cutting carrots is really a lot like meditating, don't you think?" Both these comments make such a link explicit, but they forge that link in very different ways. By extension, their divergence points to two ways of understanding how religion happens in kitchen life. Some individuals describe the religious in the kitchen as intentionally imported. Volunteers like Cynthia pull in the religious through their actions and thus act to make the space religious. In contrast, Lydia's comment suggests that spiritual sentiment or feeling arises from the action "itself," welling up unannounced. These two understandings of how religion combines with kitchen work evoke philosophical differences in the ways we understand religion as happening in, and becoming part of, daily life. Analytical understanding of religious experience has in recent years come to reject the essentializing aspects of early phenomenology, which suggest that religion descends (or arises) into our mundane lives as the wholly other, and that we are "necessarily" religious at our core, in favor of constructivist or relational interpretations. Volunteers spoke of both, however,[7] and so both need to be addressed.

Likewise, the way volunteers told the story of their religious action in the kitchen invites further analysis of the American distinction between "religious" and "spiritual" things. Those who talked about how they brought in religious practice, including Emily, Anita, and Cynthia, articulated a conscious desire to connect the sacred to their work. Not incidentally, Anita and Emily explain this intentional action as "spiritual." In so doing they draw attention to their own agency in developing this meaning in the kitchen. Volunteers who acted in this way, and who thought consciously of how their work was religious or spiritual, did not expect those around them to share their own personal ways of thinking about these connections. Viewing religiousness as a conscious act, rather than as a development of the setting itself, appeared to lead them to emphasize the variety of their fellow volunteers' religious and spiritual views. In contrast, those like Lydia, on whom the spiritual worked unexpectedly in the kitchen, or who "discovered" spirituality there, were much more likely to assume that everyone there shared their sentiments. Sandra, whose story ends this chapter, provides an example of the benefits and limitations of making such connections.

Although volunteers came from many religious backgrounds and, more important, had singular stories about how they decided to reject or claim, challenge or develop, a religious or spiritual identity, several patterns emerged in the ways they spoke about religion. In particular, the associations and connections between volunteers' interpretations of what it meant to be a religious or spiritual person (Was it general or specific? What practices were involved?) and their assumptions about what their fellow volunteers thought of these things (Did others share a general sense of the sacred? Did they care about religious things at all? Were they hostile to them?) worked together to influence the practice of religion in the kitchen.

As will become clear in this chapter and the next, these two sets of ideas and practices are linked and are likewise modified in everyday interactions, both in the kitchen and elsewhere. This chapter deals primarily with how four volunteers describe their religious agency through stories about themselves and their work at GLWD. Volunteers talked about how they understood their action as religious, what such action "looked like," and finally the limits of such action in the kitchen. As we will also see, these ideas were refracted through their understanding of the kitchen's social context as they experienced it in daily conversations and work with others. We begin with Emily, who articulated a particularly dense description of her "spiritual" activity in the kitchen.

"WORK IS PRAYER": ANATOMY OF A PRACTICE

Emily, a forty-something redhead who is a caterer and freelance writer, looked a little frazzled when we sat down to talk in the courtyard on a sunny spring morning. We had just finished our shift, and we both smelled faintly of tuna. When I thanked Emily for finding time to sit down with me, she laughed and said,

Today I really have overscheduled myself. It really would have made much more sense to go to the library and go do all these things that I really need to do [rather than coming in to volunteer]. But then I think, there are people who depend on me coming and doing my part, and I can't. I sometimes don't feel like getting on the bus to get on the train to come, but—

I said I would do it. This is life or death for someone. They can't eat if we don't make the food. So I can't think like that. . . . I just I think to myself—I think we take a lot of that for granted. . . . How can I say that I don't feel like coming? I don't think I have the right.

Emily had started volunteering at GLWD earlier the previous year after feeling at such "loose ends" about the "horrible things going on in the world" that she was finding it hard to sleep at night. Her husband suggested that volunteering might be palliative, and he reminded her of an article she had read in *People* about the "organization that makes good food for people with AIDS." With this prompting, she collected reference letters and her recent tuberculosis test results, took the subway to 103d Street, and walked into the GLWD volunteer office.

Emily considered herself a practically minded person. Asked why she thought God's Love We Deliver was such a "wonderful" program, she said, "You come in, prepare the food, they box it up, it goes out." She continued, "This seemed like a very simple thing I could do. I can't fix the whole world, but one morning a week I could go make some food for people who need it." Anticipating my next question, Emily told me that she was not volunteering in order to do something about AIDS. "I don't care what disease you have, if you're sick, you need help." As I would soon discover, Emily considered caring for the sick a duty, one deeply enmeshed with intense childhood memories.

Commenting on how volunteering has helped her, Emily said: "I still read the newspaper and I still find it upsetting, but I don't feel quite the same way I did. I don't know any other way to explain it. I can't do anything about the big things, but I can do one small thing." She continued, "There's something real basic about feeding hungry people. I wanted—I wanted to feed somebody. For lack of a better word, I think there's something spiritual that happens when you feed somebody. I think that's so basic, and because it's so basic it's so intimate, even though I don't know who it's going to."

Emily's sense that there is "something spiritual" about cooking developed through a life of caring for other people and being cared for. Although she had told me earlier in our interview that AIDS was not her "main reason" for volunteering, a coworker had died of AIDS. Emily admitted that she had gone to visit him regularly in his last months of life, even though "I didn't like him particularly." I asked her why she had visited someone she wasn't close to, and she paused to delve deeper into her past. When she was a young girl, her mother was chronically ill, and she died just as Emily entered her teenage years. Other people—women from the community and family—were always in the house, taking care of her family. She "knew things that other people didn't know about suffering," and as an adult she felt it was important to do what she "knew how to do." Visiting her coworker fulfilled a duty she had to the sick people who crossed her path.

On one of Emily's last visits to her coworker's house, about a week before he died, the weight of the moment finally caught up with her. "It was devastating—just devastating to me. I was standing there with his partner, who also had it, and I thought to myself, *'Who's going to help him?'* "

This question remained dangling, but it seemed to me that Emily was answering it in her actions. Her description of spiritual activity as an intimate and basic act developed through her own life story, returning again and again to caring for those who were suffering. Doubling back to reflect on how difficult it was for her to know how to give when she was younger, she commented that "part of being an adult is learning to give back. So in that sense I think that the emphasis of what I'm doing is to be aware of somebody other than yourself, to be aware and to be grateful for how much you have." To be aware, Emily stressed, meant making a commitment of time and effort and coming to the kitchen every week no matter how tired or overcommitted she was.

Emily's ideas of spiritual activity grew specifically out of her past, but they also hinged on the importance of discipline and commitment. In this sense she thought that "doing one small thing" was far superior to other ways of helping others. She contrasted her commitment to giving money, where "you just write the check and put it in the envelope and that's it. In a sense, it doesn't cost you anything. There's nothing of yourself there." Similarly, Emily suggested that a regular commitment was superior even to doing short-term overseas relief work, as one of her friends at church had done. Emily was not interested in taking heroic measures to help others because it would not give her the same discipline as a weekly commitment. Spiritual life was neither easy nor based on heroic deeds. Cooking food for someone who needed it cost her something; it was work, and it was her responsibility.

Commitment and discipline, of course, needed to be directed toward some "basic" problem, as Emily put it. As she said of cooking at God's Love We Deliver, "This is the experience we can have of God. . . . I think work *is* prayer, essentially. Like the Shakers said, work is prayer." But as I learned, Emily did not think all work was prayer. Certainly cooking at God's Love We Deliver was, in her lights, but cooking at home, or even on her job, was not similarly constituted in her mind as religious work. As she groused, "I had four days' catering work in a row last week. And I'd cook from nine in the morning until six at night with one twenty-minute break. All I want to do is go home and fix dinner and lie down." Unlike exhausting catering and cooking for her family, she found her work at GLWD energizing.

What, then, made cooking at GLWD a specifically spiritual practice? Certainly it was not the setting itself, at least as Emily described it. Emily considered this practice her own, brought to the kitchen and then built by her individual actions there. She did not talk about the corporate nature of such prayerful work.

What distinguished cooking at GLWD as prayer was Emily's simple intention to make it so. Catherine Bell has argued that what distinguishes "ritualized" action is the act of deciding to distinguish some activities from "ordinary" life.[8] Anything, in this light, can become meaningful if it is thought to be so by individuals or groups who assign this meaning. The process of naming an intention does not fully express the ways cooking became spiritual for Emily, however. She developed her ideas and, indeed, the ability to understand and call the work such through her connections to religious traditions she was a part of and to memories of interactions in other communities and collectivities. In effect, the act of intentionally calling her work spiritual in this context was built on prior actions, practices, and memories that made sense of it in that light.

Emily's description of cooking as religious practice gradually developed in the narrative she told about herself, and was most clearly articulated in a contrast between cooking and more traditionally defined religious practices. Emily was an active member at a large Episcopalian church, where she figured she also did about eight hours of volunteer work each week. She mentioned the kinds of prayer her church promulgated and the difficulties they posed. She sighed as she said, "I've tried off and on to meditate, but I'm just too busy. I'm too practical. If it's not in front of me, it's not real to me. . . . It just makes me antsy and I start making grocery lists in my head. I'm just no good at that." Pausing, she continued:

Both things count—I happen to be more comfortable with the doing. I would never be able to join a contemplative order. I couldn't do it. For me, that would be . . . , well, they have an experience that I know nothing about. I don't see how that would do any human good. . . . The idea that if you sit and pray for the world you've done it some good? I'm not so sure I believe that.

In contrast, working in the kitchen "is what 'God's love we deliver' " means, she said:

I don't think of God in the sense of a traditional religious kind of view. I don't think God has to be a particular, patriarchal old white man with a white beard. I'm not so sure myself how I think about God—I am more inclined to believe that God is people who do what they can do and are willing to give, to improve things. I think we do deliver God's love, because I think God's love is whatever's right in the world, whatever people make work, I think that's God.

If you do something for somebody else, I think that is whatever God is, or some

part of it. Or the experience we can have of God. And I don't think it gets any more
basic than feeding the hungry, clothing the naked, healing the sick, visiting the people
in prison.

According to Nancy Ammerman, many liberal "Golden Rule" Christians
craft a working understanding of religion where dogma is less important
than "ethics," caring for others is the highest calling in religious life, and
"God" becomes a fuzzy, albeit transcendent, concept. Ammerman argues
that such Christians have "little hope that anything very fundamental will
change in the larger world, but they are more than willing to do what small
things they can do to ameliorate suffering."[9] Emily's comments, actions,
and ideas fit this description well. She describes God as "whatever is right
in the world," admits her inability to do anything "big" to change the
world, and is a member of a theologically liberal Protestant congregation.

As we will see, Emily not only had a clear understanding of how her
work was prayer, she also could talk about this with other people, both
Christian and otherwise, at church, at home, and at God's Love We Deliver. She also acted on those opportunities, crafting her religious language to fit the context and, as she would report, finding church to be a
place where she found it hard to think about the spiritual at all. "Religion," as she saw the contrast between church and volunteering, was about
"administrative matters."[10] Before turning explicitly to these processes of
talking about religion at God's Love We Deliver, we need to look further
at what we mean by religious practice and discuss how Emily's actions and
expressions might shed light on discussions about the quality of such practice in contemporary American society.

SPIRITUAL OR RELIGIOUS:
UNRAVELING INDIVIDUALISTIC NARRATIVES

As Emily put it, spiritual practice was personal and intentional, enacted
in places where memories and past experiences compelled her to act. It
is worth noting that she called her activities at GLWD "spiritual" and
distinguished them from "religion," with which she was also actively involved. Emily was not alone in making this distinction between religion
and spirituality. Volunteers frequently described their devotions and their
experiences with the sacred as "spiritual" and used "religion" to evoke
institutions, clergy, and traditions. Given the institutional connotations
that came with religion, it is not surprising that volunteers considered
what they did at God's Love We Deliver to be spiritual. While they might

have learned that volunteering was an important spiritual practice through conversations with coreligionists, in churches and synagogues, most did not tell me that when they volunteered they were acting religiously as Presbyterians, or as Jews, or whatever. They were, instead, acting spiritually (that is, as private individuals).

While at one level it thus makes sense to say that Emily's view of her work at God's Love We Deliver as "spiritual" alludes to her individual actions, rather than the corporate ones that happen at church, it also bears noting that the distinction she makes is linked to a broader set of distinctions between these two elements. Emily's language refers to (if not actually engages) an ongoing popular critique of institutionalized religion, where American religious culture appears to be experiencing a "growing divide" or "divorce" between spirituality and religion.[11] "Spiritual" people, in this distinction, build and create their own religions in a spiritual marketplace, intentionally eschewing commitments to traditional religious communities, identities, and theologies as they do so.[12] By contrast, "religious" people find meaning in traditional communities and in congregational and denominational forms of religion. This distinction has been the subject of numerous volumes, some of which slip easily into normative critiques. Religion is negatively characterized as "dead" and as bound to outdated, sectarian, and conservative understandings of the sacred.[13] Spirituality, on the other hand, is roundly criticized for giving people what they want to hear and for being ultimately changeable and discardable and generally lacking the power to shape or change people's lives.[14]

Sociologists of religion have often located themselves in this debate with their strong critiques of individualistic spirituality and the various aspects of modern social life that make such practices hopelessly personal, overly materialistic, and limited in social power. Spirituality might be personally meaningful, but it is primarily "private" and therefore can leave little mark on social life.[15] This criticism received its early apotheosis in the form of Sheila Larson, the young nurse described in Robert Bellah's *Habits of the Heart,* who eschewed all traditional and existing religious organizations and named her religion after herself. Bellah warned that Sheila's private religion was unlikely to equip her with a moral language that she could use beyond her own musings.[16] An increasingly individualistic culture gives Sheila the language to express her faith as "Sheilaism," but her religion nevertheless begins and ends in herself.[17]

Even largely sympathetic commentators, who have been reluctant to wholly join Bellah in his criticism of Sheila[18] and who argue for more discerning interpretations of modern spiritual practices, sound similar warnings about "private" spirituality. For instance, Nancy Ammerman argues that Golden Rule Christians (those liberal Protestants who attend church but appear to have little grasp of theology or finer religious ideals) "have little opportunity for developing a sustained religious vocabulary . . . [and] this lack of ongoing religious conversation may undermine their ability to continue to practice their faith."[19] Others, echoing the themes in *Habits of the Heart,* point out that community ties, already weakened in general (owing to growing geographic mobility, increasing pluralism, and even television), are eroding to the point where it is difficult for religious communities to develop legitimate, shared languages.[20]

Missing from these arguments are attempts to trace how the individualistic or communalistic languages gleaned from interviews function in daily conversations and interactions. There are many ways to think about how narratives elicited in interviews are linked to other forms of expression and identity work. Paul Lichterman's ethnographic research with participants in a political action group, for instance, demonstrates what we often expect: individuals' discourse in interviews does not mirror their discourse in other settings.[21] We each have at our disposal multiple repertoires and ways of speaking and acting and explaining our actions.[22] We have different competencies and habits, learned in a variety of specific social contexts. We thus "choose" our language and actions in ways that take into account the complexities of the settings our language also helps to create. We take into account, in particular, whom we are addressing and the kinds of responses we hope to elicit by speaking at all. To carry this into our analysis of the language of personal spirituality often heard in interviews, we must reflect on how interviews provide contexts where we are likely to hear stories of personal freedom and choice rather than connection and conviction.[23] Narratives by "religious seekers" may obscure personal and institutional connections and ties (in fact, one suspects that the similarities in seekers' narratives point to their participation in social networks where such language is cultivated), but this does not mean such stories are the only ones seekers tell about themselves. Likewise, the measure of a narrative's force cannot be found through interviews alone but must be coupled with observations of the various contexts where we might understand how such self-descriptions shape individuals' activities, approaches, and values.

In Emily's case, invoking the spiritual allows room for personal practice and provides some critical leverage on her experience at church. Seen in this light, the firmly drawn distinctions between the "religious" and the "spiritual" begin to unravel. That is, while the links between the individual-spiritual and the institutional-religious exist in the languages we hear and use, we cannot assume that this language simply reflects indi-

viduals' positions. Language use does not in itself determine anyone's positions or identities: to make such assessments we also need to interpret
how it is used, and in what contexts.

All the same, religious and spiritual language shaped volunteers' views
of how they could cultivate religious practice in various social settings. It
is for that reason that I turn to Nancy's and Anita's descriptions of how
they practice religion and spirituality and the ways they practice (or do
not practice) it in the kitchen. In their cases the various languages of religion and spirituality reinforce and institute the current cultural understandings of the differences between institutional religion and boundless
spirituality within the fabric of daily life. Whereas Emily's narrative skirts
the edges and draws on both personal and corporate ideas of the sacred,
Nancy more fully embraces a "religious" life and Anita a "spiritual" life—
with consequences for how they practice religion in the kitchen and talk
about it with others.

"SPIRITUALITY" AND "RELIGION" IN ACTION

Anita

"Anita's a yenta," Judy said when she introduced us. Anita rolled her eyes
and stuck out her tongue. ("Courtney's pretty nosy too," Judy offered in
reply.) Anita and I soon discovered that we lived close to each other, and
she invited me over to see her artwork. Anita constructed altars and med-
itation pieces from found objects and, it turned out, thought she might
be able to sell me one. When I got to her apartment, Anita was finishing a
group of sculptures representing the life of Saint Francis of Assisi. I picked
my way through completed and half-finished projects, boxes of junk not
yet transformed into art, and hundreds of plants growing in pots, mugs,
tin cans, and glass jars. We settled down on her sofa to talk and drink
oolong tea while her large white cat tried to burrow under the cushions
behind my back.

Anita considered herself a very spiritual person. When I asked what
that meant, she said, "Spirituality is what's between you and the rest of the
world, and religion is about rules. It isn't so much about a person's being
in the world—I mean, I don't care how many rules you follow, if you don't
go out in the world and do something good for someone else, then what
are you? Spirituality is what comes from your center."

I had heard from other volunteers, I said, that spirituality was "doing
something good." "I try to do that at God's Love," she replied. "Yeah?"

"Yeah. Like—you weren't there two weeks ago. Evan [a new chef] was flirt-ing—flirting up a *storm* with this cute little young black girl. And him with a wife, and a new baby!" She took a sip of tea and continued.

"I didn't say anything at the time, because I thought she knew he was married. But then later I found out she didn't, which made it worse, of course, but I didn't know then. But then later he was up at the bulletin board when I walked up there. And he came over and said, "I need a hug." And so I gave him a hug. And I said to him, "Hey. What's going on down there?"

And he looked at me kind of sad, and he said, "Sometimes it's just nice to feel desired." And I took a step back and looked at him.

I said, "You have a long, long life ahead of you. You have a baby, you have a wife. What are you doing? You're making it really hard on yourself. You know, this is not the way to make it easier for you," And he said he knew, and you know, he thanked me for saying it.

Anita continued her story. "I just told him that he really had to be careful. I think it was important that he knew there was someone who was watching him, watching what he did. But I do that a lot. I go around the kitchen, I ask people how they're doing, I talk to them, I don't stand still. That's what I have to offer in the kitchen, I think."

As far as I could tell, Anita didn't like cooking very much. She often wandered around with a glum look on her face, and she never stayed long at one task. She admitted during the interview that if she stood in one place for an hour she would "go crazy." It took me some time to understand what Anita was doing in the kitchen: keeping her eye on people, "intuiting" their emotions, and saying "what they needed to hear."

Anita's religious practices drew on many religious teachings.[24] She bought and used the materials from Marianne Williamson's courses and alternately attended the Sunday morning services at the Episcopalian and Catholic churches on her block. She spirit channeled, took astrology courses, read Deepak Chopra, and dabbled in Catholic mysticism. She grew up in a Jewish family, but since childhood she had been attracted to the "mysterious" black habits that Catholic nuns wore. She recently learned that she had been "a nun in a past life." Anita emphatically told me that her inner spirit guided her to ideas that would be "helpful."

I asked Anita more about the many people and experiences that crowded the story of her spiritual growth. She told me about her longtime Catholic friend and about the Episcopalian priest she met at the health food store; both invited her to services, and she made mass and vespers part of her weekly schedule. Anita's favorite cousin, who died of AIDS, left her a bookshelf of New Age and astrology texts, and a former friend introduced her to her first guru and her first experience with channeling. Wasn't her story perhaps about arbitrary personal connections? I asked naively.

She shook her head and said, "You've never read the *Celestine Prophecy*, have you?" I said I hadn't. "Wait here," she said, running to her bedroom.

She brought the book back and read from a passage she had underlined: " 'There are no such things as coincidences.' Once you begin to get in touch with your own center, you see that there aren't. Everything happens for a reason. That's one of the principles in this book. You want to read it?" I took the book. "You know, some of the things are so hokey and contrived, of course, but he's trying to make a point about something that's true. Everything happens for a reason. *You* came here for a reason, Courtney," she said, giving me a penetrating stare as if by looking at me harder she could discern the cosmic reasons behind my visit.

Even though Anita emphasized that her spirituality emanated from herself, she populated her story with other people who affirmed its presence. Anita's desire to claim her spiritual life as her own shrouded some of the social aspects of her spiritual world. Her emphasis on her personal spirituality underlined what she understood to be broad, limitless contexts in which spirituality was at work. If everything was connected, and if everything happened for a reason, then no boundaries, doctrines, or buildings contained her spiritual experience. The people in her story, while important, were incidental to the webs that connected all people and connected her to them. And if everything was connected, she had every right to "intuit" things about other people's lives and tell them so. (Judy, perhaps less spiritually advanced, called this meddling.) Anita spoke up when Evan flirted. She overheard Lydia crying on the pay phone about some bad news; later she asked what was the matter and told her, "It's OK to go home, honey."

If Anita saw spirituality everywhere and could engage it everywhere she went, Emily's (and Nancy's) practices were, by comparison, much more tied to particular places and actions. In contrast to Emily, Anita placed no particular importance on cooking, even while she was at GLWD. Spirituality emanated from herself and her actions. Since she was their center, she did not expect that her religious practices would change much from one setting to another. Nancy, who described herself as religious, also did not expect her religious practices to change much from place to place—but for Nancy this suggested different limits to practice.

Nancy

Nancy thought she was a "rather religious" person: she attended mass weekly, was a eucharistic lay minister, sang in the choir, and fretted about not going to confession more often. Most of her religious practice revolved around devotional acts defined by her church; it included reciting the rosary and reading the Bible in the evenings, and prayer throughout the day.

Nancy's understanding of what it meant to be religious centered on cultivating the devotional practices prescribed by her priests. For this reason she felt "bad," as she put it, that she did not go to confession more often, and she tried often, but without much success, to develop Bible reading as part of her regular routine. Nancy's practices were, in this respect, more closely connected to a "religion" than Emily's. Emily, also a churchgoer, did not talk about struggling with the forms of contemplative prayer that she said she was "not good at." She knew that her church believed such prayer was important, but she did not view her decision not to pursue it as a serious failing.

Although Nancy's practices were more institutionally defined than Emily's, and though she struggled with them, they were also sources of dynamic engagement. She described her prayer life with a mixture of awe and pride, stating that she prayed "all the time," starting when she woke up. "I cross myself and say a few prayers—and then I put on the water for coffee." She prayed while she worked through the morning. "Where I work, there are plenty of church bells, and whenever I hear one, it reminds me to pray." She prayed as she ran through the park and in the evening before she went to bed. "I have holy things in my room," she said to me, "pictures [of saints], that kind of thing," that reminded her to pray. Except when she prayed at church, her prayers were silent. She prayed when she was alone with God and her thoughts.[25] As Nancy described her prayer life, I imagined that it, like Anita's spiritual life, knew few boundaries. But this was not so. For while Nancy said she prayed "all the time," she admitted that she found it very hard to pray in GLWD's noisy, chaotic kitchen.

Nancy dropped out of junior college in the late 1970s to start a small florist's shop with a friend, Jack. "He was gay," Nancy said, foreshadowing with the past tense what would come later in her story. On the weekends they went to parties and gay clubs. Nancy loved to dance, and she never had as much fun as when she was "partying with the boys." Everything was going well until Jack found out he had AIDS. Jack's lover abandoned him, and Nancy found herself his sole caregiver. As she recalled, "We did everything wrong." Their recreational drug use became full-blown addiction.

She bought them cocaine "to keep from thinking about the inevitable." Between the addiction and their absences at the shop, they were soon bankrupt.

One morning, with fear and worry about Jack and the bankruptcy crashing over her as she drank her coffee, she had a vision. At the precise moment she reached "rock bottom," God appeared to her. Nancy recalled, "A dove (well, actually it was only one of those white seagulls) came down—and now it doesn't even sound believable—it came to the ledge on my apartment window and looked me straight in the eye, and it was God." After seeing the dove, Nancy never touched drugs again. She quit the habit without suffering withdrawal symptoms, further confirmation that God turned her life around. "When I saw that dove, it was God telling me, 'This is it for you.' I knew it was God, that's all I can tell you. I knew he was going to be helping me. That's when I started becoming very involved in religion—you know, church, going back. Like when I was a little girl."

Nancy became a regular attender at her parish church and helped Jack die. She dissolved her business and started work as a house cleaner, later volunteering as an AIDS buddy for two other men with AIDS. She eventually landed in GLWD's kitchen after the second man died, hoping to continue doing something about AIDS. Working at GLWD placed Nancy closer to the world of drugs, gays, and partying that she had abandoned after she saw her vision of God. The kitchen thus provided a powerful mix of the familiar and the other (with a disco throb to accompany it). Nancy's inability to pray in the kitchen marks how clearly, and cleanly, she established the boundary between these parts of her history.

Despite the differences, each woman's understanding of religious practice suggested and constructed contexts where it could be practiced. Each one had a different understanding of the place of religion within the kitchen (or of her ability to place religion there) that developed before her work at GLWD. The ways individuals defined their place within this context depended on the practices they brought to it and their uneven awareness of others'. These practices defined the kitchen context, just as the kitchen itself—as a place where there were many such definitions at work—provided ongoing challenges to these definitions and to the practices that articulated them.

Notably, Anita, Emily, and Nancy each assumed (although for different reasons) that she was unique among the volunteers in her religious or spiritual practice. As it was, most volunteers shared an idea that they were different and that they had many ways to talk about, think about, and evaluate such things. Hannah, the volunteer director, talked incessantly about volunteers' diversity, causing many rolling eyes and rueful snorts.

But there was a truth in what she said that they largely accepted, at least when it came to religion. This shared assumption about religious difference influenced the ways volunteers practiced their religion in the kitchen.

Not all volunteers, however, brought religious or spiritual ideas to the kitchen. Many who considered themselves secular (and happily, positively so) found the idea of doing something religious at GLWD just not what it was all about. And another group unexpectedly found religion through their work at GLWD. Sandra, one of these, told me that GLWD's kitchen was in fact her religion. In contrast to Anita, who could practice spirituality anywhere, or Emily, who intentionally worked to make work at GLWD religious, Sandra suggested that the community in the kitchen had all the elements necessary for religion and that she experienced it that way. Sandra's claim contrasts sharply with the other volunteers' practices in that her understanding embraced a hope that the others she worked with would find God in the carrots as she had done.

FINDING GOD IN THE CARROTS

In contrast to volunteers like Anita and Emily, who brought religion to the kitchen by conscious enactment, others, like Sandra, said they discovered religion there. Lydia's question about the meditative properties of chopping carrots indicates that on occasion the work "itself" gave rise to spiritual associations. These "unexpected" discoveries posed interesting interpretive issues for the volunteers who experienced them. The ones who talked to me about such experiences were those who, like Charles, were "not particularly spiritual." Charles, musing about the power of cooking, told me, "I'm not a particularly spiritual or mystical, you know, kind of guy, but sometimes something will wash over me. The memory of it—it makes the hair on my neck stand up even now. You know that feeling? Once it was so overwhelming, I went outside for a smoke. I don't smoke, you know. It was just to get myself back together."

Charles did not conjure up these feelings, nor did he try to explain what circumstances were likely to lead to them. As he saw it, they dropped into his world as he worked at GLWD. These overwhelming, hair-raising feelings are what William James refers to as numinous experiences. James notes that there are many ways to interpret them: "It does not [necessarily] connect itself with the religious sphere. Yet it may upon occasion do so."[26]

That such powerful tingling "feelings" sometimes happen, and that it is not necessary to see them as religious, bears keeping in mind. Kate used similar language when she tried one day to explain the problems with popular psychology's understanding of "the grieving process." Using expressly nonreligious language, she told me how she missed her husband, who had died unexpectedly several years before: "There's a mailbox on the corner of Columbus and Seventy-fourth. I can't go by there. Every time I do, I think of [my husband]. I have no idea why that is. As far as I can remember, there's nothing particular about it. But the feeling is just so real—there are certain things I don't do anymore, because it brings it all back."

Kate did not interpret this forceful memory as spiritual, and her language slips uneasily between memory as thought and as feeling. Her reflection on this sensation and "thought" points to her unfinished business of understanding how we live in the world filled with such memories and unexpected encounters with emotion. As Kate put it somewhat wryly, books about grieving "tell you all about the stages of grief, as if they come in a line, one after the other. But [for] everyone I know, they usually come all at once, and then they keep coming out of order, and then when you think it's all finished, they come back again." Explanations that she had found in books and heard from the experts were inadequate. They made no sense of the memories and emotions that continued to spill over into her daily life. [27]

William James does not dwell on the "occasions" when such an experience might be interpreted as religious or otherwise. I nevertheless suspect that the presence of religious languages embedded in specific social contexts and communities makes it more likely for them to be interpreted and remembered as such. In other words, experiences are not "purely" religious but become so only with "reference to concepts, beliefs, grammatical rules, and practices." [28] Daily life presents both expected and unexpected sensations and experiences. In addition, it presents a range of concepts (sometimes meager, sometimes more lush) with which to interpret them, as well as rituals and routines that draw them together. Charles's interpretation, for instance, demonstrates his uncertainty about using "spiritual" to name what happens when his hair tingles in the kitchen at GLWD. Kate, likewise, wryly grumbled that books on grief were little help to anyone who had ever had the active experience of grieving.

God's Love We Deliver presented a number of symbols that invited spiritual interpretations, chief among them its name. For some volunteers, the "God" in God's Love We Deliver was neither diaphanous nor easily dismissed. Similarly, aspects of kitchen work conjured at least the *possibility* of interpreting otherwise mundane work as spiritually meaningful. These qualities of the work, "arising" or "appearing" unexpectedly, as they did, suggested to volunteers that others might find such things valuable and meaningful in the same way. This is where Sandra found herself, and at first happily so.

A "LITTLE RELIGION":
SANDRA'S VISIONS OF SHARED BELIEF

Sandra told me that the kitchen and the people gathered around her constituted a "little" religious community. She told me she was not religious, except insofar as GLWD helped her develop an "existential" religion of her own. At the beginning of our interview Sandra consciously used the agency's official languages and repertoires to explain her actions. Unlike the other volunteers I spoke with, she told me how important it had been to realize that "food is love," and she spoke of Ganga Stone and her ideas with reverence. Sandra's devotion to GLWD had initially grown out of the help her brother received from the agency when he was dying. Sandra told me: "I first found out about God's Love We Deliver when my brother was being released from the hospital. The social worker was asking me about meals and coverage at home, and one of the nurses asked if I knew about God's Love We Deliver—that they deliver meals. And my brother became a client. It was a little late in his illness. He wasn't really able to eat very well. I wish I had known about them earlier. But whatever did come was tremendously helpful and nutritious." Several months after he died, Sandra decided she wanted to volunteer as a "way of showing appreciation for the assistance." She became involved in fundraising and appeared in television spots for the agency.

Sandra liked to work in the kitchen, where "in some small way, I [am] still feeding my brother." As she cooked she realized she was feeding others as well. Her sense of responsibility and purpose broadened, she said, and she now realized that "if you can put a spoonful of food in someone's mouth, I think you've lived a worthwhile life. Life can't be just about feeding yourself." In fact, her understanding of the purpose of life had been translated into a food analogy, feeding others and by extension feeding herself.

The day I volunteer, I feel empowered to do just about anything. I feel empowered. It's a form of energy. It's like drinking a tonic. I remember at the beginning, there were days I came here that I just felt terrible. I would leave feeling different. On Wednesdays, that day my heart is in a very special place.

What it is, is that you shut down everything else for a few hours. Like you make your business calls in the morning, maybe you do whatever those things are that you have to do every day. But that shuts down when you're here, because this is another reality. It's a bit like going into another state. It's just another state. When that ends, at five o'clock, when you go back, you have a little edge.

Sandra compared her time in the kitchen to attending religious services. "It's a little religion on one day a week. I think religion is what you feel in your heart anyway, and this is sort of like—everyone's there for the same reason, it's like a little religion." Sandra drew this analogy deliberately. "I talked with some people who do some work for the church, and they say they 'work for the Lord.' Well, that's my father's favorite expression about what I do. And this is it! So I didn't even—I wasn't even aware of it being a religious type of feeling at first, but it's evolved into that." Seeing the kitchen *itself* as sacred space had ramifications that went beyond the simple act of preparing food to creating a "full circle" of life. God's Love We Deliver *was* religion with a community of kindred spirits. Existential as this might have been for Sandra, this religion was not a personal and private spirituality. She depended on the sense that others were there and also working "for the Lord."

When Sandra first heard the name of God's Love We Deliver, she told the nurse, "We're not religious!" She and her brother had grown up in a nonobservant Jewish household. The nurse laughed. "It's not religion, it's *food.*" Ah, Sandra said to the nurse, food she could understand.

There were days when my brother would say, "What should we do about lunch?" And I would say, "I don't know. Do you want a croissant with cream cheese, or should we get the sliced rye, with the roast—"

*A nurse once said something to us. She said, "What are you doing, talking that way about what you want for lunch? You should be talking about all the **important** things."*

And I disagreed with her, quite violently. She said, "You should be talking about the real issues." But I disagree with that, and I will until the day I die. You know, where there's life, there's hope. So we focused on the day-to-day things. Nutrition, what we could do to make this day good and comfortable.

The "real issues" were what to have for lunch. Sandra followed her brother's lead and never once talked about death. Instead, they concentrated on daily life. Food was "love," in Sandra's experience, as much as it was life itself.

Sandra explained her motivations by drawing on GLWD's formal narrative. I was taken with her articulate use of the repertoires of love and therapy, and also by her admission of how much she learned about food.

"I've learned a lot from volunteering," she told me, "and it spills into my life outside the kitchen." She continued:

I'm extremely aware now of what's good to eat. I was always a little bit careful, but I now know what's good to eat, how to present food to someone who doesn't feel well. The quantities, the display, and also that food is—is a gift of love. I know I give more food gifts now. You know, if I'm coming to someone's house, I buy them a big fish or something. I consistently see a happy reaction when someone brings food instead of the inessential tchotchke. So I think I'm becoming more aware of how food can turn around someone's spirit. And sharing food—and even cleaning vegetables. I do that at home, washing celery, and cutting it. Yes, food is love.

As Sandra came to appreciate washing celery, she also thought more about how giving food could "turn someone's spirit." She explained how the "perspective of food" at God's Love We Deliver had "changed" her: "You know, you can't put a big sixteen-ounce steak in front of someone who's sick. Maybe a little meat, a little potato, a little bit of everything. I remember in between deliveries I prepared something for my brother. I made the plate colorful and used just a little food. I spread it out on the plate. Again, mindful of the way we did things in the kitchen. A little bit of this, a little bit of that—and I remember he said, 'Ooh, that looks so appetizing!' "

"I learned that from the kitchen," she said, then pausing to remember chronology. "Or maybe it came from me. It's hard to say." Whether Sandra learned about this at GLWD or just found a way to describe it within that larger context was ultimately not important. What was important was "food is love." When I asked her what the phrase meant she said, "It's spiritual and it's practical."

*Spiritual life is based on a form of practical action. You know—I don't know which came first, but I know that Ganga was a very spiritual—the founding was very spiritual. She was going out there on her bicycle. So the spirit moved her, but she was **physically** carrying the food. You can call it spiritual, but there was food in her hand and she was delivering it. There's a real action that's a result. So, it's more than just spirit. This is real action. This is doing something about something.*

*You know, they have support groups where people talk, and that's a form of action, too. But this is **something**. You actually see food going into a container and it's sealed. The evidence is right in front of you . . . and it's a nice thing, too. Really nice food.*

By adopting the language of "food is love," Sandra explicitly linked her own concerns to those voiced by the organization: this was her community. She laughed as she said, "I sound like an evangelist now, don't I? I don't mean to give a sermon, but there's no denying that it's the right way. If you could just go through life helping one person, then you've fulfilled some purpose in life." Being at God's Love We Deliver every week was about being part of a community of "slightly tarnished souls" like herself, where on some days all she could do was "keep one foot going in front of the other."

When Sandra first described the sacred character of the kitchen as she experienced it, she used GLWD's formal languages, or repertoires. But as we talked more about what made it a "little religion" for her, it became clear that the associations around food were less important than the fact that she was able to laugh in the kitchen. Laughter played a central role in her "religious" practice there. The disjuncture between the beautiful way Sandra described her "little religion" in relation to food and her experience of laughing eventually exposed her struggle to imagine a community of kindred souls who shared experiences and hopes like her own.

LAUGHTER IN THE KITCHEN

Sandra did not go looking for religion at GLWD. In fact, at the beginning she was not even sure she wanted to volunteer. Her family was concerned: "Haven't you done enough already?" Sandra, too, worried that "I would have to keep on explaining why I was there to everyone." She found, however, that no one talked about "it," and she told her family, "It's not hurtful, it's *joyful*." Sandra said, "We put a lot of effort into having a good time. I couldn't believe it would be the one day a week that I would look forward to laughing!" According to Sandra, her newly rediscovered ability to laugh came from the kitchen's being a haven. "It's different from the rest of the world, in the kitchen." The common thread of suffering bound all their laughter together, and all their sorrows as well, at least as Sandra understood it.

When I first started to hear Sandra talk about laughter, she was still volunteering, and she clowned around every week with Judy, Libby, Melinda, and the others. Sandra made a special point of standing next to Libby, an older Jewish woman with a pronounced accent, whenever she could. They had a number of running joke based on Jewish comedy routines; Judy and the others frequently chimed in to provide punchlines or to extend the puns. Libby was forcefully opinionated, the oldest volunteer, and she rarely let the chefs direct her energies without retorting with a wisecrack. Libby had little experience with people with AIDS, but she had lost many family members in the Holocaust, something Sandra and Judy both told me several times. Libby herself frequently turned conversations with Judy and Sandra to Jewish topics and often identified the people she was talking about as survivors of the camps. She remarked several times, "It's amazing, most of them, have such a sense of humor." She thought that it was a "good attitude" that brought them through. "What else could it be? That, and luck sure, but there were many who could have survived and didn't. It was that they kept their sense of humor."

Laughing at the circumstance of living in a concentration camp struck me and many of the other volunteers as strange, if not offensive. But Libby obviously thought "humor" was a Jewish trait—a Jewish survival tactic against sadness and evil that had worked many times before and would necessarily prevail again. [29] These ideas resonated with Sandra's experiences in the kitchen and, in particular, her newfound laughter. That both Sandra and Libby were Jewish was a strong part of their common bond; Libby helped Sandra see her ability to laugh as part of her, and her religious self, in a way that other practices (including cooking) were not. Libby's efforts at humor were direct and to the point. She told me that "volunteers are boring" and suggested I instead write my thesis on Gertrude Stein, her favorite writer, who had "the best recipe for brownies." [30] A few weeks later, she came up with another topic for my dissertation: humor. "I would read a dissertation on humor," she said. "I think it's real important, don't you? Much more important than volunteers, right Judy? Feh!" Judy and I laughed out loud—Libby was trying to get me to laugh, but she was also telling me something very important.

Most of the volunteers on Wednesday afternoons, and the other evening shifts, carried on about nonsense, relentlessly cracking jokes about everything they could think of. When I asked volunteers what they liked best about the kitchen, I most frequently heard that it was that "we have so much fun there." This kind of fun was consciously constructed and at times difficult, given the circumstances. When it worked, it staved off sadness. It was not easy to be happy after losing someone to AIDS, but laughing was a way to live and to turn a hideous situation upside down. [31] Laughter was Sandra's way of working with grief. Like planning for her brother's next meal, laughter was a way of overcoming death.

Sandra so strongly linked laughing to overcoming sadness caused by AIDS that when she found herself laughing with someone who thought differently about AIDS or gays, she was shaken. One morning Sean told us that he was going to visit his mother in South Carolina. He didn't want to go, because everyone "looked at him funny" when he traveled south. He said he was happy to be in New York where there weren't any bigots. Sandra let out a snort, then told him not to get suckered into thinking that all city dwellers were open-minded.

"Just this weekend I was at a great party, really. Nice place, nice view. I was standing on the side of the room. This woman, she came over and we started having this lovely conversation. We were having great laughs—really, a great time. And then she went into this thing about gay people, and she started ranting and *raving*." She shuddered and shook her head.

Sean asked her what she did in response. Sandra put down the potato she was peeling and looked up seriously. "I told her, 'I have to leave your presence immediately,' and said that it was very hurtful, what she said [about gays]. And I just walked out of the room. It was a party at a mutual friend's house so it was a little awkward."

It disturbed Sandra to discover that she had been laughing with a real homophobe. Although she assumed that people she met on the street might be homophobic, it was another thing to encounter someone like that at a friend's house, and even worse to have been laughing *with* her. Laughter was so important that when Sandra found that some people at GLWD who she thought were "laughing with her" were not, she left the organization. The evangelist was left without a religion to preach.

The ironies of the events surrounding Sandra's departure are manifold, hinging on the chef's determination that Libby was too homophobic to remain and on the misinterpretation of several probable "jokes" between volunteers and staff. But Sandra, who had talked so strongly and clearly about the spiritual life she had created with the others in the kitchen, found that it quickly dissipated as these events came to a head, leaving me, and Sandra, to question the possibility of building "shared" spiritual meaning there.

I was not present on the otherwise typical Wednesday afternoon when Judy pulled a pineapple out of her bag to share with the other volunteers toward the end of the shift. We were not supposed to eat in the kitchen, but the rules about bringing in our own food were a bit more lax. At any rate the pineapple had to be cut. Before Judy had a chance to do so, Libby insisted they wash it off. She took the pineapple to the dishwashing area and started to scrub. Just at that moment, Bill and Perry walked around the corner, deep in conversation, and bumped into Libby. Bill asked her loudly (or yelled at her), "What are you doing? We have to be careful of germs!"

Libby, startled by the outburst, shot back, "Calm down, take it easy—I'm just washing a pineapple!" But Bill stood over the diminutive woman, telling her emphatically, "You can't wash that there!" He then asked why she was washing a pineapple at all, and Judy stepped in and told him she had brought it as a snack.

Libby was upset and accused Bill of telling her to leave and not come back. That was her last day in the kitchen, but she placed a lengthy phone call every Wednesday afternoon to talk to "her girls"—Judy, Melinda, and Sandra.

Talking about it later, Sandra shook her head, laughing wryly at the absurdity of the whole scene. "Bill kept yelling, 'The germs! The germs!' Washing the pineapple—it's like that scene in the *Caine Mutiny* with the strawberries. It's not the pineapple. They just didn't like her, and they wanted to be rid of her."

As Sandra said, the issue was not whether Libby had contaminated the dishwashing sink. Volunteers were not supposed to eat snacks in the kitchen, but it was Judy, not Libby, who brought in the offending fruit. Everyone agreed that Libby had washed it in the "wrong" sink, but everyone knew that this infraction was hardly grounds for dismissal. Judy even laughed when I mentioned it to her (she was otherwise very sober about Libby's departure). "Have you ever heard of anyone washing a pineapple?" Judy went on to add, "Libby's seventy-nine years old—of course she's not going to understand everything right away. She tends to freeze up when she gets yelled at. Why didn't they just tell her what to do, instead?" Sandra added, "She took two buses to come up there. Her heart was certainly in the right place. And she was *very* hurt."

Larger issues were at stake than the contaminating pineapple. According to the chefs, Libby made too many inappropriate comments about other volunteers. The week after the pineapple incident, Perry pulled me aside to remind me of the things Libby said, including her "astonishing" question to Chris about why people with AIDS were allowed to work in the kitchen. On no terms did he want her to come back. "Libby says things that are inappropriate, and that makes everyone else work less. Some of the other volunteers really don't like it, I know. She's come out with some doozies—there was an African American man in here for a few weeks. I heard her call him *boy*. I drew her aside and told her that he was probably offended. And she wouldn't listen. She said, "What do you mean, he's offended—that I talked to him?" And I said, "Well, Libby, how would you feel if someone called you a *kike*?" And she really went off on that. Was that the wrong thing to say! She would barely say another word to me after that, except to remind me that the Jews are the chosen people of God. So what was I supposed to do?"

Bill echoed Perry's comment the next week, when Hannah asked him to call Libby and invite her back to work: "Some people are just unacceptable as volunteers." When Hannah questioned Sandra further, she acknowledged that Libby did not always say the most appropriate thing, but she took this as a sign of age. "You know, she's seventy-nine years old, and of course she's not going to understand what's wrong—or always say the right things. But she's from a different age."

Given Sandra's fury and disappointment when she found herself laughing with a bigoted person at her friend's party, I was somewhat surprised that she easily forgave Libby for making statements that seemed to offend others. Of course, it was Libby herself who had helped Sandra to laugh again. How could she laugh now that Libby, the main generator of the kitchen's laughter, had been chased away? The irony that she viewed the chefs—mostly gay, some HIV positive—with suspicion and Libby without any was lost on Sandra, but it helped drive home the point that she was committed to laughing in the kitchen, no matter what.

Bill, Hannah, and the others understood how much Sandra was hurt by Libby's departure, and they tried to make amends. Bill eventually offered to call Libby and invite her back—on condition that Sandra or Judy always be there and always "look after" her. Despite this offer (which Libby rejected), Sandra's suspicions colored her interactions in the kitchen and made her uneasy in her position. "If they could talk that way and act that way toward Libby—well, you know . . . whenever I think of it, I think, 'There but for the grace of God go I.' What if I did something wrong, or washed something in the wrong sink?"

Sandra became increasingly frustrated with kitchen work. She started noticing the work more and laughing less. The numbers got to be more, the work got more "serious," she said. Bill continued to ask her to cut onions uniformly, but no one made jokes about it anymore. Bill treated her like an "employee" and not like a cherished, hurt soul working to put one foot in front of the other. Sandra stopped volunteering for God's Love We Deliver shortly after Libby left.

Until the pineapple incident, Sandra assumed that all the other volunteers and the chefs felt as she did about love and laughter. She took their shared laughter as evidence of a community of caring people who held something inexpressible in common. When she learned that this was not so—or rather that what she believed was shared by all was much more diffuse, much more tenuous—her sense of what the kitchen gave her fell apart. After Libby left, there was little room to laugh: no matter how much she spoke about "food is love," her work no longer gave her that "little edge" that helped her face the world.

THE LIMITS OF TALK ABOUT PRACTICE

Sandra was a native speaker of the "food is love" dialect, and she wove together stories of GLWD's founding and her brother's last months in ways that strike me as genuine. Her stories were eloquent, yet they did not sustain her after Libby left. At that point preparing the food became a grind, a chore, and barely about love at all. Sandra's religious practice was more about laughter than about food, a point that became even clearer when she started to speak of laughter in the past tense. This distinction between language and practice became even more evident several weeks after Sandra stopped volunteering, when Kate related an interchange they had earlier in the spring.

Kate was standing outside the hostel entrance finishing a cigarette when Sandra arrived. Sandra stopped to ask Kate how her daughter was faring now that she was living in her own apartment. Kate answered, "Oh, I think she likes it pretty much, but I can't stand it that she always comes home at dinnertime!"

"Well, you have to admit she has a good thing going," Sandra commented, assuming (as one might expect) that Kate cooked dinner at home.

"No, no," Kate had said, as she recalled their conversation, "I don't cook for her. I haven't cooked for her or anyone else since Larry died! For all I care, she could starve to death! I never did understand all that 'food is love' stuff. I mean, I get it intellectually, but it doesn't do anything for me. I was even more amazed when Sandra leaned in close to me and whispered, 'I know. I feel the very same way.'"

Of course, I thought. Sandra didn't know how to cook. She gave her brother sliced rye and croissants, not homemade soup. I laughed out loud: she was likely to take someone a "big fish" as a hostess gift. Sandra understood intellectually what "food is love" meant, and she had learned its language very well. She had a great desire to learn the language, given that the volunteers in the Wednesday afternoon group had quickly become her community of laughter. As Sandra ultimately acknowledged, her community was based on things other than GLWD's formal repertoires. At the same time, learning these languages had helped her think of GLWD as a religion. Sandra embraced the language that food was love. Her volunteer work outside the kitchen, on the fundraising and public relations front, gave her an opportunity to learn the language well. But learning a language was not enough to develop a practice, at least not in the two years she worked at GLWD. It had not become real to her in the same way that it was for Emily, whose desire to cook and discussion of its spiritual meanings grew in conjunction with memories and social connections specific to cooking itself. There is more to practice than learning its language. Likewise, there is more to creating a "little religion" than assuming that everyone else feels it too. In fact, such assumptions could be very problematic.

As I mulled over Sandra's disappointments and the "end" of laughter in the kitchen, my thoughts turned to Emily' frustrations with church. Emily was a faithful and active participant in her church; she and her husband were both members of its executive committee, and she headed the property committee. She estimated that she spent one day a week organizing and attending meetings, "dealing with the higher-ups, writing letters, getting tree surgeons and estimates, and turning in the paperwork." She also oversaw the catering for several fundraisers the church held each year.

Although Emily enjoyed her work for the church "most of the time," it had recently come to be more of a chore. As she said quietly, "Unfortunately there seems to be a separation between religion and spirituality too often, and one of them is about administrative matters and the other is about personal commitment." Sounding a bit like Sandra, she noted that she was feeling somewhat burned out. Her family had recently decided to attend the earlier and shorter Sunday worship service. "We spend so much time doing church through the week that Sunday is the one day we really have to ourselves," she commented.

Emily noted that her current frustrations with church had not arisen from the volunteer work she did there (after all, the practical things were what she was good at). Rather, a conflict had recently developed in the executive committee meetings. They were hotly debating whether to ask their vibrant young minister to leave the church, since many in the congregation felt he had reached the limit of his talents. The meetings had exposed fault lines between people's views, and even though Emily had close friends at church, she now knew more about them than she wanted to. "I'm not impressed with some of their motives," she said.

Emily, like Sandra, had become sorely upset over what she learned about others in the course of these disagreements. In contrast to Sandra, however, she remained committed at church. She did not reflect on the reasons for her continued commitment there, but she was adamant that church was not a spiritual place for her.[32]

If she had not made the point directly, I would have gathered this perspective from her discussion of these controversies. Emily used business terminology, experiences in the world of business, and pop psychology to explain her church's current transitions. She did not use religious or sacred language to describe them. "I was just saying this morning [with the other volunteers] that often the person who is the lightning rod to get things started . . . is not a good person to get it into its adolescence. That's a whole different set of skills. And there have been issues about that at our church. [The minister] is just wonderful at outreach and getting things started. But he's really poor in administrative skills"[33]

Emily continued, "I mean, an entrepreneur gets a company to a certain stage, and then usually has to bring in a whole level of upper management. I've worked for a number of companies run by families, and they find it really difficult to let go." A nonprofit management consultant hired by the diocese to deal with the question of leadership change confirmed Emily's sense that a church was just like a business. "The consultant said that nonprofits often have the same kind of issues a church does. A leader who won't let go for the second stage; people underneath are excluded and frustrated because they can't participate fully."

The languages Emily used to describe her church were more "administrative." Her work in the business world gave her skills she could utilize well in any committee setting. But these languages and practices had little to do with the spiritual, despite their use in a religious building. It was no wonder Emily said she would never volunteer "upstairs" at GLWD. No one talked about purposes or motives in the kitchen, leaving Emily free to pursue her own. As she said, "It's a relief to come here and not have to deal with any of that. I come and do my work—to be real direct about it, nobody would come work in a kitchen if they didn't like to cook."

Emily's frustrations at church paralleled some of Sandra's at GLWD. When Sandra learned that others did not share the same concern for the same kinds of people, her religion became harder to sustain; likewise, Emily found church to be more of a chore than a joy as she engaged in debates about staffing. Sandra left God's Love We Deliver, but Emily remained a committed member of her church. Emily, notably, had different ways to describe or practice religion. Her religious practice was dispersed across settings and developed over a longer time than Sandra's. Sandra's struggles to imagine a community that valued the transforming power of laughter demonstrate, among other things, just how much effort it takes to sustain practice.

In this respect, volunteers who counted themselves successful at practicing religion in the kitchen were those with the fewest assumptions about shared religion and spirituality. Nancy, Anita, and Emily were not disappointed to discover that others' motives were not the same. In fact, they anticipated such differences. They did not think that religion emerged organically or mystically from cooking, from the experience of caring for people with AIDS, or the like. They were active and thoughtful generators of religious practice, not its happenstance experiencers. This distinction did not mean that volunteers who were active generators of religion never had mystical experiences. Nancy, for instance, spoke of her vision of God, but this experience was one small part of her story. Most important, volunteers who cultivated religious practices and used them in the kitchen pointed to other places, sources, and planes where they could cultivate religion and act on it. Their description of the location of religion evokes an orientation they shared—that religious diversity rather than shared "sensibilities" characterized their grouping.

Volunteers who noticed and paid attention to religious differences based much of their understanding on their own sense that they brought personal spiritual experiences with them as well. In contrast to what others have suggested about the difficulty of translating "personal" or "private" spirituality to public contexts, we see here that volunteers' personal articulations allowed religious practice, and even religious talk, to thrive. Volunteers who acted on religious ideas in the kitchen understood themselves as carrying religion with them and putting it to work there more or less on their own. Making religion personal, and incorporating it into a space that they viewed as nonreligious, also made religion possible. As we will see in the next chapter, volunteers translated and expressed these embodied understandings in extended conversations that almost always lacked explicit ideological content. To speak with others about religion or spirituality in this way, however, required some further work of establishing a firm footing for such talk. This work was grounded on myriad asides and offhand comments that volunteers made in daily conversation about everything under the sun.

CHAPTER FIVE

What We Talk about When We Talk about Religion

Volunteers arrived bearing religious practices. In the previous chapter, I drew on the language and stories that they used in interviews to describe how these practices came to be meaningful to them in the kitchen. Such stories forged links between religion and volunteering and between individual biography and kitchen life. They are evocative of many things, but they leave hanging the important question: How did the kitchen's daily events and interactions give shape to volunteers' notions about the sacred and the religious?

Asking questions about how daily kitchen life shapes various expressions of the religious (and in turn how it shapes various understandings of the sacred) is a necessary step, given that we are interested in how the volunteers act in the kitchen and not only what they think about after they take off their aprons. Doing so helps us gain a better grasp of why Nancy, the practicing Catholic who said that she "did something for God" in the kitchen, also said that she never talked about religion there. Nancy explained to me (during an interview) that she did not talk about religion in the kitchen because "a lot of people down there are against the Catholic religion, pretty much. Because of the homosexual thing, that isn't permitted sexually. So there's a lot of controversy with a lot of the volunteers, with the Catholic religion." She then added, "Some people have told me that they don't believe in God, so I never get involved too much in it. It's kind of private, I guess—that type of thing. You know, I don't know how people feel about talking about it. [If] they want to talk about it, I'm open to that. You know, it's kind of quiet because of the issues that come along with the faith."

Nancy made it clear in her interview that her decision not to talk about "things that come with the faith" arose from her experience in the kitchen. She did not say that she "never" talked about her faith in public, or that she was uncertain how she would talk about it. It was in this context in particular that she did not talk about religion—even though it was a context where other practicing Catholics felt no such difficulty. She and the others who felt more comfortable worked in the "same" space, but brought different histories to the kitchen and crafted different practices and discussions there. Here I explore the nuanced ways such talk differed, and how the complexities that combined when individuals with differing notions of religious talk came to the kitchen influenced the very ground for making such talk.

It bears noting before we begin that Nancy made a subtle distinction in her comment above between two ways to "talk about religion." One is talk about morals and faith, and the other is what we might for the moment call ephemeral passing comment on religious subjects. Talk about morals and faith is usually the first thing that comes to mind when we think about "talk about religion," and most social commentators who discuss the changing place of religious public discourse focus on such moral language, appeals to higher truths, and sacred justifications.[1] Nancy (and most social commentators) tended to dismiss or glide over the passing conversational mention of religion, even though it is clear that it is just such talk that allowed her to know whether she *could* talk about "faith." If anything, Nancy's statement sends a signal that the kind of religious talk occurring in passing conversations promotes or hinders the more sweeping kinds of faith talk that commentators are most interested in assessing. For while such daily talk and action appear to be ephemeral, they nevertheless are part of what allows individuals to see faith talk as possible and imagine ways to proceed toward such discussion. In short, such passing conversation allows individuals to assess their "footing" in the course of speaking: daily conversation about "nothing" is a large part of what provides that footing.[2] Studying how daily conversations and daily actions help individuals gain their footing is a requirement for analyzing any public talk about religion.[3]

I begin by investigating the ephemeral religious talk about religion in the kitchen. I focus here, as I did throughout my fieldwork, on conversations where I heard overt references to religious symbols, signs, institutions, and people. Such references, which occurred with some regularity in the kitchen (more frequently around the holidays) were usually one of several kinds, or genres, to which I have assigned the shorthand classifications *going to church, preparing for holidays,* and *parody.* These three genres are not particularly striking except that, with few exceptions, anyone in the kitchen could identify them as containing some reference to religion (or to a specific religion). For the most part they arose naturally in conversation and were not (usually) meant to engage conversations about meaning, theology, or religious value. That said, each genre contained and elaborated a structure for conversation. Each had embedded within it expectations of appropriate ways of being religious and appropriate ways of responding. These expectations played out in daily conversations and helped to create settings where volunteers made further interpretations about how, and with whom, talk about "the faith" occurred. The second half of this chapter looks at volunteers' attempts to extend talk about morality, responsibility, and duty past daily speech genres.

These three daily speech genres were not the only talk about religion in the kitchen, but at some level they were important indicators (and creators) of extended conversation that did happen. Extensive conversation about religion among coreligionists (for instance, between two Jews, or two Presbyterians, or two "New Agers") happened only after such identifications had been made. (Even when two volunteers could safely assume they were both Jewish, there was beyond that a measure of depth of practice or involvement with religion that remained to be assessed.) Volunteers from similar religious backgrounds could then talk about religion using shared, though restricted, codes; those who did not "share" religious symbols and codes needed to find other ways to speak together across religious diversity if they wished to raise such issues. How they did so, and the ways that daily genres (religious and otherwise) are put to new uses, in new creative contexts, presents new reasons to study daily talk.

TALK ABOUT RELIGION: RELIGIOUS SPEECH GENRES

Despite the varied ways volunteers practiced religion in the kitchen (through praying, counting containers, laughing, and so on), most *talk* about religion went on in several discrete ways: talk about going to church, preparing for holidays, and parody or satire. Talk about church and holidays cropped up when volunteers talked about their daily schedules, and they indulged in parody and satire when the media and political events focused on religious groups. Many volunteers were involved in churches and synagogues or other religious or spiritual groups. Most participated in religious traditions during holidays and family life events and elaborated on their often difficult and frustrating loyalties to family and tradition. Others parodied and satirized religious groups that were "bigoted," commenting on how some religions were more "religious" than others.

This talk did not include theological reflection or discourse about moral behavior. Each, however, included some direct reference to religious or spiritual organizations, belonging, or identity. Each genre structured and suggested certain statements and responses and thus constituted expectations about the possibility and extent of talk about religion.

My interpretation of religious talk is based in Bakhtin's notion of speech genres. Speech genres, Bakhtin says, "include short rejoinders of daily dialogue (and these are extremely varied depending on the subject matter, situation, and participants) everyday narration, writing . . . the brief standard military command, the elaborate and detailed order."[4] In theory, genres are not merely an individual's utterance or statement. They anticipate, and help to shape, a certain kind of rejoinder and certain kinds of relationships. (When I greet the contractor fixing my roof with "Hi, how are you," he responds "Just fine, thanks," before we move on to practical issues. When I call my sister on the phone and ask the same question, I might expect a five-minute discourse on her miserable day at school.) Speech genres are relatively stable forms in theory, but they are not always consistent in use (the contractor might also tell me about his terrible day at work). People misunderstand each other. Individuals with different expectations and understandings of words, tones, and genres transform intended meaning into something new. Genres are probably best understood, then, not as fully structuring constraints, but as created and anticipated structuring points for conversations. They do not determine outcomes, but they do sketch out expectations for how a conversation might proceed. "Genres carry the generalizable resources of particular events; but specific actions or utterances must use those resources to accomplish new purposes in each . . . milieu."[5]

The simple religious genres I heard and recorded in the kitchen are not unique to it. If one pays attention, they can be heard in other spaces and settings in daily life. Likewise, these three genres do not exhaust the everyday religious speech genres that Americans regularly use. They were nevertheless the most common ones I recorded in the kitchen, and they were the ones volunteers used to build discursive relationships where they could also elaborate on religious ideas and values.

Going to Church

Volunteers talked about going to church or synagogue by weaving their religious affiliations into the details of conversations about other things. They thus established their religious identities in everyday chatter about schedules and plans rather than by making declarative statements such as

"I'm an Episcopalian." Even volunteers like Nancy who thought others might disparage their tradition's tenets mentioned their involvement from time to time. As far as I am aware, active members of religious groups did not censor their involvement from conversations.

Most volunteers did not associate their own or others' comments about "going to church" with meaning or faith. Religious participation was one of a number of things people did throughout the week. In this regard, going to church was similar to going to the gym. Nevertheless, talk about churchgoing placed volunteers within a web of institutional affiliations that, it seemed, mattered to them and to others. When I asked volunteers if they knew whether other volunteers attended religious services, they not only said yes but told me who was Protestant, who was Catholic, and who was Buddhist.

Talk about going to church was more complex than it first appeared, however. This genre also implicitly denoted appropriate and inappropriate religious affiliations. I became aware of this boundary when Tuesday morning volunteers made plans to attend the upcoming volunteer appreciation party together. Tanya told us she wouldn't be joining us because she was going to South America to see an "Indian spiritual guide." She was surprised when the other volunteers started to make jokes about the trip. They warned her not to be "brainwashed" and to watch out for hucksters and for anyone who offered her Kool-Aid.

Tanya was a dedicated and well-liked volunteer, and the others (I believe) did not intend to hurt her feelings. Nevertheless, their allusion to Jim Jones and the implication that she was less than rational insulted Tanya. She tried to explain that the guide was a recognized healer, but she got nowhere. Tanya's defense only made the others laugh more. Finally she said, "Well, I'm going to get a great suntan!" Julie changed direction and asked Tanya what vaccines she needed, helping her to reinterpret the trip as solely a "vacation." No further discussion followed about Tanya's guide or why he was important to her.

This interchange began quite simply, when Tanya mentioned why she would not be attending an upcoming volunteer event. Her trip was not unlike others' pilgrimages to Jerusalem, and thus similar to other conversations about going to church. Yet the others' reactions made it clear that her trip fell outside the boundaries of the "going to church" genre. Tanya had waded into murky and ill-defined spiritual commitments and energies (and curiosity).

Tanya's religious journey, in other words, brought to light spiritual experiences that defied normal boundaries of affiliation expected by others in the kitchen. Attending mass or synagogue was socially acceptable. Participating in less structured practices and quests was not so acceptable.

Acceptability was structured in part by the genre, and Tanya's decision did not fit the genre in that it raised questions that went beyond what it could answer. What did Tanya believe? What would her relationship to the guide be? All those issues of authority and belief, "settled" in commonplace talk about church, were unsettled and ambiguous when volunteers began to talk about spiritual quests and novel religious affiliations.

The boundaries of "going to church" talk became clearer when a volunteer (incorrectly) interpreted the genre to signal a willingness to discuss religious experience. One morning Harrison caught Gloria off guard as she finished telling a funny story about her friend Ann, whom she identified as "my friend from church." Harrison asked what church she went to. "Unitarian," she answered.

"What do you get out of church?" he asked.

"Well, I'm really close to the people there—closer than to any other group of people—we just share so much!" Rather than telling Harrison how they had helped her and her family get through her sister's sudden death (as she had told Susan and me several months before), she said, "It's rare that you find a group of people you can talk to, and share so many things. And when you do, that's something you have to hang on to." Gloria had been attending her church for decades and considered it her extended family.

Harrison was looking for new things to do, Susan knew, because they had talked about rejoining the "singles scene" in Manhattan. Susan, who attended a progressive Presbyterian church in lower Manhattan "on and off," asked Harrison from across a heaping pile of yucca root, "Why? Are you thinking of attending somewhere? Church is a good place to meet people, you know."

He answered with a nonanswer. "It's just that recently I've been going through this rough time. I've been pretty depressed about it, you know. And one morning, I was just sitting, and thinking—and something came over me. It was like I was looking at my life and watching it go by. It was—just a detached, calm feeling. It was just this, well, it was this intensely spiritual thing, and that has never happened to me before." Susan nodded, encouraging but noncommittal. Gloria rolled her eyes.

He continued, "It was what the Buddhists call detachment. I didn't grow up religious, and that's part of my problem, you know." He chuckled and went on to say, "But I don't want to be a Buddhist. You know, to say that what happened was detachment—it's like, who cares. Everybody's a Buddhist these days, but that's really what it was, you know?"

"There's a Zen monastery I know of—maybe you should try it out," I offered, thinking that he might want a bit more encouragement, but he said no.

"With all the violence that's been in my life recently, I don't want to be in an organized religion. They just seem to be *violent*." I asked him what he meant (I had never heard Zen called violent before). He explained, "To me it seems that organized religions are just—well, they do violence to the experience. It's your experience, and they put it into something, contain it."

"Maybe, but a church can really be a support when things are rough in your life," Gloria offered.

"Yeah, maybe, but—" Harrison trailed off.

No one else said anything.

Gloria could not have expected that mentioning Ann "from church" would lead us into such a conversation. She shied away as it took shape: rather than giving him concrete examples, she used an abstract statement that could go "anywhere" Harrison wanted it to go. She didn't really answer his question.

Taking the little we knew about Harrison, the rest of the volunteers around the table suggested several reasons for going to church that fit more neatly within the contours of the genre. But Harrison rebuffed our suggestions that church would help him meet new people or offer a community to support him in time of trouble. When he started to talk about this experience, he was looking for a way to understand it, not for some affiliation or community. By the time we recognized that Harrison was not talking about finding a church to attend, we were not sure where he was headed.

Harrison labeled his experience Buddhist even though he immediately told us he was not Buddhist. Although he was familiar with a few Buddhist categories that might explain his feeling, he seemed bothered that it could be classified so easily (as in "everyone" is a Buddhist these days). My suggestion that he check out a monastery seemed to annoy him even more.

Talking about church did not propel volunteers toward talk about belief or religious experience. On the few occasions when it was misunderstood by someone to signal talk about belief, others were confused and resistant. They switched to other genres or at the very least alluded to them in their speech. Not all individuals could follow such switches without losing their place, however; some were more adept than others. Sean found this out one afternoon as we poured salad dressing into small plastic cups with Robert and Cherry, two African American volunteers. Sean asked Cherry why she hadn't come in on her regular day.

"I'm usually coming in here on Thursdays," she said, turning to Robert to clarify Sean's question. She told Sean, "On Mondays I go to the prison to do some prison visiting. There's a seminar for training tomorrow at Bethany Baptist, so I came in today. That's what I do. I do that one day, and this one day." She started prison visiting when a friend asked her to come along, and she enjoyed volunteering so much that she decided to take on a second project at God's Love We Deliver.

Robert then told us, "I found this on my own too. I didn't have a church that helped me find something to do, but here I am. I wish I could get them at my church involved in doing this kind of work. But they aren't interested."

Cherry looked surprised. "Isn't your church an *outreach church?*" she demanded, stressing each syllable.

"Sure," he said wryly. "It's an outreach church. They open up the doors every Sunday, and the preacher is preaching. That's the way they're reaching out to the people so they come in."

"But does it do *ministry?*" she wanted to know.

"My church—the money comes in, it don't flow out," said Robert, repeating as he demonstrated the flow with his hands. "You know what I'm saying, it comes in, it don't go out."

Cherry disapproved, pursing her lips and shaking her head in disgust.

"I come here on my own. I don't come through my church," he repeated.

"So who does the outreach?" Cherry persisted.

"Nobody but me."

"Well that's no church for me. If I were at that church, I would leave."

Sean, who had been silent, leaned in to add his two cents. "You know what, I saw these churches in September when I was in Europe? They were these huge buildings, you know?" Robert and Cherry listened to him for a beat as he began to describe their cool stone interiors and stained-glass windows, then returned to their conversation. Sean then turned to me, "The buildings were just beautiful."

"I know," I said. "Too bad so few people attend them!" I thought maybe this comment would connect Cherry and Robert's conversation to Sean's interjection. But Sean just stared as if he didn't understand me. Robert and Cherry were still talking.

"Pray and stay, sister, that's what it's about," Robert was telling Cherry, still defending his church. "Pray and stay. I've got roaches, and I've got mice in my house. They come in, but that doesn't mean I go. Just the same as at church. You have to keep going, don't worry about anyone else."

I laughed at the metaphor. Seeing me smile, Robert leaned over the table toward Cherry, saying in a loud, clear voice, "You've got to know this, sister: Our Lord is a deliverer."

Cherry nodded in agreement, smiling as they each repeated several times in a cadence, putting the accent on different syllables, "Our Lord is a deliverer. Our Lord is a deliverer."

Even though Sean started this conversation, he was quickly cut from it. Cherry and Robert found they had a common experience in coming to the kitchen on "their own," yet they argued about what was important about going to church.

Robert and Cherry moved easily from talk about "going to church" to a conversation that compared churches' ministerial and outreach methods. Sean, by contrast, had little experience attending religious services. He did not immediately catch the genre switch to an evaluation of different churches, and he interjected his experience, which fit better within the regular parameters of "going to church."

I was also a spectator, albeit a more knowledgeable one than Sean. Realizing he had failed to get back into the conversation, Sean tried to strike one up with me. Pained that I could not listen to Robert and Cherry (the data lost!), I attempted to craft a topical bridge to bring Sean's comments closer to theirs, but Sean's blank look told me my tack would not work. When I started listening to Robert and Cherry again and marked my renewed attention with a laugh, they closed the conversation with a confession they both agreed to: "Our Lord is a deliverer." Then Robert laughed and digressed into further conversation about the roaches in his apartment. Sean and I could both (unfortunately) relate to roach problems.

Although the genre seemed trivial when I first noted its use, I soon learned otherwise. Talk about going to church not only established religious identities but distinguished "normal" religious activity from less normal, personal kinds. It made space where the former could be discussed more easily and where the latter had to be translated if others were to respond favorably. Whether or not volunteers were religiously or spiritually tolerant, the genre excluded talk about less traditionally defined spiritual journeys.

Preparing for Holidays

Talk about going to church was frequent. Talk about holidays punctuated kitchen conversation in seasonal spurts. Holidays structured the kitchen calendar, with its most festive and frantic time stretching between Halloween and New Year's Eve. Volunteers helped cook multicourse meals for Thanksgiving and Christmas (called the "Holiday Feast"), picking up extra shifts as they were needed. While talk about going to church often imparted facts about volunteers' identities and affiliations, talk about holidays positioned them in relation to their families, to traditions, and to religious observance in more detailed ways. In talking about holidays, they could voice their ideas about religious tradition, interweaving them with stories about family and about food.

In the ongoing holiday hubbub, volunteers discussed their own heroic preparations for their families and the inevitable strains that family get-togethers produced. We compared recipes and family traditions and sometimes discussed holidays' "meanings." These discussions let them talk about their religious beliefs in more open-ended ways than the genre of "going to church" presented.

A few weeks before Passover, Judy asked Sean for a recipe for a "vegetable dish" she could take to a seder. She groaned that she would rather be anywhere than at her sister-in-law's house that night. But she would go and would even bring a vegetable dish, though this wasn't what she usually brought. "Usually my sister-in-law just tells me to bring a fruit platter—real straightforward, just cut up the fruit and go. But this year she asked my other sister-in-law's daughter to do the fruit. She told me, 'Why don't you bring a vegetable?' At least I got it easier than my other sister-in-law. She has to bring 'something in a sweet potato'!"

Sean suggested a baked asparagus dish. As he explained how to make it she interrupted. "I can't do that, it's not kosher," she said.

Melinda asked why not. "The bread crumbs? You could leave those off you know," she offered.

"Yeah, but I wouldn't put them in anyway, too heavy," Judy said. "It's the Parmesan cheese. Not kosher. I'd like to take something lighter." She wrinkled her nose, turning to me. "The whole meal is usually casseroles. The last thing I want to see is another casserole. Yech."

Sean had walked away, so Melinda and I helped Judy decide on an asparagus dish that would be easy to make for thirty people, could be served cold—and was kosher. I mentioned that my family always had asparagus on Easter.

"Do you have it with ham?" Judy asked.

"No, we usually have lamb or salmon," I said, "and a little Virginia country ham on the side, but that's just because we're southern." Judy was surprised at our "traditional" Easter main course. "I thought everyone had ham at Easter."

"No, that's just the white bread Americans," Melinda broke in, amused at Judy's stereotype. "That's what we always had, with the pineapple slices and cherries and the whole works. But the Italians have lamb, I think."

"Ah, but Courtney's not Italian!" Judy noted.

We continued talking about Easter meals, with Judy quizzing Melinda and me on what we would do on Easter Sunday. "Well, I won't go to church," Melinda said after hearing that I would attend an early morning service with my extended family. "We used to go on Easter, but that's the only day we ever went, besides Christmas. After I got married again we just decided it was silly to go once a year. So we stopped."

"So you don't do anything—you don't even go to the Easter parade?" Judy probed.

"No—I don't know, do they still have the Easter parade?"

Judy made it clear that she was not happy to take part in her holiday. "Next year, Tahiti," she said, changing the traditional phrase "Next year in Jerusalem" to an even more remote location. (Judy followed through on this pledge: the following year she spent the week of Passover in the Caribbean. I asked her what, if anything, she had done to mark the holiday. "Oh, we observed it. We had our white wine, a piece of baguette, and toasted 'Next year in Jerusalem.' That was it!")

Judy participated because her husband and children expected her to, not because she was observant. She was told what to do and how to do it: in this case her sister-in-law dictated what she was to bring. Judy was annoyed that she was being bumped further up the ladder of responsibility for the meal. It was certainly more work to fix a "hot" vegetable as part of the meal than to make a platter of fruit for noshing. Judy compromised by preparing a vegetable that was "light" and that she could serve cold, subverting the unspoken expectation of family order that an array of hot and cold dishes helped reproduce. She told us later that "everyone" loved the asparagus, even though her sister-in-law was shocked that she had brought something cold.

Judy's gripes about Passover plans led not only to a more subtle interpretation of how religion, family, and food fit together in her life, but also to further commentary about how food factored in the ways Melinda and I celebrated the Easter season. Judy told us she thought Easter was "going to church and the Easter egg hunt—chocolate bunnies, y'know."

When I first told Judy that my extended family did not have a standard Easter meal, she gave me a knowing wink, incorrectly equating our "lack" of a set, traditional menu with a lack of observance. I continued by saying that my uncle and father prepared most of the meal. "I'm gonna come to your house," she said in disbelief. Reflecting that our menu changed from year to year, I also mentioned that a smaller family group also had a celebratory meal the night before Easter that we called "the rites of spring." Unlike the noon Easter "dinner" that we ate with my abstaining grandparents, the rites of spring included excellent wine. The menu of shad roe with crabmeat and fresh asparagus had been set years before. Judy continued to ask questions about my family's "rites of spring" week after week. As she winked and grinned, I realized how surreptitious and secular the "rites" seemed when I talked about it (even the name connoted an illicit frolic in a starry field), especially when compared with the Easter meal shared after an early morning church service in the broad spring sunlight.

The easy confluence of holiday and food talk led others to discuss holidays' religious meanings (and often their confusion about those meanings). Charlene boasted, for instance, that she could teach us the "four questions" asked at a seder, but she blushed when she got stuck after the second. When Julie invited Mort "down to her place" for the second night of Passover, Mort asked no one in particular, "Why *are* there two nights of Passover?"

"I don't know either." Julie mused. She turned to ask Barbara, "Do you know why?"

Tamar broke in. "They only have one night in Israel."

"So why do we have two nights here?"

Tamar had the definitive answer; she was Israeli, and the others deferred to her on Jewish culture issues. "It's because of the Diaspora. The Jews in Europe didn't know which night it was because the calendars got confused. They did two nights to make sure they got the right time one of the nights."

"Really, that's quite interesting," said Barbara. "I always thought it was something religious. It wasn't originally that they had two nights?"

"No, it's not religious," repeated Tamar. "It's tradition."

"So now do we know the right day?" asked Julie, frowning.

"They do in Israel," answered Tamar.

"I wish we only did it once," Mort said.

"Come on—if we only did it one night then you couldn't come down to my house. Or you'd have to decide between your parents and me!" Julie laughed, patting him on the back.

Barbara mulled over Tamar's report, saying almost to herself, "Larry would probably do without the second night. But I've already invited everyone—I like to do it." Before she retired as a cooking instructor, Barbara taught countless Jewish women how to make brisket "like their mothers and grandmothers" and how to prepare gefilte fish and haroseth. She was not about to give up preparing her own table once a year, even on the "second night." Religious and ethnic or cultural reasons for celebrating holidays intertwined in exchanges like these, solidifying the importance of traditional and family rites.

Jewish volunteers—Julie, Judy, Mort, Barbara, and many others I met—volunteered on Christmas Day, recognizing that many Christian volunteers would be celebrating with family. Likewise, non-Jewish volunteers picked up the slack during the Passover season and around Yom Kippur and Rosh Hashanah. Hannah told me that volunteers' awareness of holidays, and their willingness to "pick up the slack" when others were observing, circumvented most scheduling problems. But it did not escape anyone's attention that GLWD paid more attention to Christian holidays. It sent Easter candy on Good Friday but not hamantaschen during Purim. It wrapped "Holiday" presents to deliver to clients on December 25 but did not tuck Hanukkah gelt into its deliveries.

Christian holidays thus presented situations where volunteers questioned the agency's "religiousness." According to the chefs and Barb, the client services coordinator, GLWD celebrated any day that it could, to make the clients' lives happier. So, in addition to birthday cakes for clients, the agency prepared elaborate celebrations on Thanksgiving and Christmas and delivered special treats on other holidays. It also delivered candy on Valentine's Day and Halloween and strawberry shortcake on the Fourth of July. Staff members maintained that the agency did not celebrate Christian holidays in a religious manner—or denied that they celebrated them at all.

One of my office duties was to coordinate and update the constantly changing client list for Thanksgiving and Christmas meal deliveries. When I was talking to Chris, a specials chef, about how many modified meals he would make at Christmas, we both became confused. Chris tried to convince me that GLWD had not prepared a special delivery for clients on Christmas Day in past years. "It's Thanksgiving that we celebrate here, Courtney," he told me. He was right, at least in some respects. Thanksgiving was the more prominent holiday. Religious meanings did not stick to Thanksgiving, allowing the agency to celebrate it without the sidestepping and reinterpreting that Christmas required. Nevertheless, the agency made a big deal of Christmas every year, albeit as the "Holiday Feast." I don't know why Chris forgot about the prime rib he carved on Christmases past, but our interchange highlighted some of the contradictions that holidays posed for kitchen workers.

These contradictions nonetheless made for fruitful and interesting conversations where GLWD's volunteers and staff tried to interpret the unsteady boundary between Christian holidays rooted in religious doctrine and the consumer and civic celebrations that accompanied (or engulfed) them. Whether God's Love We Deliver should deliver a full Christmas experience, replete with presents and a meal inspired by Scrooge's Christmas morning extravagance was another issue. Rather than asking staff directly why the agency celebrated these holidays, volunteers focused on the symbols themselves. Why all the trimmings for Christmas, and why notice Easter at all?

Faced with dyeing twelve hundred eggs during Easter week, Judy asked Bill, "What do eggs symbolize?" He said authoritatively, "Easter is a pagan holiday, it's the spring fertility feast. That's what it was originally. Eggs were a sign of fertility." She rolled her eyes, saying, "Yeah, yeah, I got you." The answer was not quite untrue, but Bill and Judy both knew it was not really an answer. The question of why we paid any attention to Easter was left dangling.

Earlier in the spring, on Valentine's Day, Barb, who came down for a piece of red velvet cake, mentioned in passing that she spent the previous evening clipping tracts off eight hundred Valentine's Day wreaths donated by a local florist. Emily asked what was in them. On hearing that they were Psalms, she said, "Why did you take them off? Maybe someone would have liked one!"

Barb replied, "Not all of our clients are Christian, you know. The meals are the only thing we send out. We don't send out anything that's Christian, Jewish, or whatever."

"So what about Christmas Day? Why do we do that?" Emily asked.

"That's our *Holiday Feast,*" Barb answered, correcting Emily. "We send it out that day because it's when some of our clients expect to have gifts and stuff, and since it's such a big delivery, we can get the extra volunteers we need to do it." Barb continued to call the December 25 delivery a Holiday Feast, but everyone else called it Christmas. Barb was less vigilant in ferreting out the religious message one might decipher from a dyed Easter egg. And she worked diligently to make sure that GLWD delivered the fanciest Christmas gift basket of all New York's AIDS organizations.

Volunteers developed their understanding of their own and others' religious views and obligations as they talked about holidays. Similarly, GLWD's expression of holiday cheer prompted them to raise questions about how the agency should celebrate and, by extension, how it should mark the boundaries of the religious and the cultural. Talk about the place of religion in public life received more play, however, in conversations about the Catholic Church and the "religious right." These two groups received much attention in the kitchen, most of it as parody and cutting commentary.

Parody, or What to Do with Squeezie Pope Cups

Traffic snarled to a stop in mid-Manhattan for almost a week when John Paul II visited New York in 1995. Given the daily disruptions the visit caused for many city dwellers and the constant media attention, it was small wonder the pope was a constant topic of conversation. Volunteers complained about the pope's large security detail and the tax dollars the mayor was spending. They commented favorably on the Swiss guardsmen's physiques. In this milieu, several ex-Catholic volunteers expressed their biting disdain for all things Catholic.

The parodies and satiric comments about religious groups and figures composed a third religious speech genre. Off-color jokes about the pope and cutting judgments about the religious right were quite different from talking about church affiliations or about preparing for the holidays. While satire was a constant feature of kitchen talk and volunteers left no topic unscathed, parodies of conservative religious groups often seemed to touch a deeper nerve. I noted that former Catholics were more likely to make jokes about John Cardinal O'Connor than were non-Catholics, and that those who had the most experience with conservative Protestants performed the most bawdy caricatures of television preachers.

Parody, though sometimes grotesque and scatological, usually included some judgment about what religion could or should be in a perfect world. Parody provided opportunities for volunteers rejected by these groups to turn their words around, whether by profaning the pope's image or by affecting a southern accent.[6] In other words, volunteers implied *why* they felt others' positions were wrong or even immoral. As Sean often asked with great indignation and knowing self-righteousness, "Isn't religion supposed to be about love?"

The pope's visit provided opportunities for commentary on the Catholic Church's official positions on homosexuality and birth control. On Tuesday morning, some volunteers laughed about the pro-condom banner someone had unfurled directly across from Saint Patrick's Cathedral the previous morning, just as mass ended. No one had taken credit for the banner, but Charles said he'd be happy to claim it, "as long as no one sends me to jail."

Parodies extended beyond criticism of the organizations to include those who participated in them. Vivian, a pregnant twenty-seven-year-old, started to recite a list of pope-related souvenirs she had picked up or seen: "Y'know, the little medallions, the stuff your grandmother loves." A few of us joined in, laughing about the jackets, baseball hats, and key rings that vendors hawked on the corners. Hip and funny, Vivian had most of us laughing as she described all the kitsch. But she continued on and on past the point of humor, mockingly telling us that she had bought four plastic cups with screw tops and straws decorated with the pope's picture. Her mother, a "good Catholic lady" who wished Vivian would marry her boyfriend before she delivered the baby, would be visiting New York for the first time at Thanksgiving. Vivian told us she planned to set out the "pope squeezie cups" amid the good china, "fill 'em with Bud," and "have a few good toasts to that asshole. I can't wait to see my mother's face!"

Sean and several other volunteers laughed along, not noticing, as Judy had, that Nancy and Clara had neither joined in nor looked up during the entire conversation. Judy caught my eye and looked over toward the two Catholic women. I felt a pang of guilt for laughing at all. I felt even worse when Judy leaned over and said in a stage whisper, "I don't like him either, but if he's the head of a religion, you oughta respect him a little, don't you think?" Having witnessed Judy's indifferent appraisals of reactions to things religious, I was surprised that she was the one to stick up for the pope. But Judy's comment appeared to be a cautionary comment directed at Vivian rather than a defense of Catholicism. The stage whisper worked, because when Sean started to take up the conversation again, Vivian waved him off.

Many volunteers would have answered Judy's question about respecting the pope with a vigorous no. Many had found themselves, or people close to them, subject to what they felt was religiously based bigotry. Kate often reminded me that "organized religion is organized hatred." Gaining psychic and geographic distance from her Catholic family in Oregon by moving to New York and marrying a Jewish man, she counted herself lucky to have "escaped all that Catholic bullshit." Signs of religious fervor and fanaticism creeping into the secular urban world troubled Kate greatly. Volunteers and staff fretted together over the November 1994 elections, when Republicans gained a majority of seats in the House of Representatives. Coupled with the 1993 election of Rudolph Giuliani, they suggested, things did not bode well for the moral tone of the country.

Volunteers thus blithely poked fun at political and "Christian" conservatives (whom they appeared, for the most part, to consider the same group) for their "blind ideologies," "stupidity," and general "ignorance." For instance, whenever Sean started talking about religious conservatives he affected a hillbilly accent, associating stupidity and simple-mindedness with the South and with Christians. "People stare at you just because you're different. How can they call themselves Christian?" Christians, others suggested, were beset with the same problems that their so-called moral rectitude supposedly kept at bay. Charles, who also grew up in the "South," often told us how "hypocritical" Christians were, pointing to, among other things, the many AIDS cases in his home county. "My mother works with the county clinic," Charles said, "and you would never believe how many people they have out there. They don't even know what they have, and they're so prejudiced and stupid that they spread it all over."

If the presence of practicing and nonpracticing Catholics kept caricatures of believing Catholics and their leaders at a comparatively low level, the absence of "fundamentalists" allowed lampoons of the religious right to flourish. Few volunteers had any direct experience with the Christian conservatives they vilified, and those who had were not cautious in their remarks. Shelly, a new volunteer, told us she was from Alabama and did not appreciate antisouthern humor. "There are a lot of good people in the South, and they aren't all stupid," she commented dryly. Sean was shocked, then tried to explain. He really did know what he was talking about. He grew up in a small North Carolina town and ran away to the big city at fifteen when he realized that everyone, "even some of my uncles and aunts," thought he was going to hell because he was gay. "I have nothing against southerners," he told Shelly, "just the religious bigots who live there."

Roughly sketched caricatures of public figures did not presume or even allow a value in investigating the claims conservatives make. The strength or truth of these caricatures was rarely at issue. As subtle as satire can be in the hands of a clever and informed individual, in the kitchen it was more often a blunt instrument.

Given the way parody worked, it seems natural that from time to time volunteers used the genre to close off discussions about religion. As Tanya discovered, it was easy to cross the boundary between earnest conversation and ironic commentary. Volunteers did not sustain conversations about religion and spirituality precisely because parodic and "joking" comments were easy to make and available to anyone who was uneasy when someone else started to speak of such things.

One evening John asked Rick, a former monk, what he knew about a "fourteenth-century nun" his coworker was "really into." When Rick appeared stumped, other volunteers standing between them started to call out saints' names.[7]

John was more interested in talking about the saint's visions than in making a list of saints, however. Across the clamor of comments about Teresa of Avila and Julian of Norwich, John told Rick about the visions and how the saint had apparently felt "unworthy" to receive them. The visions were about Joseph. "That's interesting," Rick interjected. "Most people had visions about Mary. Whenever you see Mary in pictures she's this beautiful young thing, but when you see Joseph, he's always old and *worked*," he added. John nodded and continued, "She had visions about Joseph. They were visions of him forgiving Mary for being pregnant."

Rick stuck his knife into the pile of beef in front of him. "You know, "Mary probably wasn't even fourteen, that's when girls got married in that culture—"

"—and Joseph was a old man by then, and could have had her killed," said the woman next to me.

Betsy, a young advertising executive standing next to Rick, added in a loud and sarcastic voice, "Yeah. He must have been *pretty horny.*" Everyone paused for a split second, then erupted into laughter—and someone turned up the disco.

These three genres said different things about religion and spirituality. Or rather, they let volunteers say different things about what religion was. Volunteers similarly made clear what talk about religion was *not* when they moved over the boundaries of each religious speech genre. As volunteers used these genres they marked the limits of most talk about the faith.

Returning to Nancy's initial comments, we see that she developed her idea of whether she could talk about religion through interpreting and remembering others' remarks. She picked up on parody, heard Vivian deride Catholics, and saw the rest of us laughing. These experiences, together with her history of living the "high life" with gay friends and then, after her salvation and return to the Catholic Church, watching many of them die, reinforced her notion that GLWD was not a place where her kind of religion would be easily accepted. Her interpretation and vision of events in the kitchen was built into her own story, both in the genres she used and in the contingencies of her life.

Not all Catholics felt the way Nancy did. The language and practice of "being Catholic" did not in itself influence how people interpreted and lived within religious speech genres in the kitchen. For example, Lucy, another practicing Catholic and a lifelong New Yorker, said her conversations with other volunteers confirmed that "everyone in the kitchen" shared a "certain spirit." She said, "You can call it the spirit of cooperation or the spirit of a cause, or the Holy Spirit, or whatever kind of spirit you would think about calling it. There's definitely a spirit there." Unlike Nancy, Lucy found it relatively easy to talk about religion in the kitchen. These two women, who attended similar parish churches and were committed to similar political positions, nevertheless heard conversations in different ways. What each heard was built as much on her biography and practice as on some objective interpretation of what was "actually" going on in the kitchen.

While the expected, ordinary speech genres provided groundwork for volunteers to understand religion and its place within the kitchen, they did not fully structure talk about religion. Such genres worked in tandem with personal memories and individually held and formed genres (being Catholic, a New Yorker, and the like) even as those were informed, and sometimes changed, by the genres common in the kitchen. Speech genres did not set objective territory for conversation about religion that all volunteers understood and lived by.

In living with, and through, genres of this kind, volunteers found relatively stable ground on which to address issues that mattered to them.
Much of this work happened within genres, but at times volunteers worked
at their boundaries, introducing new meanings, values, and expectations
into their social interactions. This more creative work of introducing unexpected purpose, or new expectations, into commonplace conversation
was risky. As individuals brought their own histories and unique inflec-
tions into the conversations they recognized, they often also drew in other
meanings and associations. The "surplus" in daily conversation that alluded to the ways people might use the same genre, or same phrases, in
other settings made it possible for extended conversations about religion
to take place.[8]

EMILY AND "GOOD MANNERS": RELIGIOUS TALK

The creative surplus of meanings embedded in daily conversations allowed
some volunteers to develop conversations about things that "come with the
faith," such as moral evaluations and differences, personally held principles, and motivations. Most of these conversations were indirect, in that
they were built on allusions rather than statements and depended (sometimes with great uncertainty) on others' hearing and picking up on such
implications. For example, Cherry and Robert, the two African American
volunteers who attended similar churches, expanded their conversation
quickly from a commonplace genre to direct language that made judgments of religious bodies and leaders. Turning their conversation about
churchgoing into one about the worthiness of churches seemed seam-
less, even as it developed out of their quick recognition that they shared
still other codes and genres, built up in similar social settings (and institutions). In comparison, most conversations between volunteers that
touched on religious motivations and authority were initiated with great
circumspection and some trepidation. In talking about religion, volunteers from different religious traditions built on their familiarity with
common religious speech genres and on their ability to use what they
knew about others, collected and remembered through the daily interchanges.[9]

The approaches to conversation that went beyond simple genres might
be described as what Mikhail Bakhtin calls "double-directed" or double-
voiced discourse.[10] It occurs as people bring in comments, asides, and
references that refer to or represent more elaborate articulations and explanations. Double-voiced discourse develops when individuals recogniz-
ably draw on others' language or phrasing and turn it toward their own

ends; that is, when they take someone else's phrase and give it new meaning in a new conversational setting. As a rule, Bakhtin notes, "practical . . . speech is full of other people's words: with some of them we completely merge our own voice, forgetting whose they are; others, which we take as authoritative, we use to reinforce our own words; still others, finally, we populate with our own aspirations, alien or hostile to them."[11] We "populate" our language and expand the number of ways it can be interpreted. In translating and reiterating others' words or putting our own words into new settings, we transform ideas. In this way religious language can "happen" without direct reference to any religious symbols at all, but rather through indirect phrasing, allusions, or patterned similarities. Bakhtin suggests that double-voiced discourse, which combines speech types and inflects standard genres with new meaning, is commonplace throughout daily life. For instance, it is not always clear what a speaker intends; common language and metaphors can be interpreted in several ways, and speakers listen and respond with differing degrees of interest and emotion.[12]

Double-voiced discourse is different from what some have termed restricted or encoded language, which develops in small communities or subcultures and can be identified by insiders through its various symbols, linguistic shorthand, and the like. Whether intentionally or not, it is hybrid language, which draws from various "languages" and thus crosses the boundaries of various genres and kinds of speech. Double-voiced discourse allows for communicating across difference, without reducing a lack of similarity to a "new" shared culture. Such translation and revising is active and creative, even as it happens within a number of specific constraints, including the actors' positions relative to one another and to the social setting, and their familiarity with various genres. In this respect, double-voiced discourse is not the last resort of the weak or powerless. Nor is it only the privilege of the powerful or those who are usually perceived to control language.[13] Interpreting double-voiced discourse exclusively in one of these frames limits our ability to even see everyday undertakings of nondirect speech or the variety of settings where it is at work. We use nondirect, double-voiced discourse for many reasons, and we employ different speech genres with an eye to what we want to communicate, and to whom.

Bakhtin focuses primarily on the unintentional aspects of hybridization of language, which he incidentally views as a major source of social change.[14] But double-voiced discourse is, in addition, a form of speech that can be intentional. In the rest of this chapter I consider intentional hybridization, where volunteers worked consciously to develop ways of understanding each other within the kitchen's bounded speech contexts. One place where double-voiced, indirect discourse might be useful is a setting where people do not assume shared language or belief. Expectations of diversity may therefore situate speakers in such a way that they already expect to have to translate or resituate their own meanings from familiar genres to some other one if they want to communicate.

In the kitchen, volunteers operated with the assumption that the others they worked with did not in general share their beliefs or views about religion. If they thought they shared the "same spirit," they were often rather circumspect about assuming they shared the same language to express it. (Those who did assume it sometimes met terrible disappointment, as Sandra did when Bill became furious because Libby washed the pineapple in the wrong sink.) In the story that follows, Emily, the Episcopalian who said that "work is prayer," and Julie, the Jewish woman who fussed over the learning disabled group, fashioned indirect discourse about personal duty and responsibility by developing a theme of "good manners." Their ongoing conversation developed strong religious resonance and meaning for both women. It took me some time to "hear" what they were telling each other, however. (In fact, without the interviews with both women, I might have guessed, but could not know, what each brought to, and took from, these conversations.) Over time, Emily also developed the notions and language contained in her conversations with Julie and in actions and conversations in her church. And in so doing she sustained talk about religion across several settings, enlivening the meanings of her actions (and others') in each.

I first heard Emily talk about good manners when she told Julie, Mort, and me how her family took its turn working at their church's soup kitchen. As a member of the church's executive committee, Emily was expected to take a turn every so often. Emily said she didn't like the soup kitchen work very much, and Mort asked why. "Oh, I don't know," Emily shrugged. "Maybe it's just that I had such a bad experience this week."

"And what was that?" Julie asked.

Emily began to tell us how she worked on the breakfast serving line while her husband flipped banana and plain pancakes. Toward the end of the serving time a woman brought a plate of half-eaten pancakes to Emily and asked her to finish cooking them, because they were raw inside. Emily gave the plate to her husband, who dumped the pancakes in the trash and gave her fresh pancakes a minute later. The woman became irate when she saw the new pancakes.

Emily mimicked the woman: "I want *my* pancakes!"

"I told her I was sorry, but that they'd been thrown away—her original pancakes were all syrupy and we couldn't put them back on the grill."

Wouldn't she like fresh ones better anyway? "I mean, they were *covered* with syrup."

No, the woman said. The fresh ones were *banana* pancakes, and she hated banana. She wanted *plain* pancakes. Emily conferred with her husband, who said there was no more batter for plain pancakes. The woman threw down the plate and stormed off to the table, where several seated women glared over at Emily.

Emily became upset as she told us this story. Her hand tightened on her knife as she continued. "I know I was there to serve her," she said, "but shouldn't she have been *grateful* for what we were giving her? First of all, it was free. And it was good food, too. And no one else got a second helping, but we were offering one to her. I couldn't believe how rude she was!"

We kept chopping, giving Emily some sympathetic nods. A moment later she added, "Sometimes it's hard to have good manners." Mort and Julie nodded, knowingly. "Sometimes it is," Mort echoed.

Unlike Mort and Julie, I thought Emily's comments about "good manners" were rather judgmental. How could Emily blame a homeless woman for not having good manners? Condemning a woman for not acting with the middle-class standards that Emily herself thought important seemed to go against the aphorisms she often used in the kitchen. Mort's and Julie's ready agreement with Emily's assessment similarly confused me. I had the strong sense that I had missed something in the conversation, but it would be weeks before I recognized what that was.

A few weeks after Emily told the story about the pancakes, she and I sat outside in the courtyard drinking coffee, resting for a few minutes after the morning shift. She was telling me again how busy she was that day, and I remarked that I was surprised she had shown up at all. She shrugged and said that coming was "her responsibility."

"To me, it's like, take Julie. Julie brings her grandchildren in [to the kitchen], to show them what it's like to give to other people. She thinks that's just part of good manners, like someone not sticking their gum on the subway, on the seats. and I think she's right." She paused before adding, "That's true spirituality."

I realized then that I had misinterpreted Emily's story about the pancakes and the homeless woman at the soup kitchen. She had been critically assessing her *own* reaction to the woman she was serving, not the woman's reaction. Having "good manners" was a spiritual responsibility that involved being civil toward others. And it was an ongoing concern throughout each day. Although it was about "good manners" in the narrow sense, it was also about the struggle to be gracious and giving toward others, especially when it became difficult.

Even though I knew I had misunderstood Emily's initial comment about good manners, I felt that I still didn't know how manners were related to spirituality and how that related to volunteering. In contrast to the soup kitchen where Emily met the woman who didn't like her pancakes, GLWD's kitchen kept the cooks separated from the clients. Was it difficult to have good manners toward the clients when volunteers could imagine them and their tastes and requests in any way they wanted? I found that most volunteers assumed the clients were grateful and appreciative. The notes from clients that were tacked to the kitchen bulletin board reaffirmed their sentiments that they were doing something intimate, basic, and good for others. Yet these intimacies and care toward others were not based on face-to-face interactions. No angry clients threw the food back at them.

So, I thought, while Emily did not want to compare volunteering with "just writing a check," at GLWD she was not forced to tailor her cooking practices (to "remake the pancakes" as it were). Rather, she could act on her desires and on her sense of what cooking well was all about. Emily was not alone in describing cooking like this or imagining that the way she preferred food was the way the clients would.

Although comparing spiritual commitment to "good manners" made it seem not much different from not sticking gum on a subway seat, the stories Emily told had deeper resonance among the volunteers she knew and talked with every week. There was more to good manners than met the eye. Emily, I realized, had been using Julie's meaning to talk to me. She was, in fact, quoting Julie.

"DOING GOOD THINGS": DECIPHERING THE MEANINGS OF MANNERS

Julie's ideas about giving were grounded in ideas about what it meant to be Jewish. Julie did not think of volunteering as a "spiritual" practice per se. That was not part of her vocabulary—it did not have any mystical import. Unlike Emily, who embraced cooking as enriching, Julie did not cook very often. Now that her children were grown, she rarely made a meal at home. But as they worked beside each other week after week and talked about their struggles to teach their children to do the right things, they probed each others' stories and came to understand each other through the language of "good manners."

When Julie talked about good manners, she had a sense that doing good should be second nature. Practicing Judaism was not so much about going

to synagogue or believing in God (neither of which she did) as about lead-
ing a life that was essentially Jewish in identity and in action. For Julie,
there was "no separation between being Jewish and doing good for others, wherever you are." Doing good did not *follow* belief. Doing things for
others was religious practice.

Many Jewish volunteers were quick to tell me that in their tradition
it is less important to believe in God than to "practice." Alexis, a young
woman who grew up in a conservative Jewish family, thought that her faith
required action more than discussion. When I asked why she was involved
in countless volunteer projects in high school, she said, "I don't know
why. . . . It was just there to do, with the expectation that it would be done.
It was 'Go do it.' " This expectation had more to do with social justice
than with biblical laws. It was Passover week; we were both drinking coffee,
and she was eating scrambled eggs with whole wheat toast. She picked up
the toast and without irony said, "I don't have to believe that eating this
piece of bread on Passover is going to make God strike me down. I don't
have to believe that, but I have to do it anyway. I mean—Judaism could be
contrasted to a sort of mainline Protestant tradition, where you could be
a good Christian just by believing; you don't even have to do anything."
Catching herself, remembering that I was not Jewish, she said, "Maybe you
think I'm wrong, but then in a lot of denominations you can just believe
and that's sufficient. And in Judaism it doesn't matter whether you believe
or not. You've just got to do it. You have to be counted, and be public."

This conversation about good manners took me back to my first day in
the kitchen, when the learning disabled adults had turned things upside
down. Julie arrived after we were already upset. She reprimanded Lee for
not having more foresight, but then she made the best of the situation.
Julie was gentle and encouraging with them, even though she made it clear
to me that she was not happy.

After the group left, Julie went upstairs to talk to Hannah about what
had happened, then came back down to report to us. She told Hannah
it was not good for the clients or for the volunteers to have to baby-sit.
Hannah did not agree with Julie, but she admitted she could not ask the
group to return, given the situation with the sunglasses. Julie also admitted, when she returned, that she was not happy with the way the group
had left. She agreed with Hannah that Tom had overstepped his authority
when he searched the group's bags. "It turned out for the good in the long
run," Julie opined, finishing her story.

Sharon joined in. "Yeah, well really I'm sure that what happened was
just that she saw [the glasses] and thought they were nice." Julie nodded.
"It's just like a little kid would do, not really meaning to do it."

"I suppose I can see their point in a way, that Tom didn't ask, or tell them first," I offered, but Julie broke in. "But it wasn't that he singled them out—he went through everyone's bags, not just theirs. I'm glad that got settled without having to make a scene, because we just can't have people who are like that down here. We'll never get the work done. This isn't about making people feel like they're contributing. It just isn't appropriate, and it isn't fair to them, either."

When Julie talked about having good manners she did not mean only being kind and gentle and civil. Good manners also meant sensing the big picture and weighing what was best for all of those in need. It meant telling Hannah that some volunteers were inappropriate workers, yet also making do and pitching in when the situation required. It meant being fair and doing right no matter how you felt.

Although I heard these resonances in Julie's talk about good manners, it took me longer to understand how Julie's talk resonated with Emily's spirituality. Later when Emily translated "good manners" into a children's lesson I understood better.

Several months after she started volunteering, Emily said, she had the inspiration that she should teach a church school lesson. Her congregation had recently had a potluck meal, and it bothered her that the children pushed to the head of the line, grabbing at the food without regard for the carefully laid out tables or for others around them. This wasn't new, she said.

"*Every* time we have potlucks at church, the kids push and shove, so I spoke to the Sunday school instructor and said, 'You know, I think I'd like to do an active project with the kids and have them prepare food for others.' So often they have no concept of the amount of work that is involved with that. Besides, I never met a kid who didn't want to cook—they all like it. Let them cook and let them serve it, so they can have the experience of giving. Even though they're only five or six, they can put a muffin on a plate, they can wash grapes. I spent about three minutes talking to the kids beforehand. I said, 'One of the stories we always hear with Jesus was that he ate with other people, and that he thought it was important to share food together, and that's what we're going to do this morning. We are going to do something very grown-up this morning.'"

She continued, "It only took an hour. My husband has had lots of dealings with kids, so he helped me scale it down into what I could reasonably do in an hour. It was really successful. I think it's important—it's sort of part of manners. If you sit down and try to tell kids about manners, that doesn't work very well. It's better to just have them do it, and talk about how you let other people go first, and you don't take seconds before everybody else has firsts. That's the kind way to do it, and that's what Jesus told us to do—make sure everybody has some."

Emily's appreciation for good manners combined teaching through example and sharing with others. Her lesson on "good manners" was about service and why eating together was special. In telling Bible stories, she connected respecting others in the potluck line with Jesus' concrete example of eating with others. In telling these stories, Emily also signaled their importance in her understanding of Jesus.

Talking with other volunteers about good manners gave Emily a way to translate these ideas into church settings. When she decided to teach children's church, she redrew the practices she learned and practiced at GLWD in Christian—even biblical—terms. Even though church was more about "religion" than spirituality, she still found room there to talk about what she did at God's Love We Deliver and to teach children about spirituality through preparing meals for others. She also said that she talked about "the context of cooking" at God's Love We Deliver with her friends at church. Once, in the middle of a conversation she said, "It dawned on me that I really didn't want another full-time job because it would be very difficult to do something like this. We had a conversation about how important it was to have time in your life, in a full life to be able to do this. Now this is a given."

Volunteers used daily speech genres to signal their commitments and to make space for extended conversations. In these uses their meanings, and the genres themselves, were transformed. Such transformations are ongoing; in this case they not only made space for volunteers to talk to each other across perceived differences but also brought into the kitchen a range of interpretations, meanings, and language that helped volunteers understand their practice. In this particular case, Emily and Julie continued to make good manners into religious practice, even though the resonance and connected associations for each continued to differ.

CONCLUSION

Navigating the shoals of kitchen conversation often required deliberate attention. Volunteers did pay attention to each others' words, particularly when they related to things like religion, because they were aware of (or at least presumed) a certain difference in religious ideas and beliefs. Talking with each other about religion, whether in double-voiced ways or in commonplace genres, was itself a kind of religious practice. We often distinguish talk from action—after all, praying and talking about praying are not the same thing. Yet both parts work to define prayer and to establish it as an activity with social meaning.

Similarly, talk about going to church, talk about the holidays, and parody are not the same as actually attending church or making a seder meal. In the kitchen, however, such talk made space for conversations about religion to happen by providing unorganized, but apparent, grist for volunteers who wanted to talk about things that mattered to them. The genres in use there marked boundaries of appropriate (or respectable) religious practice, challenged the authenticity and authority of some religious groups, and also heightened volunteers' already developed sense of religious diversity. Much of volunteers' "moral" talk that took place in double-voiced and indirect conversation developed on such ground. As they worked to talk about things that mattered in a context where straightforward discussion about moral or ethical issues was not the norm, they developed ways to communicate and also creative reinterpretations of their own practices. In this setting, an absence of straightforward discourse signaled neither the total absence of moral discourse nor empty or ineffectual religious talk. This suggests new possibilities for understanding the shape of moral discourse in daily public life.

As I have said many times, both in these chapters on religion and in the chapter on cooking, many volunteers perceived—or came to understand—that they did not share many practices or ideas about their work. When volunteers cooked together, for instance, constant conflicts about how to cut onions or wash dishes demonstrated unanticipated differences in basic understandings of what the meals were for and what they meant. In the case of religious practices and beliefs, volunteers were more likely to anticipate differences, but many were also open to exploring those, or at least to offering them in daily conversation. Most entered the kitchen with an assumption that the others they worked with probably believed and practiced differently. In comparison, they all assumed that they shared a deep understanding of the importance of doing something for people with AIDS. In contrast to volunteers' notions about their cooking practices, which they routinely found not to be true, this greater assumption about shared purpose held fast. It held fast because volunteers did not talk about it. As I discuss next, the (perhaps understandably) limited conversation about AIDS in the kitchen made for an interesting social context—and ultimately invited comparison with volunteers' ability to talk about religion.

CHAPTER SIX

Doing Something about AIDS

Simon, my friend Simon, is the one who put up—on the bulletin board area—the thing for the AIDS Walk. It's for if you want to do the AIDS Walk with God's Love. Simon, he's one of those people who dominates the conversation, and he's very entertaining. I know him from [abortion] clinic escorting. That's when he told me about God's Love. So, he's doing the AIDS Walk. And I have to admit, when I first saw it on the bulletin board, I had this thought of, "Oh, why should we do this with God's Love?"

I forgot for a minute that we were an AIDS organization. *I remember, I was with Simon and I said, "Oh, maybe the people from the clinic should have a group," that we should all do it—because you know, we're friends, and we should walk together. And then I said "Oh! Oh, but wait, we're an **AIDS** organization, gotcha—the **AIDS** Walk, gotcha."*

. . . It really took me a minute to put it together, why I would walk with God's Love, as opposed to any other group of friends and acquaintances.

As Alexis came to the end of this story, we both paused for a minute to ponder the question it posed: Why had it taken her a minute to "put together" that GLWD was an AIDS organization? How was it, indeed, that *anyone* could forget that God's Love We Deliver was an AIDS organization? The simple answer was that volunteers did not talk together about AIDS. In the course of regular kitchen work, there were few direct comments about AIDS; the word AIDS was rarely said. In its absence, other things took center stage. It was not until Alexis told me she had actually forgotten what GLWD did that I realized how much I took this particular silence for granted. I had explained it to myself through a variety of blanket assumptions rather than understanding how volunteers created and maintained it—and for what purposes.

Americans do not talk much about death, particularly their own deaths. Many have written of the "conspiracy of silence" surrounding death in American culture: grief and bereavement are largely expected to be contained in public funerary rituals and then managed within therapeutic settings.[1] Given these cultural silences, the lack of talk about death in the kitchen was not of much note. Speaking about AIDS, one might presume, would conjure up emotions and memories that were not to be broached in public: therefore, one could reason, volunteers did not talk about new therapies announced in the news or the problems the Ryan White Comprehensive Care Act encountered in Congress. But an absence of talk about AIDS also extended, as I mentioned in chapter 3, to limited talk about who received the meals. AIDS hovered like a specter, of course, in volunteers' concerns about blood and contamination, in allusions to and arguments about food quality, and in other ways as well. Nevertheless, volunteers did not talk openly about AIDS, and they made no overt statements of their personal connection to GLWD's mission. They rarely signaled their political engagement with the issues related to the social and medical treatment of people with AIDS.

The extent of these silences and the particularity of AIDS-related death, however, made the pat explanations about Americans' failure to talk about death unsatisfactory. God's Love We Deliver was an AIDS organization, after all, and within the subcultures most strongly affected by AIDS, death had become a part of daily life, something that was unavoidable, highly politicized, and (nonetheless) emotionally charged. Death from AIDS is as much public as private: conspiracies of silence surrounding death were often strongly challenged in practice.[2] Alexis and I had both been schooled in activist AIDS discourse before showing up at GLWD, she through participation in politically focused gay and lesbian groups, I through conversation with activist friends. Alexis carried a messenger bag that sported the ubiquitous ACT UP slogan proclaiming "Silence = Death."[3] This statement made it clear that as the closet and social stigma had earlier deprived gays of rights and agency as full human beings, AIDS now threatened to do the same.[4] In our understanding, then, AIDS volunteering was an important way to "bear witness" to the social stigma and isolation experienced by people with AIDS. It was public, just as the many deaths from AIDS had been made visible by AIDS groups through the AIDS Memorial Quilt, the annual AIDS Walk, ACT UP's "die-ins," and other public performances.[5] Working for people with AIDS—people dying with AIDS—included an expectation of going public, and that meant talking.

Even though I, like Alexis, had noted that the silence about AIDS seemed curious, I had other reasons for not investigating it further. Unlike (I assumed) most kitchen volunteers, I did not know anyone who had died of AIDS, nor had I been intimately involved in any person's death. I did not live in Chelsea or any of the other gay neighborhoods in the city, and I do not work in any of the industries that have a strong gay presence or aesthetic. In short, I was only tangentially connected to the settings and associations where I suspected such talk about AIDS was most clearly expressed. If ways of talking are learned in institutions (for instance, if bureaucratic language is "learned" in offices and religious language in synagogues and churches), then since I was not an active participant in any other AIDS organizations I had no opportunity to become familiar with the relevant genres. The silence I heard was an artifact of my position, I assumed. I realized it was quite possible that I was not picking up the cues others heard.[6] This was quite possible (and indeed held some element of truth), especially given the complexities of double-voiced, double-directed talk about religion that occasionally occurred in the kitchen.

This assumption about my own tone- and speech-deaf position would have stayed in place had Alexis not voiced her concern. Hearing a young, fairly hip bisexual woman who was firmly entrenched in the subcultures that I assumed taught the languages and codes I (imagined I) did not know well forced me to rethink my assumptions concerning talk about AIDS in the kitchen. It forced me to listen more clearly to what volunteers like Nancy, Sandra, John, and Kate told me about what they were doing when they came to chop and dice.

CREATING SAFE SPACE: SOME USES OF DOING

Volunteers in the kitchen consciously chose to "do something" rather than to "talk about" AIDS. With clients' faces and bodies absent from the kitchen, volunteers could focus on the cooking, and many lost themselves in the work. The practical tasks at hand, the order of the kitchen's day, and the limited number of decisions required of volunteers allowed them to concentrate on chopping or scrubbing in a very local way. As Emily quipped, "When you're standing there on the line [packing out meals] you don't have a real deep conversation." The basic, uncontroversial work of feeding people who were sick and hungry kept public discussion about purpose, or decisions about the worthiness of recipients, far from the kitchen.

Volunteers I spoke with rarely dwelled on the things they were not saying to each other. They talked instead about what a surprisingly happy place the kitchen was. When I remarked that some of my friends thought God's Love We Deliver must be depressing, Kate laughed and replied, "Well that's a curious thing, isn't it? Actually, it's not curious. It's because we're *doing something*, not looking at statistics or talking about what we have to do or what's going to happen. Now, that's *really* depressing."[7]

Volunteers' actions offered an alternative to New York's public AIDS culture, which suggested that people with AIDS and their families had no choice *but* to speak. This alternative also presented an implicit challenge to a culture of bereavement in which talking out (or about) one's feelings is the most appropriate (and healthiest) way to work through grief.[8] Although many volunteers participated in therapy or counseling, in the kitchen they remained silent. In so doing, they both established and preserved personal and private parts of death and thus personal and private ways of doing something about their emotions and memories. In such a way, some of these practices can be seen not as powerlessness but as their own "idiom of resistance," where through certain kinds of work grief can become a source of strength. The decision not to speak can thus be viewed as an open challenge to those who said there was no other choice.[9]

Volunteers sometimes felt this empowerment acutely. Sandra, who spoke of the "little edge" that kitchen work gave her, told me how she had coaxed and prodded her father to join her for an afternoon in the kitchen. He resisted her invitation for some time until Sandra finally told him, " 'Dad—everybody feels what you feel.' I think because he's so private and of course feels terrible grief about he death of his son, he said, 'Well, I don't want to talk about it.' And I said, 'You won't talk about it, you'll see. . . .' I said, 'Daddy, *no one talks about it there, no one ever mentions it,* you'll see, we talk about everything, everything but *that.*' "

He finally joined her. Sandra laughed and said, "He never had such a good time! He told me, 'Everybody there is so *un-mean.*' And I knew, of course, exactly what he meant. He said, 'I knew that they knew, and I know [that they know].' It was something." Sandra was whispering to me through her tears. She loved her father so much, and she felt how hard it was for him to live in "his generation" with the memory of a son who had died of AIDS. She continued after a long pause: "He didn't have a secret that day. Even though he didn't discuss it, he was, I think, free that day."

To be freed of the "secrets" and of grief was possible in the kitchen precisely because everyone "knew" what everyone else had felt and because everyone was "doing something" about AIDS. What was shared in the kitchen was possible only when volunteers refused to speak. They shared this silence, and these secrets, by doing something about AIDS rather than talking about it. Kitchen work made this possible, of course. Those volunteers who arrived in the kitchen "all talked out" could don an apron and turn to the work at hand. When on one of my first evenings in the kitchen I asked John why he decided to cook rather than deliver meals for GLWD (breaching conversational protocols as I did), he said, "Well it's because I don't have a usual lunch hour at my work. And this is a good place to meet people." But then he looked around and lowered his voice to a whisper: "Actually, I don't think I want to be emotionally ripped up again, right now." Several weeks later, Christopher mentioned in passing that John's partner of ten years had died only months before.[10]

The kitchen also put some physical distance between volunteers and people with AIDS. John, Sandra, Nancy, and other volunteers told me that they decided to work there because they couldn't look someone with AIDS in the face. Sandra discovered just how hard this was only after she finished training as a delivery volunteer. On her first day, she delivered a meal to a man who "could barely make it to the door." He smiled warmly when he met her and worried over Sandra, whose cheeks were raw from the bitter wind. "Oh, it must be so cold for you!" he exclaimed. Sandra became very upset that he was concerned about her. "I was too emotional to be helpful, [and] I didn't want to be indulgent of my feelings, because they're the ones who need help." She switched to kitchen volunteering the following week. Nancy likewise started in the kitchen after the deaths of several buddies left her "emotionally devastated." She thought she might eventually become a volunteer buddy again, but that work was so "demanding and overwhelming, psychologically, that I needed a rest."

Volunteers' silence about AIDS was intentional. It was built on their *refusal* to speak.[11] Silence around AIDS was not "merely" the default mode that built on a range of things that volunteers assumed they shared. Volunteers consciously constructed it as one practice of doing something about AIDS, as I discovered after I started paying attention to this silence that I had initially felt was mine alone. It was, as a practice, also full of ambiguities and highly charged. It was not easy to maintain. Talk about AIDS leaked indirectly into the various arguments about how to cook and how to chop, and it resonated in concerns about blood contamination in the kitchen. Volunteers privately harbored concerns about the health of their fellow volunteers, and they whispered to each other on the way up the stairs. On rare occasions volunteers like Libby, whom Sandra loved so much, would transgress the boundary and would no longer be tolerated. The idea, and the reality, of AIDS reverberated in the undertones of action and some conversation. Nevertheless, volunteers' silence effectively shrouded daily talk from any personal connection to AIDS: no daily speech genres about AIDS were at work in the kitchen.

ENGAGING AIDS TALK, ENCOUNTERING SILENCE

Volunteers' corporate refusal to speak created and maintained a culture in which they could do something about AIDS, at the same time creating a space devoid of speech genres to which conversation about AIDS could be related even indirectly.

The only regular daily speech genre that directly mentioned AIDS was talk about current events. But even this did not happen often, and such talk never led to a political discussion about the pros and cons of a particular policy. As Nancy said, "One [person] or another might say something . . . like about the drugs they think might help. You know, things you read about in the paper, like the cutback issue we were talking about last week, things like that." This one recurrent, bounded speech genre did little to highlight or evoke a person's unique interest in AIDS. That is, talk about funding cutbacks did not lead to discussion of how such cutbacks might affect a particular family or person. Talk about new drugs that "might help" some condition found no connection, in open conversation, to any person's condition. Even though many volunteers left their shift at God's Love We Deliver to be someone's primary caregiver, or to attend a death and dying support group, or to lead a meeting at Gay Men's Health Crisis, the daily speech genres about AIDS did not signal such connections.

This distinction bears noting, given that it enforced (or reinforced) volunteers' assumptions that everyone in the kitchen shared experience with AIDS. Whereas talk about going to church or preparing for the holidays linked volunteers within a web of relationships and institutional commitments and worked to mark distinctions between those from different traditions and with different loyalties, talk about the news allowed no such distinctions to arise. Talking about new AIDS treatments might have been more telling around the water cooler at work, but in an organization where everyone "assumed" that others had a connection to AIDS, such comments did not signal a unique or personal connection. If anything, these and similar passing comments reinforced (yet left unproved) volunteers' feelings of solidarity. As Mort said, "everyone [here] is in the same situation—or at least seemingly. You know if they weren't personally, in the immediate family, then it was a friend, or maybe they were just sympathetic to the cause."

Our refusal to speak allowed us to assume that others shared in a universe of tragic personal experiences and simultaneously limited any further investigation into what those experiences might be. I protested in vain when Sandra confided, "I can tell you personal things that I just don't dare tell anyone else, Courtney, because I suspect you've had something happen that's made you more sensitive to this. Either observed or lived through or—it's not important, it's just something has touched your life . . . and it's usually not something pleasant. We've all had something happen. Everybody." I gently told Sandra she had read me wrong, but she gave me a look, as if she knew there was something I didn't want to speak about and she found this perfectly understandable.

The winks and nods of affirmed, shared experience were frustrating to Alexis, who confided, "In part I went to God's Love looking for some catharsis. You know, looking for a way to—to find a place in this, in the plague, and *say* I'm doing something and *this* is what it means. I guess when I read articles [about AIDS] what I read about was activism. You know, thinking 'where we stand now, when we look back on this time in the future.' "

Alexis, who was active in several gay and lesbian organizations and volunteered as an escort at an abortion clinic, had worked in settings where she openly talked about her identity and her reasons for doing what she did. She found the kitchen volunteers' silence on these issues confusing. "I think in a way that everyone who volunteers in the kitchen wants to be a little bit—well, no one wants to talk about *why*." She said, "I guess what I mean [about God's Love We Deliver] is that there's not any chance to say that you grieve as a group. . . . I know that everyone's lost somebody, and you have your own personal point of grief. But I—my favorite, a friend of a friend, after he died, at his memorial service they read one of the last things that he had written—he was an actor—'I can't believe I'm dead and *Cats* is still running.' Yes, we don't talk about it and we choose not to, and I don't quite know why."

Maybe people were grieving while they chopped carrots. Or maybe they were grieving as they talked about movies and work and softball or for that matter when they talked about the wretched musical *Cats*. This set Alexis to wondering what she was missing and prompted her to listen more closely to what people were saying.

As we wrapped up our long breakfast, Alexis asked me what I knew about "the group of older women who predominate while I'm there. What's their connection—assuming, you know, that there are many reasons—but why?" She wondered if she should she give them space to grieve or whether they, like her, also assumed that everyone else was grieving. I shrugged and said something general, trying to remain as neutral as I could about what I knew of the others' lives. In the weeks that followed, Alexis tried to find out for herself, introducing AIDS obliquely into several conversations with this "group of older women."

The older women Alexis wondered about were the Jewish women in our group, including Julie and Barbara. Alexis told me as we walked up the street that she thought they were highly responsible people, and she imagined (because she did not know for sure) that they had taken care of people with AIDS, perhaps even their own children. She wanted to believe that they made sacrifices in their lives and still remained as powerful and happy as they seemed to be. Julie and Barbara were wealthy and enjoyed life. They came to the kitchen every week when they were in town; they both spent several months of the year in Florida, Europe, or Long Island. Alexis had been talking with them for several weeks about her summer plans to travel in Israel. Julie had traveled extensively through the Middle East, so she told Alexis why it was not advisable to stay in kibbutzim and which towns she shouldn't miss.

When Alexis asked Julie one morning whether it would be feasible to take a dog to Israel, the older woman raised an eyebrow. Julie (to my surprise) appeared to know a fair bit about quarantine rules and started to offer her advice. But when she found out that Alexis's dog was a large Labrador mix, she said, "You really don't want that big dog to be with you. Leave it at home."

"I might end up doing that, yeah." Alexis said, "But I'd like to try first to take him along. I don't want to leave him in a kennel here for that long."

"But it is *such* a pain to travel with an animal," Julie said. "You have to think about it all the time. You aren't—you can't be as mobile. Do you have a travel agent?"

"Yeah, I'm looking for one. One that will help me accommodate—"

"—There are some places that do take animals, you know, but what if you want to take a day trip, or an overnight trip to see something?"

"I know, I know," Alexis answered. The conversation went in loops. Julie thought Alexis wasn't being very smart. She couldn't figure out what the big deal was. Couldn't a friend take care of it? Alexis continued to insist that she was very attached to the dog. Exasperated, and perhaps working to change the subject, Barbara interjected, "Have you ever been to Israel?"

"No," Alexis said.

"Well, it's wonderful. You're lucky to be able to go for such a long time. Will you be traveling through the country much?"

"It depends on the dog," Alexis answered. Barbara shot Julie a look and went back to the pile of vegetables on her board.

When Alexis left, Julie repeated her advice to Barbara and everyone else who was standing at the table, "You shouldn't give up an opportunity to go to Israel to look after a dog." Barbara asked Julie if she thought she had come on too strong. "No," Julie said, pausing, "it just seems like such a burden. I just wanted to let her know it was all right to just go ahead and enjoy her vacation."

A week later I met Alexis for a quick coffee. In the middle of griping about the housing market in Manhattan Alexis told me about her housing woes: "I'm subletting from a man who is dying of AIDS. I'm taking his apartment, because he's moved in with his sister in Albany. I feel like I'm doing something good that way. The main thing is that I have his dog—you know, the 'big dog' [she said, laughing, using Julie's phrase]. I've adopted this dog and am very attached to it and plan to keep it for the rest of its life and—my friends sort of joke about my AIDS-orphaned dog."

It all became clear to me then why Alexis had been fumbling for a way to talk with Julie and Barbara about her commitments to caring for something, in a way that would connect her experience to what she imagined was theirs. It appears that she failed in this attempt to communicate and to develop a meaningful conversation about AIDS. Julie and Barbara did not grasp Alexis's point—nor could they, given that there had been few conversational clues to link the dog to caring for a person with AIDS. Alexis did not tell the women how she had come to have her dog, feeling acutely the pressures in the kitchen not to talk about the specifics of her commitments. They were left wondering why a young single woman might ruin her vacation by dragging along a dog. Alexis, likewise, was left with her questions: Why were Barbara and Julie volunteering, and what were their points of grief? Alexis, as far as I know, did not receive answers to her questions before she kenneled her dog and set off for Israel later that spring.

WORKING AROUND SILENCE

As Alexis and I discovered, using double-voiced discourse to talk about AIDS meant communicating without the ground of AIDS-related referents, asides, and implied conversational parameters. Not only did this make talk about AIDS difficult for volunteers like Alexis and me, it also made it hard for volunteers who engaged in such indirect talk to describe it. As it was, even though volunteers such as Sandra told me that "no one" talked about AIDS, others, including Nancy, told me they talked about AIDS in the kitchen "all the time." Given that I myself had heard little direct or indirect talk about AIDS in the kitchen, I asked those volunteers who said they talked about it to give me a recent example. They struggled to recount what had taken place: their conversations seemed to slip from straightforward and open discussion to something else. Nancy, who told me she did not talk about religion in the kitchen (but who said she talked about AIDS "all the time") paused for a long moment before proceeding cautiously:

An example. Yes, when someone who I've been volunteering with all of a sudden would confide in me and it would just—and I—and for me, I've had problems with stigma, with the guys I've dated, you know, the "straight world," for my involvement with AIDS. But people who work around AIDS and are straight are different. And usually, you see, I don't react in a straight way, so I've dealt with it. It's not a surprise in that way, when they tell me that they are HIV positive. It's just a surprise that that particular person has it.

So then I just—we usually end up discussing it a little bit. And I'm pretty much listening and they're pretty much [doing all the talking], because a lot of times people with AIDS need to talk, and it's not easy to find somebody to talk to.

Nancy's answer was typical in its opacity. Aside from wanting to protect the identity of the person she had spoken with, her language about this conversation was empty of an actual "example." The conversation is just "listening and talking"; it happened "all of a sudden." Nancy knew that something had happened between the two of them that signaled the possibility of confiding about AIDS. In Nancy's parlance, this "something" appears to be connected with not acting in a "straight way." She did not specify exactly what this meant, although I was reminded of what she had told me about her long friendship and business partnership with a gay man who had died of AIDS in the late 1980s. Nancy had taken care of four men who died of AIDS; she knew how to talk about "it" even though she could not easily distill what that knowledge was in our interview. In short, Nancy had mastered talking about AIDS, even though she could not clearly articulate what this meant or pinpoint how such conversations began. Nancy's mastery was built on experience of caring for dying people, notably, and not from participation in AIDS activism or political involvement. She was not politically active with AIDS, and she continued, in our conversations, to call people with AIDS "AIDS patients." Whatever she had said, whatever her actions, something had clicked between two people. Nothing had been said outright, Nancy told me, but when this person confided in her "all of a sudden," she suggested they go get a soda and take the conversation about AIDS out of the kitchen, into the courtyard behind GLWD.

The silences around AIDS were not complete. Silence, furthermore, did not suggest by any measure that those in the kitchen could not talk about AIDS or lacked a language for doing so. The lack of talk about AIDS did not denote failure to make a moral argument: in its own way it was a moral stance. [12] A conscious effort of not speaking about AIDS did not rule out indirect or double-directed discourse, although it did make it more difficult, and less certain when it did occur, even for those who (unlike Alexis and me) had firsthand experience with caring for people with AIDS.

MAKING SENSE OF TALK ABOUT RELIGION AND AIDS

The silence around AIDS in the kitchen and volunteers' specific refusal to speak about AIDS there are interesting in their own right, and in some ways they mirror findings from other recent ethnographies dealing with voluntary and religious organizations. For instance, Jody Shapiro Davie learned that every member of a Protestant women's spirituality group claimed an intense spiritual experience (including near-death experiences and visions of angels) that loomed large in each woman's decision to participate in the group. Yet she also noted that none of them had ever spoken of these experiences with others in the group, even though it had been meeting for over ten years. Davie suggests that these Protestant women find talking about spiritual experience, even with a group of coreligionists, a "dangerous game." [13]

Similarly, Nina Eliasoph's ethnographic research with volunteers in political and community groups uncovers little political talk among them. People do not talk about the things that bring them together or the commitments they believe they share. [14] Eliasoph takes the absence of such discussion as a sign that volunteers and activists value civility and maintaining group ties more than what might be gained from broaching issues that might disrupt them. Both Eliasoph and Davie focus on group etiquette and manners and on the danger participants feel they court by bringing up the very experiences and issues that (ostensibly) draw them together.

Eliasoph's and Davie's studies emphasize the importance of talk and express a concern that an absence of political or religious talk in political and religious groups signals a dwindling level of engagement with those very issues in some parts of American society. If we consider such groups as anchoring institutions, where individuals gather and learn how to speak and identify religiously, politically, or in other public ways, then such concern is indeed well placed. Where do people learn to speak about religion, and gain practice at doing so, if not in religious collectives? The notion that cultural scripts are generated only (or solely) in the daily goings-on in organizations is of course too facile. We know that much talk in groups and organizations focuses on problem solving and so on rather than on articulating formal and purposive statements, and that much of it is free-wheeling and relatively disorganized. [15]

With this in mind, concerns stemming from the absence of direct talk about religion or politics in religious and political organizations may well be misplaced. We should not expect to find direct, public "talk about AIDS" in the kitchen of an AIDS organization, and we might in fact find little talk about religion (or at least certain kinds of religious experience) in some religious institutions. Absence of talk thus does not mark an absence of practice: an exclusive focus on actors' direct talk pulls attention away from a range of actions, as well as the many inferences, metaphors, and indirect speech that combine in various "practices." At GLWD, for instance, volunteers consciously used the power of their shared silence around AIDS to fiercely defend the spaces of grief that could not be spoken. In the space of this silence, volunteers cultivated and directed their personal practices of cooking and caring for people with AIDS.

In addition to noting that practice does not require talk to be what it is, we also see that an emphasis on what is, or should be, shared in any organization (and the tacit meanings apparently associated with that) curtails talk about it but nevertheless leaves some room open for discussion of those things that are not shared. If it is difficult or dangerous to speak of religion or AIDS where ideas about those things are supposed to be shared, other contexts may present themselves as places where such talk can occur—in indirect and direct conversations. That is, I might be more likely to hear volunteers talk about AIDS in other contexts and in institutions that were not devoted to doing something about AIDS. We might likewise find that people who want to talk about religion find multiple settings in which to sustain such conversation. Seen in this light, the sporadic talk about religion in the kitchen's daily freewheeling conversation takes on a different import. The ways volunteers understood, exploited, or ignored daily talk about religion, and the ways they understood others' talk (or their own) as setting implicit boundaries to limit or allow for such conversation, take more of a central place in the ways we understand the lived practice of religion. Volunteers used their interactions to inflect offhand comments with values, and they creatively engaged the possibility of religious conversation with others: they were able to do this precisely because religion and religious ideas occupied a tertiary place in the presumed shared culture of kitchen life. Its apparent inconsequentiality allowed room for its creative practice.

Hints Followed by Guesses

We build and practice our selves through ongoing interaction in multiple worlds. We all draw from and develop many scripts, stories, and actions that we communicate with and that shape what others perceive us to be. This is no less true for how people demonstrate that they are religious than for any other part of cultural and social life. As such, the questions in this book have concerned not whether Americans practice religion, but how and when they do and how such practice contributes to our understanding of the category itself.

I was well warned that an observational study of religious talk and practice outside religious organizations might mean spending days in the field without hearing or seeing anything "religious." This was not a problem in itself, given that my point has not been to "prove" the existence or the sustainability of religion in any particular setting or kind of interaction (or, on the contrary, to document its absence from daily life). My purpose has been to understand the social processes that surrounded and made room for its occasional (or more frequent) appearances, and likewise to understand how various religious practices structured interactions in the kitchen. It was certainly true that volunteers did not often talk about religion at this nonreligious urban AIDS organization. Even those who thought of their work as religious rarely called attention to their practices. Volunteers explicitly did *not* share religious culture, and those few who, like Sandra, imagined they did were sometimes disappointed to discover otherwise.

The specific contours of religious practice and talk that I observed and participated in hinged on the particular cultural and social ecology of the kitchen, and it is easy to imagine, or observe, other sites where religious talk is organized differently. I chose to conduct field research at GLWD because volunteers had plenty of time to talk with each other about things that did not directly relate to what we chopped and stirred. Many other locations would have allowed me to make a similar study of how religious talk and action happened in the course of daily talk and action among nonreligiously connected acquaintances. I imagine that in some settings I would have seen "more" religion, and in others much less. Rather than focusing on these issues, I have worked to explicate a perspective that will help us see how and when more and less religious practice might be understood, analyzed, and actuated by individuals. In any social context (even those we might consider to be "religious" institutions, including congregations) these questions remain pertinent: How and when did volunteers decide to talk about religion—their own or others? When did "situations occur" in which people talked about it? How did people recognize others' talk, or practice, as religious? How did otherwise mundane practices influence this talk?

KITCHEN WORK:
CULTURE IN PRACTICE AT GOD'S LOVE WE DELIVER

Volunteers did not engage in many overt discussions about deep, meaningful things. They claimed that the work they did together was self-evidently important and valuable, and they questioned anyone's attempt to ground it in something obviously ideological. They answered my queries about why they did the work with another question: Why would anyone need to justify work that was so "basic" and obviously necessary? The barriers volunteers created to talking about our reasons for being in the kitchen extended to other issues as well. Yet such rhetorical questions notwithstanding, they brought to the kitchen habits and practices that reproduced and called to mind moral, aesthetic, and personal values. Such "individual" memories and values developed in other social settings were enacted through the very practices of cooking, and at times they resonated strongly and were brought to the surface in daily arguments about the most mundane issues.[1] The perpetual "argument" about how to cut onions was only one example of how volunteers became aware of, and sought indirect ways to defend, their own expertise in cooking for others (or for people with AIDS) and the all-important practices they used to do this well.

The volunteers I worked with were on the whole quite savvy. They regularly received GLWD public relations information in the mail, and some who worked in the kitchen also volunteered to speak about the agency, worked in the offices, and had dinner with "upstairs" staff responsible for imbuing the meals with meaning. Volunteers often framed their kitchen arguments, then, in terms of the organization's repertoires. They argued with each other using terms like love and therapy, though often with an ironic and bemused air. Their uses of GLWD's most authoritative scripts bolstered their own actions (and hid their "truer" purposes) and, at the same time, pointed clearly to the underlying surge of personally articulated values that buoyed them up.

The heat of arguments that sometimes erupted around small issues of kitchen procedure pointed toward ways of understanding how talk and practice worked in the kitchen. This first became explicit as I thought about how volunteers worked to do something "so basic" about AIDS. The memories and practices they carried with them and used in the kitchen, either consciously or habitually, often conjured up memories of things they had done for people who died. Volunteers intentions to "do something" about AIDS, however, were not accompanied by direct discussion of what this "something" was. In fact, as Alexis, the young bisexual activist and volunteer, reported in a shocked voice, "No one talks about AIDS [in the kitchen]."

Alexis's comment pointed to the absence of direct talk—the kind of talk that is unequivocally about AIDS in the same way that, say, rehashing an Agassi versus Sampras match is unequivocally talk about tennis or mentioning attending church is unequivocally about religion. I quickly noted that volunteers were more likely to talk about religion in such a "direct" way than they were to talk about AIDS. Religious participation was not something that most volunteers felt they needed to keep to themselves. It did not, on the whole, seem to engender the fear of emotional outburst that talk about AIDS did for some. Religion was much less dangerous to speak of than AIDS, and though it certainly created its own spaces of silence and confusion, volunteers were still more likely to mention participating in a local congregation than in an AIDS bereavement support group.

Nevertheless, the absence of direct, obvious talk did not signal an absence of significant talk about AIDS in the kitchen. I could describe how volunteers' discussions about cutting onions and keeping the kitchen clean indirectly engaged arguments about how to care for people with AIDS, even though I could not simply make the same connections between cooking and religion. In fact, it became clear that volunteers' ways of "doing something about AIDS" were organized very differently than were their assumptions and patterns of religious action. It is true that some volunteers felt they had a religious calling to work in the kitchen and that others spoke of what they came to understand as the sacramental logic of making meals. But beyond this, religion was organized, as a category of activity, in a much different way than cooking or "doing something" about AIDS. Volunteers assumed religious difference, not similarity, meaning they presumed they had different religious backgrounds and experiences and different commitments (or hostilities) to things religious. As such, their understanding and practice of religion in the kitchen provided the beginning of a portrait of how religion is lived in a setting that its actors understand as religiously plural. The picture that develops here confirms some recent understandings of religion in contemporary America and challenges others.

RELIGION IN DAILY LIFE

We can say several things about how volunteers practiced religion in the kitchen at God's Love We Deliver. First, most of the talk about religion was commonplace, conducted within the confines of three daily speech genres. Talk about going to church, talk about preparing for holidays, and parody of conservative religious figures constituted identity talk, marking out appropriate and inappropriate religions and appropriate and inappropriate religious activities. As Tanya discovered when she mentioned her upcoming trip to visit a South American spiritual guide, such talk could in fact be dangerous or demeaning. Nancy, a practicing Catholic, interpreted parodies of John Cardinal O'Connor as evidence that the others were "against the Catholic religion" (even though other practicing Catholics did not make such judgments). Perhaps not unexpectedly, religious identity was more acceptable when it could be named (Presbyterian, for instance) and when it was not associated directly with institutions that preached against homosexuality. These three daily genres, then, marked out the space of religious talk and activity and made it difficult to speak or act religiously in ways that extended beyond these boundaries.

Furthermore, despite the barriers to extending religious talk beyond common genres, the commonplace talk about religion made such "difficult" talk possible. Sometimes people misunderstood what others meant (or even what they were talking about) and demanded qualifications and explanations. These interactions extended (or at least exposed) the limits of everyday talk. In other circumstances the more generically bounded talk about going to church and celebrating holidays provided an endlessly growing set of context points and shared events that volunteers could use to build further conversations. In this sense everyday small talk was necessary—it constructed contexts in which future talk could go on. Volunteers could draw on the elements they had learned or the stories they had narrated to develop indirect speech about religion. They could use such language to highlight the aspects of their work that they viewed as religious, even if no one necessarily called such talk religious. Although such talk was not frequent, and although it was specific to the situations and persons involved, it was also language that could travel under the right conditions. Emily's story, which recounts how she developed the idea of teaching manners in a Sunday school lesson after talking to Julie, is one such instance.

Religious talk was far from being private or hidden, yet it was also far from being public and part of straightforward conversations. Volunteers talked about religion, playing the "dangerous game" by picking up hints from everyday talk and making guesses about the best ways to communicate. Sometimes individuals learned that they shared a religious background and could convey meaning without stating it explicitly, much as some volunteers spoke indirectly about AIDS. However, some learned from daily talk that they did not share religious stories or meaning with others. To talk about religion, then, they translated and resituated their ideas and languages, testing the waters of conversation. This talk required mastery of several kinds of discourse. Emily and Julie's discussion of "good manners" is one example of the double voicing that happens in indirect speech. Much talk about religion was, to use T. S. Eliot's phrase, built on "hints and guesses."[2] Not all hints and guesses were correctly interpreted or given the meaning their authors intended, but even misinterpretations were often instructive. Despite the constancy of errors and corrections, the hints followed by guesses marked volunteers' attempts to keep the conversation going at all costs.

That said, there were silences in volunteers' talk about religion, both direct and indirect. They skirted talk that may have marked strong differences between them, with one conspicuous exception. Explicit negative critiques of Roman Catholicism and the nebulous "religious right" (Jerry Falwell in particular) developed from time to time in the kitchen. Both traditions, as volunteers told each other, were bound by antiquated and oppressive teachings, ruled by authoritarian leaders, and filled with homophobes. These were not progressive religions or schools of thought (to say the least). As such, this exception confirmed volunteers' unspoken understanding that religion could in fact alienate. Those who wanted to talk about religion did not deny that they were playing a "dangerous game" in which disclosures made to the wrong person might be misunderstood (or worse).

This tangle of daily speech genres and indirect talk about religion in the kitchen suggests that religious practice and talk in daily life are far from being diffuse and vague, as some have suggested. They are, on the contrary, highly context specific. While the prospects of communicating, and the possibility of failing to communicate, are quite real in this kind of conversation, nevertheless one cannot say that such talk is empty or abstract. Volunteers drew on the very specific resources built within shared conversations to make sense of their activities together. It bears noting that the specificity of such language could limit its value to outsiders or to anyone who had not taken part in its construction. To such observers and participants, a conversation might not appear to have anything at all to do with religion. This sort of indirect religious language developing among specific volunteers bears little similarity to the public rhetoric that we hear ministers and politicians (and other public figures) using in debates and in claims of moral certitude. That volunteers draw on their own experiences in their various daily worlds to communicate religious meaning suggests powerful ways that moral arguments are made. In short, people use styles and modes of speech that are very distant from those forms that are most relevant to most recent discussions of public religious discourse.

What, then, are the consequences of such talk? Volunteers' indirect conversations lead us to consider how average Americans both understand and engage what they perceive as religious pluralism, as well as some of the strategies they use to communicate across perceived difference. By all estimations, Americans are experiencing a ground shift from understanding their country as a "Christian nation" to living in a "nation of religions." Religious pluralism, while not necessarily experienced more deeply by contemporary Americans than by their predecessors, is nevertheless now part of our collective religious landscape. We are just beginning to see the impact of this reimagining on the position of religion in American culture; and judging by conversation at GLWD, it is quite different from what other commentators have suggested. Peter Berger famously argued that religious pluralism will cause people to doubt the verities of their own traditions, consequently making faith weak or, at best, forcing its retreat into small private enclaves. And while Berger has largely abandoned this position, the idea persists that people cannot talk about religion together if they do not share a common language. In this line of reasoning, some have recently pointed to the growth of empty, abstract "spiritual" language as a popular, though unsatisfactory, attempt to find the lowest common denominator, a language in which everyone can participate. Such "religionless" religion lacks force and roots, given that it emphasizes personal spirituality, process, love, and service rather than tradition, continuity, and particularistic beliefs.[3]

When we look at the lived religious practices of volunteers, these interpretations and predictions are not fulfilled. Rather than shrinking from discussion because they lacked a shared language, volunteers at God's Love We Deliver navigated a plurality of religious and spiritual beliefs and practices, both experienced and imagined. They found ways to speak together about these ideas that were built on common daily genres, both religious and nonreligious. Rather than appealing to language that was diffuse, empty, and abstract or based on the lowest common denominator, volunteers built particular ways of talking with each other through specific encounters. Their translations and indirect language conveyed meaning across differences and also actively revised and expanded definitions of religious practice.

Volunteers' indirect talk about religion, occurring in spaces where pluralism and difference (rather than similarity) are assumed, nevertheless does entail a trade-off. In speaking indirectly about religious ideas, they ran the very real risk of not being heard at all. Their metaphors or allusions might be overlooked or not recognized. They might find themselves misunderstood and their ideas ridiculed. In this context volunteers clearly understood that in speaking directly and openly about religious motivations or evaluations they risked alienating others by drawing on unknown languages, metaphors, and spiritual experiences. Such direct talk would have closed off further discussion about things that mattered.

STUDYING RELIGION IN EVERYDAY LIFE:
BRINGING CONTEXT BACK IN

What, then, are we to make of the diffuse and general abstract language that other scholars have heard regular people using when they talk about religion? How can we make sense of "Golden Rule Christians" or thin spiritual talk? To begin with, we can see that much of the "general" and abstract spiritual language that scholars have heard occurs in interviews. I too heard more general, open-ended talk in interviews with volunteers. Even though my questions were constructed not as "whys" but rather as "whats" and "hows," volunteers often backtracked and second-guessed their own responses. Some, like Emily, would answer a single question with several metaphors or examples, thus drawing attention to the numerous interpretations and understandings—theirs and others'—that could apply as answers. Others, like Sandra, relied on GLWD's institutional scripts to talk about their work in the kitchen, even though they never used that language there. Lucy, a practicing Catholic, was eager to broaden her language and avoid particularities in the interview. She told me, for instance, that the Holy Spirit was at work in the kitchen, but that the Spirit could also be "the spirit of cooperation, whatever you want to call it." Likewise, when I asked in interviews what the "God" in God's Love We Deliver meant, volunteers often listed several ideas about the name that they had heard, had thought about, or thought might be useful. Their ability to describe and talk about the God in God's Love We Deliver in a number of ways allows me to paraphrase Ann Swidler: volunteers knew more religion than they used.[4] Their general rather than specific answers highlighted not their "general" way of thinking but some uncertainty about how they should answer and their flexibility in trying to find the best way.

The limitations of interviews for studying how scripts, repertoires, and practices are put to use is well documented in cultural sociology.[5] Interviews alone cannot assess how or whether respondents use the very scripts and stories they tell us in other settings, or when they decide to do so. Some critics have pointed to the rather surreal context of an interview, where respondents are asked to reflect and to choose their language more carefully than if they were, say, talking about the same subject at the neighborhood pub. Yet interview contexts are no less "real" than any other conversation or observation: they merely provide a different context, where those involved utilize some of the scripts and repertoires they have on hand rather than others. Rather than abandoning interview studies altogether, then, I suggest we pay closer attention to the specifics of all discursive contexts. This will require methods that not only analyze how different actors talk about religion in the same space (as I have done here) but also investigate how those same actors then speak about religion in various social and cultural worlds.

Although I have not followed volunteers through various institutional contexts (say, from GLWD's kitchen to church to work), it is possible to consider what we might learn by thinking of GLWD's kitchen conversation and activities as harboring multiple speech contexts.[6] Multiplicity implies not only the coexistence of various ways of speaking within a single setting but the interaction of those various manners of talk. These interchanges and interactions are the most rudimentary resources and sites for social and cultural change. In the strictest sense, every interpersonal interaction is a unique context, where people must navigate the horizons of known meaning, anticipated responses, and the possibility of others' creative (as opposed to stock) responses and rejoinders. Every unique context, however, develops from, and in relation to, previous interactions both remembered and encapsulated within the structures of talk and action. The glut of genres, memories, and experiences shapes each new setting in particular ways. We must pay attention to the history of any interaction, as far as we can, and attend to the particular interactions that precede each, if we are to understand how culture operates and, in this case, how religion is at work in daily life.

Take the interchange between Harrison and Gloria in chapter 5. After she mentioned her friend Ann, Harrison asked Gloria why she went to church. Asking her to give a reason caught Gloria off guard; she made a general response that only hinted at the stories she told Susan and me. It was not so much that she had never heard the question before or that she had no answer as that the context was unusual. Volunteers rarely asked each other direct questions to begin with. Harrison, as a new volunteer, did not know Gloria well, making such direct questioning necessary but simultaneously troubling for the rest of us. Harrison had been in the kitchen only a few weeks, and we had not interacted with him enough to know what he was driving at. Was he antireligious and getting ready to challenge her participation? Was he going to compare notes about his church? Was he looking for a church to join? Gloria could have answered Harrison's question by responding to any of these questions, but none of us had enough information to guess which one he intended. Gloria did not know where Harrison meant to take the conversation, so she responded with abstract language that anticipated any number of possible questions.

Having a sense of the context was important for the way Gloria (and then Susan and I) responded. This "sense" means reading a particular situation, in a particular setting where certain things are topics of conversation and others are not, where certain things are not often spoken of directly, and so on. As an ethnographer, I needed to take into account the particularities of my previous conversation with Gloria to determine why she answered Harrison as she did. Although I imagine this is self-evident, consider the contrary position. Had I assumed that this was a "typical" interchange in the kitchen about religion, or one of Gloria's "typical" responses, I might have concluded that Gloria was uncomfortable in speaking about religion and that the kitchen was a place hostile to open talk about it. If we develop a reading of social settings where we expect to find general "rules of the game" that are played out regardless of the actors involved, such an interpretation would be more viable.[7] But this interpretation seems weak when we put Gloria's talk about religion into its lived context. Gloria did not lack the nerve or the ability to talk in more specific ways about church. She was reading the context: her responses were specific, based on what she knew, and developed through daily conversation.

While we cannot fill out the entire context and history of any single event, we can nevertheless go forward with the analytical position that such context is essential to interpretation. That is, while we all sometimes use stock responses, we do so in particular events that can (and do) transform them from "general" into specific uses. We respond not to general questions from others, but to specific ones: in so doing, we take account of the broader horizons of knowledge and emotion in those settings. Volunteers' involvement in conversation was never general, even if it was habitual. Their stories and ways of talking about themselves and things that mattered to them were multiple: what mattered in any particular interaction was their ability to read a context, an ability that was without question created in interactions that preceded it.

If specificity of context is an integral part of the shape that talk and practice take in everyday life, then we are left with further questions about findings on religious practice and talk that come from interview studies alone. What we hear people say in interviews does not necessarily have a clear analogue or connection to everyday discourse in other settings. Taken on their own, without broader attempts at contextualization, it is impossible to know how artifactual, or central, any person's comments and responses are. Ethnography provides methods for seeing how the relations between people's languages, scripts, and frames are put to use within specific contexts. The ethnography of religious action will, in the future, require not just analysis of the way people are religious in one religious setting, but observations of how they use the same practices and languages across multiple institutional and conversational contexts.

EVERYDAY LIFE AS HETEROGLOSSIC CONTEXT

I have argued that we are often aware of how little we can assume that we share meaning or interpretation with others or understand how their interpretations may differ from ours. The various social contexts we are engaged in affect our evaluations of difference and similarity and shape our strategies for communication. Our worlds are heteroglossic: they are populated with multiple languages, genres, and the like that *speak to each other* in the course of daily matters. The specific organization of various genres and ideas, and the ways individuals are likely to evaluate them, differs from one setting to another and from one period to the next. At GLWD, volunteers largely assumed that they shared a connection with people with AIDS; at a church, people generally assume that all gathered there will commit to a shared understanding of a faith or religious principles. Many things happened (or can happen) within both contexts to challenge these assumptions: no set of assumptions, or genres, is very stable when we begin to view interactions at this level.

We act in the world with a healthy dose of doubt about what we have in common with others and whether they understand what we are saying. This doubt arises from experience. It extends inward as well. We are aware of the number of languages we speak, our ability to use them in different ways, and the ways they fail to hold together (at least at times) in some concentrated and condensed "self." We experience our own lives and acts, shaped by the structures we participate in, and recognize in this course of life just how incomplete they are. We juggle a range of possible and necessary practices. Doing so makes everyday life what it is—made up of decisions about how to communicate or respond based on what we know about the discursive contexts we enter and what we want to make of them. Engaging the study of everyday life as the study of a dialogue between multiple languages and practices repositions a basic sociological gloss that equates "daily life" with the mundane and taken-for-granted, churning along without forethought or conscious adjustment.

Emphasizing the specificity of contexts and interactions is an obvious extension of current work in the sociology of culture. We no longer take it for granted that religious ideas constructed in one context are put to use in others without modification or change. This permits further analyses of the ways contexts and concrete events, themselves the products of a variety of practices, influence how practices are put into play.[8] Others have also demonstrated how ideological positions that seem diametrically opposed include a range of overlap and flexibility.[9] We have access to a wide range of practices, certainly more than we use in any given day or context: volunteers' ability to give multiple, analogous interpretations of the meanings of "God" in "God's Love We Deliver" is one example of this. Sociologists have abandoned the idea that people subjectively carry religion or other culture internally in ways that do not change much from setting to setting. They have also laid aside the simplistic notion that action in a single institution is shaped purely by the contingencies and rules of that setting. These unsettled currents in cultural sociology surrounding the relation between individuals' discursive styles and practices, and the contexts where they live and work, talk and play, point toward the need to better understand the creative forces set in motion through unrelenting encounters with multiple others, multiple ways of responding, and a lack of stock certainty about how to respond.

I have focused here on how multiple potential ways of speaking and communicating make people aware of the need to choose language, but much everyday activity is not conducted on a conscious level. I hope it is clear that volunteers went to the kitchen with no intention of making meaning or negotiating the value of their work. And though establishing the value of our work was often part of the job, cooking was often habitual, repetitive, and done without thinking. Sometimes cutting carrots was just cutting carrots. Volunteers regularly ignored or overlooked chances to explore the complexities of the meanings and purposes that individuals engaged. Nevertheless, they sometimes remarked on how meaning sneaked up on them unawares, as when Charles's hair stood up.

It would be easy to suggest, as others have, that the experience Charles described as the unexpected confrontation with the meaningful reasserts a mysterious but real distinction between mundane life and a more mystical and meaningful plane. But articulating such experiences as the descent (or irruption) of meaning into the ongoing whole of an individual's activities would require an exposition much different from the one I have considered here. If we begin instead with a view that the languages we speak (some more expectedly than others) speak to each other, we begin to see what Bakhtin suggested—that the pure everyday life "is a fiction, a product of the intellect. Human life is always shaped and this shaping is always ritualistic."[10]

In short, then, experiences like Charles's suggest how meaning is sometimes developed through the histories of habits and the particularities of experience combining in new ways. Everyday life is neither a habitual sphere lacking in meaning and thought into which meaning descends nor a sphere that is always given to transformation, value, and symbolic weight. Daily life's potential for both can, perhaps, be best described as a loosely organized polyglot, an ever changing set of social contexts made by individuals who draw on and develop practices of meaning. Daily life's potential for both compels us to reconsider its varied spaces, and it charges us to look carefully once more at these practices as they continue to structure action in our multiple worlds.

APPENDIX:
STUDYING RELIGION AT GOD'S LOVE WE DELIVER

I first heard about God's Love We Deliver at a dinner party. Over dessert, I discussed my intended research with my husband's thesis adviser, who told me about Ganga Stone, the daughter of a longtime family acquaintance, and "her organization." A bit of investigating the next day confirmed that GLWD's kitchen was a potential site for research. Though I harbored some concerns about what Stone's spiritual views might be and whether GLWD was "religious," I drafted a letter stating my interest in studying "volunteer motivations" and how volunteers "talk to each other." As it happened, Stone (as well as the photographs of Swami Muktananda and most of the "spiritual" language Stone had fostered) had left the agency several months earlier. My inquiry found its way to Hannah, the volunteer director, who invited me come have a look around.

I started research in September 1994 and continued through December 1995, with a three-month hiatus during summer 1995. I typically spent three seven-hour days each week at the agency. I delivered meals to clients in Manhattan and rode on the vans through the outer boroughs, dispatched delivery volunteers from a phone in the client services office, organized files, sold Christmas ornaments in the cafeteria at MTV, checked volunteers' references, and helped rearrange office furniture. And of course I worked in the kitchen.

DISCLOSURES
I told people I met at God's Love We Deliver that I was interested in studying volunteers' moral languages and practices. While this was not exactly an untruth, I expressly did not tell anyone there that I was studying religious

languages and practices. In choosing to cloak this interest, I dealt every day
with the possible consequences of harboring secrets in the field. This was
a new research prospect: in my previous ethnographies (on Mennonite
charismatic churches) I told the congregations and their leaders what I
was studying. They knew I was interested in how individuals dealt with two
contrasting (and some said antithetical) religious identities and that I was
not evangelical or charismatic myself. In these studies I explicitly invited
my respondents to think about the questions that concerned me. Although
my respondents and acquaintances at these churches were not privy to the
technical terms I used with my scholarly peers, they were aware of what I
was studying, and I was not guarded about what I wanted to know. These
encounters were more in line with typical ethnographic research, but the
same methods would not work in my favor at God's Love We Deliver.

I chose not to disclose my interest in religion for fear of radically alter-
ing the place where I conducted research. Although my presence, my talk,
my questions, and my practices ultimately did "change" the kitchen (how
could they not?), I took the position that stating my interest would have
changed the way volunteers talked to me (and each other) about religion.
I occasionally fantasized about making comments to other volunteers that
might have spurred corporate, extended conversations about the role of
religion in society. But the volunteers were not a focus group, and my
goal was not to find as much religion as possible but to see how religious
talk and practice occurred in everyday situations. I may have diminished
my returns on learning about volunteers' spiritual and religious lives. I
undoubtedly could have heard more, learned more, and written more
about religion had I been more forthcoming about my primary interest
and talked openly with volunteers about it. But doing so would have produced a very different project.

Despite my certainty that not disclosing my primary interest was the
only way to execute the study, my secret initially put me on edge. In introducing my project, I told Hannah I was interested in studying volunteers' motivations, and she was extremely enthusiastic. As she explained
the agency's work to me and told me about the diverse volunteers and the
importance of doing something for people with AIDS, I was prompted
to disclose that I had no personal experience with people with AIDS. In
retrospect, I realize that my need to disclose this was spurred by the analogous fact that at the time I had no particular interest in AIDS. I had
chosen GLWD because of its kitchen, not because it was an AIDS organization. Hannah brushed aside my admission with the comment, "Oh, we
have all kinds of volunteers, from every walk of life—you know, AIDS is in
everyone's life, it isn't just one community anymore." In summer 1994,

GLWD was turning away prospective volunteers: AIDS was such a trendy charity cause that I was not unusual.

I spent my first day at GLWD in the kitchen, but on the second day Hannah made it clear that she had other things in mind. She explained that she wanted me to get a feel for the work of the "entire agency" and introduced me to staff members in several departments. Each one had a project for me to do. At first I set to work on them willingly, reasoning that it was important to demonstrate my sincerity and credibility. A week sitting at a lonely desk checking clients' ZIP codes against their addresses gave me plenty of time to realize that my hazily explicated research goals had led Hannah to concoct her own agenda for me as her personal intern. As I slowly started to find ways to establish and defend my priorities while still demonstrating my willingness to help out, I began to assert my role of "social scientist." In this capacity I extracted myself from desk work by assisting staff in reviewing client statistics and grant proposals and designing research protocols to measure clients' eating habits. Although I eventually shifted most of my hours to the kitchen, staff members continued to call on me to pitch in with office work, and I occasionally lent a hand with photocopying and filing. I did not realize how much the staff considered me one of them until the head of human resources offered me the position of payroll director (which I politely declined) and I started to receive invitations to staff parties and "staff only" invitations to GLWD soirees.

Kitchen volunteers were not as confused about what I was doing as the office staff, most likely because it was clear to me and to them that they were the primary subjects of my study. On my first day in the kitchen Hannah took me down to introduce me—a gesture I assumed was typical (but soon learned was not). Already unwittingly marked as "different" and not like the "regular volunteers," I conscientiously explained to each person I met that I was a sociologist observing conversations and interactions I heard and saw. The volunteers immediately rose to the challenge, questioning my motives for coming to the kitchen. Sharon and the others made it very clear they would judge me by the sweat of my brow. She told me about another sociologist who had not spent enough time in the kitchen to really learn anything. One needed to stick with the work to find out about kitchen life.

Volunteers talked about themselves and their lives all the time as we worked together. Nevertheless, this talk did not offer an open invitation for me to ask them questions. As long as my questions were about the work at hand (such as why we washed spinach one way and lettuce another), volunteers answered them readily. Personal questions, however, were off limits. As long as I persisted in asking them, I was shut out of the laughing, intimate groups that gathered around the big stainless steel tables. To learn more about the other volunteers, I had to disclose things about myself as they did. I had to enter the stream of conversation.

The volunteers' insistence that I join them in the work as they experienced it marked the beginning of my journey into true participation. Within this world, my secret interest in religion initially fell into the background. I focused, necessarily, on forming relationships with the people I worked beside from week to week. I told volunteers about my project when I introduced myself, and I found that some were intensely interested in my agenda (and others were utterly indifferent). But more often, conversation was less about my project than about my other hobbies and interests. Some volunteers learned that I enjoy cooking but did not have much experience dealing with large quantities, that I am not gay, that I am a Mennonite, and that my parents live in "Pennsylvania Dutch Country." Others learned that my boyfriend (now husband) is a scientist, that I am not a lifelong New Yorker, that I was a graduate student at Princeton, and that I have two sisters, one of whom studied opera. I did not calculate these varied disclosures: I did not hide information from some volunteers and divulge it to others. On the contrary, some things just never came up— not that they could not or should not have been mentioned. Such details set me in different relationships with different volunteers. Such details gave me "expertise" in some situations, such as when volunteers wanted to know about the best restaurants in Lancaster County, and made me a marginal figure in others. When others talked about the opening of a new gay discotheque or reminisced about the dance scene in San Francisco in the 1970s, I could only listen. I imagine this was true for other volunteers as well. Our presentations to each other were partial, and there was always more to say about ourselves and to learn from each other.

The fragmentary yet ordinary ways that volunteers talked about themselves and their interests, coupled with my growing interest in the practices of cooking and in volunteers' approval of "diversity," alleviated many of my worries about hiding my interest in religion. That volunteers rarely talked about what motivated them within the course of kitchen work meant that they never asked me to disclose my research agenda. That their daily conversations occasionally included some hints about religion additionally reduced my fears that any inadvertent slip I might make about religion would not be viewed as strange.

I eventually came to know the kitchen as well as most volunteers and was conversant in "what we knew to do." My knife skills improved markedly, and the chefs asked me to show new volunteers around. I complained with the others like an old hand about the jobs Monique or Bill asked us to do. I even started to appraise new volunteers in much the same way that Sharon had appraised my work. One morning in January I found myself facing Deborah Gibson. The onetime teen pop star had just finished a run in the London production of *Grease* and had returned to New York to start a new recording venture. In her "time off" she was "doing some charity work." We chatted idly about the agency; I answered her questions about the clients and the food, and she told me about the charity organization she founded for teenagers on Long Island. I asked if she was going to work in the kitchen regularly, and she said she thought she would like to. Catching her wistful and hesitant tone, I commented that"a lot of celebrities come in just once, for the publicity" and noted favorably that the paparazzi had not followed her to the agency. She smiled and laughed. When I told this story to Christopher later that day, I was embarrassed to recognize the insincerity of my praise and my judgmental attitude. I remembered how uneasy Charles's comments about that "other" sociologist had made me feel on my first day in the kitchen, and after that morning I was careful to keep such thoughts to myself.

Despite the willingness of most to accept me as just another kitchen volunteer, I was never typical. Because I spent long hours at GLWD, I had more time to witness the swirl of kitchen and office gossip and intrigue than almost any other volunteer. While most heard about arguments between staff and volunteers at second or third hand, I often saw them happen. Given that I regularly spent time in the offices, I was often in a position to answer other kitchen volunteers' questions about the current number of clients we served, to give updates on GLWD's new building renovation, and to identify new staff members who came into the kitchen for their lunches. Rather than asking Sean or Perry or Bill, volunteers started to ask me what I knew. While I sometimes demurred, finding it more helpful to my project to hear others say what they knew (or thought they knew), I nonetheless often added my two cents.

My position as researcher also meant I *could* ask questions that others could not, at least in interviews. Volunteers who agreed to sit for an interview told me details of their lives that I doubt they would have divulged to other new acquaintances. My interviews were very loosely structured, beginning with a question about how people found their way to God's Love We Deliver. Volunteers' stories usually disclosed a connection to AIDS and some articulation of their "motives" or reasons for volunteering. In keeping with my desire not to disclose my interest in religion, I asked about spiritual or religious issues only after volunteers' own statements or asides showed me some way to probe. Where volunteers did not make some linkage explicit, I introduced the theme by asking them what they thought "God's Love We Deliver" meant and whether they felt any personal connection to the name.

As a result of these interviews, I had true sets of confidences to harbor while working in the kitchen. None of the things I learned in interviews could be discussed during kitchen work: ethnographers do not disclose confidential stories without disguising informants' identities. Fortunately, there were few opportunities or windows in daily kitchen life where such disclosures might have even been considered. And as Charles said to me on my first day, volunteers do not tell each others' secrets. Learning individuals' stories and their ways of talking made me much more alert to double-voiced discourse, hints and guesses, and allusions.

Some of the most interesting conversations I had with volunteers at God's Love We Deliver happened at the now defunct City Diner on One Hundredth and Broadway, and at Ollie's Chinese Restaurant at Eighty-third and Broadway. Several volunteers I made friends of and regularly had dinner or lunch with often asked how my work was coming and what I was finding. These queries about "my work" provided the opportunity to test my interpretations of what I saw against volunteers' perceptions and elicited true dialogues where they used their knowledge and expertise to critique my fledgling reports. This book is stronger because of their thoughtful comments. My world is broader and my life richer for their friendship as well. I continued to meet with them well after I stopped my formal volunteer work, and I drew on their resources and expertise as I planned my wedding in December 1996. Many of our conversations turned to unadulterated gossip; others included incredibly intense moments as we divulged emotions, opinions, and stories of the kind only intimates know. I never wrote detailed notes about these events, since the boundaries between my positions as ethnographer, volunteer, and friend were less well drawn than when I was in the kitchen. Nevertheless, these dialogues could not help but inform my understanding of my journey.

DIALOGUE

Ethnography is about human relationships: it is built (or broken) through trust and through barter and exchange of various kinds. Although we focus on fieldwork relationships, ethnographers carry on simultaneous dialogue and exchange (and human relations) with the scholarly community and other texts as well. These concurrent dialogues make ethnographic research unique among investigative journeys.

In exchange for telling me about their lives, volunteers at God's Love We Deliver demanded that I pull my weight in both kitchen work and daily conversation. When I passed through the kitchen doorway, I stepped into an ongoing stream of events and conversation that they demanded I join. Choosing not to join in meant asserting an outsider status that they would have no part of. Joining them, making their talk into "our" talk, necessarily wiped out much of the distance that an ethnographic gaze developed. Volunteers were wary of my own silences, and they began to speak, to assert what was going on, only when I joined in the conversations and shared what I was doing. Ethnography happened as I let myself speak and stopped merely listening.

This is not to say that I lost a critical perspective while in the field. Joining in dialogue with volunteers did not lead to my "going native." Those dialogues that continued within my scholarly community required that I pay certain, constant attention to volunteers' dialogue (our dialogue). I continued to listen not only to what was said but to the ways my own moods, and previous conversations and events, influenced my understanding. I noted the things people did and analyzed the ways they were commented on, disputed, and ignored. I analyzed how people interpreted others' comments and reactions and how they interpreted their own actions and comments over time, taking into account some of the many practices of kitchen life.[1] I have attempted to describe particular interactions in as much detail as possible, incorporating volunteers' tones and voices and, where possible, alluding to conversational history.

Nevertheless, I am fully aware that my text does not reproduce others' voices. The events I recorded were inevitably shaped by my peculiar position and perspective in the kitchen. My field notes are not verbatim transcripts (transcripts, in any case, only partially record emotion and tone). One way to at least hint at volunteers' perspectives, and how they inevitably differ from my own, was to include as much material as possible from the events I discuss. Including "surplus" material suggests, at the very least, that other interpretations and explications of events swirled around my own.

"Dialogue" in ethnographic texts, writes James Clifford, occurs as ethnographers "try on" different languages and perspectives. As he says, "Dialogic textual production goes well beyond the more or less artful presentation of 'actual' encounters. It locates cultural interpretations in many sorts of reciprocal contexts, and it obliges writers to find diverse ways of rendering negotiated realities as multi-subjective, power-laden, and incongruent."[2]

Put a bit more plainly, dialogic methods and writing styles contain more meaning than the author intends: respondents' words fit with what an author wants to convey, but they also include enough "surplus" to call such interpretations into question. This destabilizes the interpretation an ethnographer puts forward by including or alluding to parallel interpretations. At the very least, such a perspective keeps in check the ethnographer's attempts to *explain* respondents' subjectivities, moods, and motivations.[3] This definition of "dialogue" does not require or assert equality of position among speakers: in fact it does not assume that equality between speaking subjects is even possible.[4] At their best, ethnographic texts establish their own authority yet hint at and speak of alternative interpretations through humble explications of others' words, thus prompting readers to query what has not been yet said.

Making the dialogue of daily life part of the text has also helped me recognize the limits of the cases I explain and expand on. Ethnographers tend to focus on single events in their writing rather than on many. However, the cases they use are often decontextualized and read for "deep meanings."[5] We live through stories, of course, and it is inevitable that some stories take on great resonance. As such, however, ethnographic events often adopt the character of unchanging or "typical" events. By using dialogue and including the same volunteers speaking in different contexts, I have hoped to dispel the aura that might elevate the stories I tell from their provisional, singular, and ordinary contexts. Dialogic methods are necessary to the study of ordinary conversations, since they remind readers and writers of the situated and incomplete interpretations that ethnographers give to the settings of daily life.

This book is built on dialogues with flesh-and-blood respondents, with flesh-and-blood scholars, and with the dry and brittle bones of text and theory that brought me closer to ideas of dialogue. It was also, unexpectedly, built on a dialogue with my own body. As volunteers hinted from my first day in the kitchen, becoming a volunteer meant learning from the physical work we engaged in. Work in the kitchen was about bodies. We fed sick bodies and hoped to nurse them to health with our labor. Volunteers relished the "dirty" work we did, even as they complained about aching backs and sore feet. Some transformed this physical labor into a spiritual or bodily good. After hours of hard work in the kitchen, they felt an "edge" that helped them face the world with renewed strength. I became a true volunteer when I too focused on my body. At first this focus was unavoidable: I ached. On occasion I could not bear the thought of forcing my exhausted limbs to write up field notes. As my arms cried out for rest, they demanded I think about the limits of my discursive focus in this project. They demanded I search for a more balanced portrait of kitchen work (not just kitchen talk) and led eventually to a deeper appreciation of how the unspoken (and at some points, unspeakable) parts of "doing something" at GLWD made space for everything else to happen.

This unexpected development within my ethnographic travels, on the page and in the field, solidified my growing sense that ethnographic work is a hybrid journey.

TWO KINDS OF JOURNEYS

An astute mentor once remarked that most books boil down to one of two narrative themes: "a stranger comes to town" or "someone goes on a journey." In this framework, ethnography almost always finds itself in the second category, and the ethnographer is always in some ways a pilgrim (or in the words of some of my respondents, a "seeker"). We go on trips to undiscovered countries or, armed with notepads and a "critical eye," we make our own countries strange.

There are several kinds of journeys a pilgrim can undertake. Some quests move the seeker forward linearly, toward a clear end point. Others are undertaken not so much to attain some particular "end" as for the journey itself. Such journeys may have a more circular pattern, and the traveler ends where she started, although it is no longer the "same" place, since she views it from a new perspective, with a new body, and within a newly framed horizon of meaning.[6] Ethnography, if it is a journey, is a hybrid of these forms. All successful ethnography is guided by goals that must be sought after, premises that must be addressed, and implicit arguments that must be answered. Nevertheless, ethnographers often speak in their writings of the necessity that the work itself imposes—to cease moving toward the goal, to look around, to use a different set of eyes and senses. This part is often discussed in almost mystical language; it is what makes sociologists speak of the "art" of ethnography. Ethnographers talk of immersion, of "going native," of finding what was not sought: these ideas and words elicit dangerous thoughts and provoke worries. Yet no matter how it is cloaked, fieldwork compels us to circle back on ourselves, our ideas, and our worlds, just as it also compels us to keep moving toward answers to our questions about the worlds of those around us.

Both elements of journeying enter into ethnographic work: the tensions of settling in the moment and getting to know others are magnified by the knowledge that we will move on. We know that the events we record will continue to live on in our minds and on the page (and within our ethnographic selves) in quite a different way than in the communities and individuals where we first heard them. Ethnographic transformation occurs within these tensions and opens up space between what is expected and what just "happens." It is in this space that the next dialogue can emerge.

NOTES

1. "Jackie" and "Hannah" are pseudonyms. I have changed the names of all the volunteers and staff members I worked with at God's Love We Deliver. I have also changed some of the most identifying parts of their stories, to preserve their anonymity. I use the actual name of the organization and the names of its executive director (Kathy Spahn) and its founder (Ganga Stone), as well as those of board members and others who appear in the history of GLWD (chapter 2). This information is a matter of public record, and their positions make them recognizable immediately to those familiar with AIDS organizations in New York City.

2. "Everyday life" has a varied history as a concept (see Norbert Elias, "On the Concept of Everyday Life," in *The Norbert Elias Reader,* ed. Johan Goudsblom and Stephen Mennell [Oxford: Basil Blackwell, 1998]). In using the term here, I want to call attention to—and thereby challenge—its common interpretation as routine behavior that is taken for granted as individuals move through the world with tacit agreement on the shared operative meanings of things. The problems that arise when a firm line is drawn between everyday activity and meaningful activity, or mundane activity and sacred activity, is recognized by many yet is implicitly reproduced in the choices that sociologists of religion make in determining areas of social life that are worthy of study.

3. The most common sociological measures of religious practice in America come from surveys that ask respondents about a preset collection of devotional practices such as church attendance and prayer. Although surveys report how much people pray (and in the United States these numbers frequently are high), they tell us little of what people think about prayer, why they pray, what it feels like to pray, or why they pray at all. Large-scale surveys likewise have limited

ability to discern other activities that individuals might assign religious or spiritual meaning to, and that they might find even more valuable than prayer or church attendance. In other words, surveys, taken in sum, at the least fail to capture a full array of religious practice, and they may even obscure features of the religious landscape.

For this reason, many researchers who use surveys (and others who do not) conduct interview-based studies to learn more about individuals' and groups' religious experiences (for instance, Alan Wolfe, *One Nation, after All* [New York: Viking, 1998]; Christian Smith and Michael Emerson, *American Evangelicalism: Embattled and Thriving* [Chicago: University of Chicago Press, 1998]; Robert Wuthnow, *Sharing the Journey: Support Groups and America's New Quest for Community* [New York: Free Press, 1994]). Interview studies take into account many of the limitations of surveys: they allow individuals to talk about what role religion plays in their lives and allow us to develop and analyze more detailed portraits of their religious lives. Nevertheless, interview settings are not everyday contexts and are not perceived as such by either interviewers or respondents (Michael Bell, *Childerley: Nature and Morality in a Country Village* [Chicago: University of Chicago Press, 1994], 248–50). Therefore interviews provide *accounts* of religious practice that may indeed be remembered differently from the way it was practiced. We use interviews to understand the cultural repertoires, languages, and interpretations that people make of the stories they tell, but these nevertheless remain partial accounts (Paul Lichterman, *The Search for Political Community: American Activists Reinventing Commitment* [Cambridge: Cambridge University Press, 1996], 237–42).

Ethnographic studies of religion take such broader contexts into account, but with few exceptions they focus solely on interactions within religious organizations (one counterexample is Judith Stacey's *Brave New Families* [New York: Basic Books, 1993]). The numerous ethnographies of religious institutions and collectivities often juxtapose the orthodox religious worldviews in such collectivities with the lived religious expressions and meanings of participants (Nancy Ammerman, *Bible Believers* [New Brunswick, N.J.: Rutgers University Press, 1987]; Lynn Davidman, *Tradition in a Rootless World* [Berkeley: University of California Press, 1991]; Nancy L. Eiesland, *A Particular Place* [New Brunswick, N.J.: Rutgers University Press, 1999]; Michael McNally, *Ojibwa Singers* [New York: Oxford University Press, 2000]; R. Stephen Warner, *New Wine in Old Wineskins: Evangelicals and Liberals in a Small-Town Church* [Berkeley: University of California Press, 1988]; R. Marie Griffith, *God's Daughters: Evangelical Women and the Power of Submission* [Berkeley: University of California Press, 1997]). This work demonstrates clearly that lived religious practice involves putting together responses to particular social circumstances, which often appear to be quite different in action than in the stories and narratives that participants tell about them after the fact. The next step, which I take in this book, is to take such ethnographic methods and conventions and apply them to religious practice outside religious institutions.

4. GLWD is not a religious organization: it is not connected formally to any religious groups, its staff and volunteers do not understand it to be a religious organization, and it does not articulate its mission in religious or spiritual terms (at least not in most venues). I discuss GLWD's name, its organizational development, and its curious relationship with religion in chapter 2.

5. For a historical overview of popular and religious notions about the place of religion in urban settings and the place of the city in Americans' imaginations about religion, see Robert Orsi, "Crossing the City Line," in *Gods of the City*, ed. Robert Orsi (Bloomington: Indiana University Press, 1999), 1–78. See also Harvey Cox, *The Secular City* (New York: Macmillan, 1967), and John K. Roth, *Private Needs, Public Selves* (Urbana: University of Illinois Press, 1997).

6. Barry A. Kosmin and Seymour P. Lachman, *One Nation under God* (New York: Harmony Books, 1993).

7. For instance, Rodney Stark, "Secularization R.I.P.," *Sociology of Religion* 60 (fall 1999): 249–73; Peter Berger, "Reflections on the Sociology of Religion Today," *Sociology of Religion* 62 (winter 2001): 443–54.

8. Wade Clark Roof, *A Generation of Seekers: The Spiritual Journeys of the Baby Boom Generation* (San Francisco: HarperSanFrancisco, 1993); Robert Wuthnow, *After Heaven: Spirituality in America since the 1960s* (Berkeley: University of California Press, 1998). A growing body of evidence from historians and anthropologists suggests that individuals' work of blending disparate (and unorthodox) practices, or shopping for such, is not a recent innovation. See Leigh Eric Schmidt, *Holy Fairs: Scottish Communions and American Revivals in the Early Modern Period* (Princeton: Princeton University Press, 1989), and the papers in David Hall, ed., *Lived Religion in America* (Princeton: Princeton University Press, 1997).

9. Nancy Ammerman, "Golden Rule Christians," in *Lived Religion in America*, ed. David Hall (Princeton: Princeton University Press, 1997), 196–216.

10. Robert Wuthnow, *The Restructuring of American Religion* (Princeton: Princeton University Press, 1988), 108–9.

11. Rhys Williams, "Constructing the Public Good: Social Movements and Cultural Resources," *Social Problems* 42, 1 (1995): 124–44; John Evans, *Playing God: Human Genetic Engineering and the Rationalization of Bioethics* (Chicago: University of Chicago Press, 2002).

12. Robert D. Putnam, *Bowling Alone: The Collapse and Revival of American Community* (New York: Simon and Schuster, 2000); Theda Skocpol, Marshall Ganz, and Ziad Munson, "A Nation of Organizers: The Institutional Origins of Civic Voluntarism in the United States," *American Political Science Review* 94 (September 2000): 527–46.

13. Nina Eliasoph, *Avoiding Politics: How Americans Produce Apathy in Everyday Life* (Cambridge: Cambridge University Press, 1998).

14. Within this line of argument, there have been two main emphases on what people must share if communication is to happen. The first approach focuses

on shared content or substance of shared values. Within a culture, individuals share the meaning of particular objects, rituals, parables, and history that resonate across any particular person's experience (Jeffrey Alexander and Phillip Smith, "The Discourse of American Civil Society: A New Proposal for Cultural Studies," *Theory and Society* 22 [1993]: 157–207; Steven Tipton, *Getting Saved from the Sixties: Moral Meaning in Conversion and Cultural Change* [Berkeley: University of California Press, 1982]; Robert Bellah et al., *Habits of the Heart: Individualism and Commitment in American Life* [Berkeley: University of California Press, 1985]). Subcultures and resistant groups exist within any culture, of course, but even individuals and groups that stand in opposition to the dominant culture acknowledge its artifacts and languages, even if only to rail against them (James C. Scott, *Weapons of the Weak: Everyday Forms of Peasant Resistance* [New Haven: Yale University Press, 1985]; Dick Hebdige, *Subculture: The Meaning of Style* [London: Methuen, 1979]).

A second group of scholars suggests that it is not so much cultural content (scripts and vocabularies) as styles (manners and approaches to interacting) that we must share if communication is to happen. This strain of thought emphasizes that ways of talking (styles or practices) are cultural forms in themselves (Pierre Bourdieu, *The Logic of Practice*, trans. Richard Nice [Stanford: Stanford University Press, 1990]; Nina Eliasoph and Paul Lichterman, "The Practice of Meaning in Civil Society," paper presented at the American Sociological Association annual meetings, New York, August 1996). It allows that individuals need not share the meaning of words and ideas so much as a general sense of how interaction progresses. This second, stylistic approach rectifies some of the epistemological problems presented in studies that focus on shared content, in that it emphasizes acts of communicating rather than the content of communication. Nevertheless, as in its counterpart view, a lack of shared stylistic practices can cause "hostility and confusion," which signals "a failure of meaning" in a group (Eliasoph and Lichterman, "Practice of Meaning," 32).

15. This perspective (e.g., Daniel Bell, *The Cultural Contradictions of Capitalism* [New York: Basic Books, 1976]; Phillip Rieff, *The Triumph of the Therapeutic* [London: Chatto and Windus, 1966]) suggests that increased diversity and personalism are coupled with dwindling commitment to community life and are thus highly problematic for democratic society. Of course others have countered these claims: speaking from a liberal multiculturalist perspective, Joseph Raz envisions a society where the variety of "diverse values embodied in the practices of different societies" interlace to make democracy and society stronger, yet where each hangs in a balance of an underlying "common culture" of mutual respect and tolerance (Raz, "Multiculturalism: A Liberal Perspective," *Dissent* 41 [winter 1994]: 67–79). Jürgen Habermas suggests that critical, reasoned thinking can overcome differences and can subvert personalism (Habermas, *The Theory of Communicative Action*, vol. 1 [Boston: Beacon Press, 1984]). Both of these liberal perspectives nevertheless

also assume the presence of an underlying substrate of shared cultural styles (see preceding note) that privilege tolerance and reason. Feminist political theorists have criticized this position, suggesting that these forms of communication hold their own cultural histories that keep individuals (women, minorities, and others who are to be included in "multicultural" forums) from expressing their own competing styles of interacting, thus diminishing their personal positions (Nancy Fraser, "Rethinking the Public Sphere: A Contribution to the Critique of Actually Existing Democracy," *Social Text* 25–26 [1990]: 56–80).

Acknowledging cultural diversity shifts sociologists' (and political theorists') attention from shared content to shared styles of acting. Nevertheless, this shift in emphasis tends to ignore how cultural "styles" are connected in practice. Juxtaposing the ways members of the same group of volunteers, in the same social space, talk about different issues as I do in this book makes this clearer.

16. Garfinkel established how valuable assumptions are in social interactions, demonstrating that in social life our assumptions about how people will understand and respond to our actions and language often form the basis of social interactions. Indeed, we could not interact without such expectations (Harold Garfinkel, *Studies in Ethnomethodology* [Englewood Cliffs, N.J.: Prentice-Hall, 1967]). I do not mean these assumptions are not an integral part of our daily existence, but I do argue that not all daily action is governed by them. We have as many skills and tools that bar us from making assumptions within conversation as skills that help us to make them. Without such skills, communication and social life would also be impossible.

17. As Peter Berger and Thomas Luckmann note, emphasis on patterns can be taken too far: the whole culture of any institution is available only "upon reflection" and cannot be found in the actual living out of any particular group. They state that "great care is required in any statements one makes about the 'logic' of institutions. The logic does not reside in the institutions and their external functions, but in the ways these are treated in reflection about them. Put differently, reflective consciousness superimposes the quality of logic on the institutional order" (Berger and Luckmann, *The Social Construction of Reality* [Garden City, N.Y.: Doubleday, 1966], 64). They nevertheless also argue that it is important to act as if such logic did exist in everyday life, for without such order, our ability to interact would be diminished.

18. We will also have to shift from using methods that gird up the expectation that people in groups hold shared cultures to using methods that incorporate the idea that shared culture "happens" to varying degrees. See James Clifford, "On Ethnographic Authority," in *The Predicament of Culture,* ed. James Clifford (Cambridge: Harvard University Press, 1988), and his "Introduction: Partial Truths," in *Writing Culture: The Poetics and Politics of Ethnography,* ed. James Clifford and George E. Marcus (Berkeley: University of California Press, 1986).

19. In particular, I draw here on the conversations about practice found in Bourdieu, *Logic of Practice;* Ann Swidler, "Culture in Action: Symbols and Strategies," *American Sociological Review* 51 (1986): 273–86; Sherry Ortner, "Theory in Anthropology since the Sixties," *Comparative Studies in Society and History* 26, 1 (1988): 126–66; Charles Camic, "The Matter of Habit," *American Journal of Sociology* 91 (March 1986): 1039–87); and Catherine Bell, *Ritual Theory, Ritual Practice* (New York: Oxford University Press, 1992).

In addition, Mikhail Bakhtin's theory of speech genres (*"Speech Genres" and Other Late Essays* [Austin: University of Texas Press, 1986]) lends complementary understanding to practice. His theories add some necessary flexibility and mobility to the structuring properties (both intended and unintended) of practice. See Jeffrey Olick, "Genre Memories and Memory Genres: A Dialogical Analysis of May 8 1945 Commemorations in the Federal Republic of Germany," *American Sociological Review* 64 (1999): 381–402.

20. Individuals and groups within traditions craft responses specific to their circumstances, often recasting or transforming the official meanings in the course of their daily traffic in those symbols and rituals. A collection of projects that use "lived religion" as an orienting term is found in Hall, *Lived Religion in America.* See also Griffith, *God's Daughters;* Robert Orsi, *Thank You St. Jude: Women's Devotion to the Patron Saint of Hopeless Causes* (New Haven: Yale University Press, 1996); and Leigh Eric Schmidt, *Consumer Rites: The Buying and Selling of American Holidays* (Princeton: Princeton University Press, 1995).

21. McNally, *Ojibwa Singers.*

22. For instance, Michel de Certeau, *The Practice of Everyday Life* (Berkeley: University of California Press, 1984); Anthony Giddens, *New Rules of Sociological Method,* 2d ed. (Stanford: Stanford University Press, 1993); Judith Butler, *Bodies That Matter: On the Discursive Limits of "Sex"* (London: Routledge, 1993).

23. Roger Friedland and Robert Alford, "Bringing Society Back In: Symbols, Practices, and Institutional Contradictions," in *The New Institutionalism in Organizational Analysis,* ed. Walter W. Powell and Paul DiMaggio (Chicago: University of Chicago Press, 1991).

24. Berger and Luckmann, *Social Construction of Reality,* for example, argue that a religious sphere by definition is a distinct sphere of consciousness that individuals use to reflect on action in more mundane spheres of life and consciousness but that does not interact with others. In contrast, Mikhail Bakhtin notes: "Pure everyday life is a fiction, a product of the intellect. Human life is always shaped and this shaping is always ritualistic (even if only 'aesthetically' so)" ("From Notes Made 1970–71," in *"Speech Genres" and Other Late Essays,* 154).

25. Berger and Luckmann, *Social Construction of Reality,* 44, describe the serial use of mental orientations as such: "For instance, as a businessman I know that it pays to be inconsiderate of others. I may laugh at a joke in which this maxim

leads to failure, I may be moved by an actor or a preacher extolling the virtues of consideration, and I may concede in a philosophical mood that all social relations should be governed by the Golden Rule. Having laughed, having been moved and having philosophized, I return to the 'serious' world of business, once more recognize the logic of its maxims, and act accordingly. Only when my maxims fail to 'deliver the goods' in the world to which they are intended to apply are they likely to become problematic to me 'in earnest.' "

26. Paul DiMaggio, "Culture and Cognition: An Interdisciplinary Review," *Annual Review of Sociology* 23 (1997): 263–87.

27. And so, Bakhtin says, the "inviolability and predetermined quality of these languages came to an end, and the necessity of actively choosing one's orientation among them began" (Mikhail Bakhtin, *The Dialogic Imagination: Four Essays,* trans. Caryl Emerson and Michael Holquist [Austin: University of Texas Press, 1981], 296).

28. All conversation in this book is reconstructed from field notes except where I specify otherwise (as in interviews).

29. One of the many ironies of the Christmas delivery was that many Jewish volunteers worked on Christmas Day so Christians could have "their holiday" off.

30. M. A. K. Halliday, *Language as Social Semiotic: The Social Interpretation of Language and Meaning* (London: Edward Arnold, 1978), esp. 154–64. Halliday's argument draws from research conducted in the 1960s and 1970s, which demonstrates that the heterogeneity of speech is noted, and evident to, the "average New Yorker . . . [who] not only does not speak like all other New Yorkers . . . [but] does not even speak like himself. He may be consistent in his judgement on others . . . but he is far from being consistent in his own practice. What is more, he is often aware of not being consistent" (155). This description holds, I believe (as, with some variation, does his suggestion that New Yorkers' attitudes toward speaking are more similar than what is actually said—that is, their dialects).

31. This pattern of volunteer participation is typical of AIDS organizations. See Philip Kayal, *Bearing Witness: Gay Men's Health Crisis and the Politics of AIDS* (Boulder, Colo.: Westview Press, 1993); Susan Chambré, "Being Needful: Family, Love, and Prayer among AIDS Volunteers," *Research in the Sociology of Health Care* 12 (1995): 113–39; and Allen M. Omoto and Mark Snyder, "AIDS Volunteers and Their Motivations: Theoretical Issues and Practical Concerns," *Nonprofit Management and Leadership* 4 (winter 1993): 157–76.

CHAPTER TWO

Epigraph: Mikhail Bakhtin, *Rabelais and His World* (Bloomington: Indiana University Press, 1986), 291.

1. I use "repertoire" here to mean a collected and changing set of symbols, actions, and language (William Sewell, "A Theory of Structure: Duality, Agency, and Transformation," *American Journal of Sociology* 98 [July 1992]: 1–29; Swidler, "Cul-

ture in Action"). There are manifold ways of defining and referring to the culturally constructed systems or collections of somewhat consistent symbols, stories,
and expressions that articulate positions and, at some level, galvanize action or
responses by individuals or groups. I take my cues from Pierre Bourdieu's notion of practice and Mikhail Bakhtin's complementary notion of "speech genres"
(Bourdieu, *Logic of Practice;* Bakhtin, *Problems of Dostoevsky's Poetics,* ed. and trans. Caryl
Emerson [Minneapolis: University of Minnesota Press, 1984]; Bakhtin, *"Speech
Genres" and Other Late Essays*). Each focuses on the historically created and largely un-
reflective expression of cultural forms, justifications, and explanations.

I assume that cultural repertoires become articulated within contingent and
nonstrategic "daily" local cultures and that they gain authority through connections to more broadly apparent "institutional logics" (Friedland and Alford,
"Bringing Society Back In"; David Stark, "Work, Worth and Justice in a Socialist
Mixed Economy," Working Paper 5, Harvard University Center for Eastern European Studies, 1988). In this respect, repertoires within an organization may
conflict insofar as they are directed toward different goals and ends.

2. Charles Perrow makes the distinction between "formal" and "operative"
goals. Formal goals are articulated by leaders and organizers of an organization
and are distinct from the daily practical goals (and knowledge) that workers within
the organization use to get their work done (Perrow, *Complex Organizations: A Critical
Essay,* 3d ed. [New York: Random House, 1986]). John Meyer and Brian Rowan
similarly argue that formal structures "dramatically reflect the myths of their institutional environments instead of the demands of their work activities" (Meyer
and Rowan, "Institutionalized Organizations: Formal Structure as Myth and Ceremony," *American Sociological Review* 83 [1977]: 340–63). Both perspectives suggest
that formal ideologies, goals, or structures are decoupled from necessary daily
pursuits. Yet these myths and ceremonies are also necessary.

3. As Rhys Williams and Jeffrey Blackburn have observed in the case of Operation Rescue, regular rank-and-file members do not necessarily commit to a social
movement's official positions, and when queried they may take positions that directly conflict with those of the groups they work for. This makes "generalizations
about . . . membership and commitment more, rather than less, problematic"
(Williams and Blackburn, "Many Are Called but Few Obey: Ideological Commitment and Activism in Operation Rescue," in *Disruptive Religion,* ed. Christian Smith
[New York: Routledge, 1996], 194).

4. Beth Roy, *Some Trouble with Cows: Making Sense of Social Conflict* (Berkeley: University of California Press, 1994), 163. Although hearing actors use a particular bit
of language or ideology mischievously does not imply that they do not "believe"
what they say, it calls attention to the various stances an actor can take toward it.

5. God's Love We Deliver, promotional flier, ca. 1993.

6. For instance, GLWD's incorporation documents reveal a broader history

than the origin story tells. They list Stone, Stone's lawyer, and Jane Ellen Best as founders. Best is mentioned in documents from the early years as the agency's "co-founder," but her name drops out after 1987. No one I spoke with at GLWD in 1994 knew who she was. Similarly, GLWD's papers state two equal goals: delivering meals and starting a hospice. The hospice idea also drops out of GLWD literature after 1987, even though it seems that Stone and some others continued to think about adding other services. For instance, GLWD advertised "upcoming" services such as an oral history project and housecleaning in 1988 client newsletters.

7. Stone's departure was cause for speculation in city tabloids about possible mismanagement at GLWD during her tenure. It is evident, rather, that she had reached the end of her interest in the daily running of the agency, especially after the purchase of the SoHo building in 1993. Renovations were projected at $4 million, and the board insisted on mounting a capital campaign and raising a large portion of the funds before beginning the necessary work. Stone's replacement was a seasoned nonprofit management professional with extensive experience in fundraising.

8. Submerged meanings are reinvigorated through enactment in particular contingent contexts. "Even past meanings can never be stable . . . they will always change in the process of subsequent, future development of the dialogue. At any moment in the development of the dialogue there are immense, boundless masses of forgotten contextual meanings, but at certain moments . . . along the way they are recalled and invigorated in a new form (in a new context)" (Mikhail Bakhtin, "Methodology for the Human Sciences," in *"Speech Genres" and other Late Essays,* 170).

9. God's Love We Deliver promotional flier, ca. 1988.

10. Swami Muktananda was founder and leader of the Siddha Yoga Dham Association of America (SYDA) until his death. Based in Hindu traditions, SYDA teaches that a spiritual leader helps followers progress to full development of the inner self. Stone was (and is) a devoted follower and did not hide her allegiance: while she was at God's Love We Deliver, a large portrait of Muktananda hung behind her desk.

11. "God's Love We Deliver," *New Yorker,* February 25, 1991, 28–29. .

12. God's Love We Deliver, promotional information flier, ca. 1988.

13. K. Cronstrom, "Ganga Stone, Samaritan," *Egg,* May 1990, as quoted in Susan Chambré, "Uncertainty, Diversity, and Change: The AIDS Community in New York City," *Research in Community Sociology* 6 (1996): 149–90.

14. As symbols go, "God" is certainly one of the most unambiguously religious ones there is. But "God" has qualities similar to a Rorschach ink blot in an era when, as Wade Clark Roof argues, "God" is increasingly associated with a diaphanous and "weightless" sense of the sacred than any traditional, patriarchal sense of deity (Roof, *Spiritual Marketplace* [Princeton: Princeton University Press, 1999], 100–101, 129–30).

15. Thomas Jeavons provides a helpful set of questions to ascertain whether an organization is more or less religious. These questions assess self-identity, the religiousness of its participants (and the relative homogeneity of their beliefs), its goals and products, its decision-making processes, and its connections with other organizational fields. God's Love We Deliver has fluctuated on a religious to nonreligious scale along almost all these lines (Jeavons, "Identifying Character-istics of 'Religious' Organizations: An Exploratory Proposal," in *Sacred Companies: Organizational Aspects of Religion and Religious Aspects of Organizations,* ed. N. J. Demerath et al. [New York: Oxford University Press, 1998], 79–96).

16. Susan Chambré notes that many early organized responses to AIDS in New York were faith based, involving "existing congregations, gay religious groups and people influenced by spiritual concerns," even as many other religious responses to AIDS condemned homosexuality and suggested that AIDS was punishment for sin (Chambré, "The Secularization of Faith-Based Organizations: Case Studies of Four New York City Organizations," paper presented at the Association for Research on Nonprofit Organizations and Voluntary Action, November 2000).

17. By placing religious language in a client's voice (rather than a staff member's or the organization's own language) GLWD created an "intentional hybrid" form, where two worldviews, two "epochs . . . come together and consciously fight it out in the territory of the utterance" (Bakhtin, "Discourse in the Novel," in *The Dialogic Imagination,* 358–60).

18. "God's Love We Deliver: A Lifeline for AIDS Victims," *New York Times,* No-vember 14, 1993, advertising insert by Charge against Hunger/American Express; italics added.

19. Teresa Carpenter, "A Certifiable Saint," *Harper's Bazaar,* no. 3382 (Septem-ber 1993): 418–21.

20. "Twenty Dollars Feeds a Homebound Person with AIDS for One Week. Will You Pick up the Tab?" *Good News Letter,* 1988.

21. *Good News Letter,* 1988. The quilt piece depicted the original GLWD logo (a turquoise oval framing two hands and a heart, with the phrase "Hands to Help").

22. "No meal can be sad. Sadness and food are incompatible (while death and food are perfectly compatible). The banquet always celebrates a victory and this is part of its very nature. . . . It is the triumph of life over death" (Bakhtin, *Rabelais and His World,* 283).

23. Susan M. Chambré, "Volunteers as Witnesses: The Mobilization of AIDS Volunteers in New York City, 1981–1988," *Social Service Review* 65 (December 1991): 533–47.

24. In contrast, many AIDS organizations, including Gay Men's Health Crisis (GMHC), ACT UP, and the like were founded by gay men or by people with AIDS. Many of these groups struggled quite openly over whether political or succoring endeavors should receive first priority. See Philip M. Kayal, "Gay AIDS Volun-tarism as Political Activity," *Nonprofit and Voluntary Sector Quarterly* 20 (fall 1991): 289–

312; Charles Perrow and Mauro F. Guillén, *The AIDS Disaster: The Failure of Organizations in New York and the Nation* (New Haven: Yale University Press, 1990); Joshua Gamson, "Silence, Death, and the Invisible Enemy: AIDS Activism and Social Movement 'Newness,' " in *Ethnography Unbound: Power and Resistance in the Modern Metropolis,* ed. Michael Burawoy et al. (Berkeley: University of California Press, 1991).

25. God's Love We Deliver held a second auction in 1993, raising close to $500,000. In 1995 the God's Love We Deliver auction was superseded by a four-organization benefit auction spearheaded and organized by GMHC at the request of Robert Wooley, the auctioneer in whose honor the auction was mounted (Wooley had retired with full-blown AIDS). The 1995 auction raised $1.2 million for GLWD, GMHC, two other AIDS organizations.

26. Perrow and Guillén, *AIDS Disaster,* 17–23. Several studies have chronicled the overwhelming hurdles that AIDS service organizations faced in gaining funding in the mid-1980s. They encountered not only the stigma and lack of public support that came with the epidemic, but also structural barriers to gaining financial and other support. These initial barriers became less of a problem as the AIDS epidemic wore on. See also Randy Shilts, *And the Band Played On: Politics, People, and the AIDS Epidemic* (New York: Penguin, 1988); Susan Chambré, "Creating New Nonprofit Organizations as Responses to Social Change: HIV/AIDS Organizations in New York City," *Policy Studies Review* 14 (spring–summer 1995): 117–26; Roy Cain, "Managing Impressions of an AIDS Service Organization: Into the Mainstream or out of the Closet?" *Qualitative Sociology* 17, 1 (1994): 43–61.

27. With the introduction of the federally sponsored Ryan White CARE Act in 1990, AIDS funding in New York City grew considerably. By fiscal year 1993–94, GLWD received just over $1.4 million through government contracts (accounting for a little more than one-quarter of its budget), including money from Ryan White, SNAP, and the Federal Emergency Management Association.

28. Courtney Bender, "The Meals Are the Message: The Growth and Congestion of an AIDS Service Organization's Mission in Multiple Organizational Fields," Working Paper 221, Program on Non-Profit Organizations, Yale University, 1995).

29. "God's Love We Deliver: A Lifeline for AIDS Victims."

30. God's Love We Deliver, Report to the New York State Department of Health, Homeless and Destitute Program Bureau of Nutrition, 1990.

31. Of course, a person with AIDS who is not at home is not technically "homebound." In its first years, GLWD policy stated that when clients had medical appointments, they had to provide proof. During my fieldwork, clients could call twenty-four hours in advance to notify client services that they would be away for the day, whether they had an appointment with a masseuse, a chiropractor, or a doctor. This muddied the definition of "homebound." Several years after my field research, the "homebound" requirement was dropped altogether.

32. *Good News Letter,* 1988.

33. Throughout this period, God's Love We Deliver also was a major actor in the growth of a countrywide group of AIDS food service organizations. One of two such organizations to get off the ground in 1985 (the other, Project Open Hand, is in San Francisco), it was soon followed by MANNA in Philadelphia, Project Angel Food in Los Angeles, Chicken Soup Brigade in Seattle, and Mama's Kitchen in San Diego. These organizations also provide nutritious home meals to people with AIDS. GLWD contributed to the growth of this field by developing and distributing technical assistance manuals on setting up meal distribution networks, providing nutritional counseling, and recruiting community-based volunteers.

34. Mary Romeyn, *Nutrition and HIV: A New Model for Treatment* (San Francisco: Jossey-Bass, 1995).

35. God's Love We Deliver, Report to the New York State Department of Health, Homeless and Destitute Program Bureau of Nutrition, 1990.

36. "Nutrition Means More Than Food," *Good News Letter,* fall 1994, 7.

37. "God's Love We Deliver," *New Yorker,* February 25, 1991, 28–29.

38. Daniel Sack, *Whitebread Protestants: Food and Religion in American Culture* (New York: St. Martin's Press, 2000).

39. "God's Love We Deliver is reaching out and branching out," the 1988 *Good News Letter* proclaimed. Expansion into the outer boroughs marked the beginning of an ongoing commitment to serve people who were outside established AIDS networks. This expansion began two years before the Ryan White CARE Act (1990), which encouraged and mandated such expansions in AIDS service organizations.

40. "Languages do not exclude each other but intersect with each other in many different ways," Bakhtin writes (*Dialogic Imagination,* 291). In other words, language is always ambiguous, symbolic, filled with potential meanings that rub up against each other. If we say this, however, we are in danger of saying that "it might even seem that the very word 'language' loses all meaning . . . for there is no single plane on which all these 'languages' might be juxtaposed."

Of course there is a common plane—their use in social contexts. "External markers" (the symbolic interactions and connections we map out in chapters like this, that is, the entire group of "potential" meanings and connections that can be made), Bakhtin says, "cannot in themselves be understood or studied without understanding the specific conceptualization they have been given by an intention" (*Dialogic Imagination,* 292). See also Marc Steinberg, "Dialogic Analysis of Repertoires of Discourse among Nineteenth-Century English Cotton Spinners," *American Journal of Sociology* 105 (November 1999): 736–80.

41. Rosabeth Moss Kantor and David V. Summers, "Doing Well While Doing Good: Dilemmas of Performance Measurement in Nonprofit Organizations and the Need for a Multiple-Constituency Approach," in *The Nonprofit Sector: A Research Handbook,* ed. Walter W. Powell (New Haven: Yale University Press, 1987), 155–56.

See also Joseph A. Kotarba and Darlene Hurt, "An Ethnography of an AIDS Hospice: Toward a Theory of Organizational Pastiche," *Symbolic Interaction* 18, 4 (1995): 413–38.

42. Every meal that diverged in any way from a regular entrée, in contents or portion size, was designated with a special sticker. This helped van drivers and delivery volunteers deliver the correct meal to the correct person. All these meals were called "specials."

43. The chefs did accept donations of packaged frozen desserts, like crates of Sara Lee cakes and packaged Pepperidge Farm cookies, and gave them to the clients when the baker was on vacation or out sick. Other food donations were either declined (politely) or sometimes set out for the volunteers to snack on. The kitchen also once accepted several cases of premium berry preserves. The baker used them to make linzer torte.

44. Fred H. Goldner, R. Richard Ritti, and Thomas P. Ference, "The Production of Cynical Knowledge in Organizations," *American Sociological Review* 42 (1977): 539–51.

CHAPTER THREE

1. Gary Alan Fine, *Kitchens: The Culture of Restaurant Work* (Berkeley: University of California Press, 1996); Sharon Zukin, "Artists and Immigrants in New York City Restaurants," in *The Cultures of Cities,* by Sharon Zukin (Cambridge, Mass.: Blackwell, 1995), 153–86.

2. The "rules" were not formally written down. (The few that I gleaned from reading volunteer orientation material included requirements for attire, kitchen safety, and cleanliness [cleaning up one's own work area].) These rules, of course, did not even begin to cover what Emily meant when she said she knew exactly what to do, knowledge that covered a set of shared expectations, "rules of the game," and relationships that made a kitchen community. See George Herbert Mead, *Mind, Self, and Society,* ed. C. W. Morris (Chicago: University of Chicago Press, 1962), 152–60.

3. Sociologists and anthropologists have long noted that pollution and contamination are culturally defined and enacted categories. For example, eating pork may be taboo and "unclean" in one culture but perfectly acceptable in another. The cultural consequences of some forms of contamination or boundary crossing are often more clearly understood in these writings than are the "material" and physiological outcomes. See Mary Douglas, *Purity and Danger: An Analysis of the Concepts of Pollution and Taboo* (1966; reprint, New York: Routledge, 1991); Gaye Tuchman and Harry Levine, "New York Jews and Chinese Food: The Social Construction of an Ethnic Pattern," *Journal of Contemporary Ethnography* 22 (1993): 382–407.

4. Much of the concern about food contamination focused on food delivery.

For instance, delivery volunteers were instructed never to leave a meal at a client's home if a client was not there because the food could begin to spoil if not eaten or refrigerated immediately. (I found this policy sad, given that most of the neediest clients living in single room occupancy hotels had no access to refrigeration anyway.) In addition, client services sent periodic reminders to clients on how to properly store and reheat meals. The meals were stamped with a "throw away date."

Mary Romeyn, an HIV nutrition specialist, provides guidelines on how people with AIDS should cook and store vegetables and meat: "Even if you cook contaminated food long enough to kill the germs, there may be toxins from bacterial growth that can cause food poisoning" (Romeyn, *Nutrition and HIV: A New Model for Treatment*, 84).

5. Pierre Bourdieu, *Outline of a Theory of Practice*, trans. Richard Nice (Cambridge: Cambridge University Press, 1977); Bourdieu, *Logic of Practice*; Camic, "Matter of Habit."

6. Quoted from letters from former volunteers to Ganga Stone, dated February 28 to March 10, 1994.

7. Fine, *Kitchens*, 33–34.

8. Erving Goffman, *The Presentation of Self in Everyday Life* (New York: Doubleday, 1959).

9. Another possible, tentative interpretation of volunteers' disregard for contamination comes from Emily Martin's description of changes in common understandings of contamination and disease. Martin shows how our understanding of infection has moved from one of boundaries that must be protected from incursions to one in which "flexible bodies" can absorb infectious agents and do away from them (Martin, *Flexible Bodies* [Boston: Beacon Press, 1994]). Within this model of contamination, the "contaminating" agents would have to be large or dispersed throughout the dishes: one piece of hair in three hundred pounds of egg salad would probably not "infect" the salad. Likewise, picking out tiny pieces of dirt or sand that inadvertently made their way into the roasted potatoes would not be worth doing, since they would not pose a threat of any substance.

10. The introduction of other unofficial languages is ongoing, commonplace, and disorganized. It is not a "unified" opposition to the official (as Marxist readings of Bakhtin have suggested) but rather a response to the ordinary heterogeneous elements of everyday life that do not fit within the official. Bakhtin suggests that centripetal, organizing forces always work to disrupt the centrifugal tendencies of everyday life: "The centripetal forces of the life of language, embodied in a 'unitary language,' operate in the midst of heteroglossia" (Bakhtin, *Dialogic Imagination*, 271, 272). See Gary Saul Morson and Caryl Emerson, *Mikhail Bakhtin: Creation of a Prosaics* (Stanford: Stanford University Press, 1990), 30–35, 139–40. Bakhtin suggests that certain circumstances can be more or less weighted toward centrifugal

disorder or centripetal order but that, as with the second law of thermodynamics, it takes work to create order, and order is always being achieved and is never given. This standpoint is similar to the one made by ethnomethodologists and (at least in passing) by Berger and Luckmann, *Social Construction of Reality,* among others. See also Courtney Bender, "Bakhtinian Perspectives on Everyday Life Sociology," in *Bakhtin and the Human Sciences: No Last Words,* ed. Michael Gardiner and Michael Bell (Thousand Oaks, Calif.: Sage, 1998).

11. For instance, Bourdieu's (1990) analysis of practice has come under criticism for being too static. William Sewell Jr. argues that Bourdieu's "schemas and resources so powerfully reproduce one another that even the most cunning or improvisational actions undertaken by agents necessarily reproduce the structure" (Sewell, "Theory of Structure: Duality, Agency, and Transformation," 15). He argues that Bourdieu fails to provide us with a definition of practice that truly mediates between structure and agency. Sewell proposes several mechanisms in which agency can occur (and by which practices and structures change over time), including multiplicity, transposability, unpredictability, polysemy, and the intersection of structures. These words all imply the use of metaphors, multivalent symbols, and translations. As such, they suggest the availability of a wide range of discursive styles that conjure up visions of practices mixing and commingling.

CHAPTER FOUR

1. Robert Wuthnow, *Acts of Compassion: Caring for Others and Helping Ourselves* (Princeton: Princeton University Press, 1991); for a historical account, see Peter Dobkin Hall, *Inventing the Nonprofit Sector and Other Essays on Philanthropy, Voluntarism, and Nonprofit Organizations* (Baltimore: Johns Hopkins University Press, 1992). For an early analysis of AIDS volunteers and their religious affiliations, see Omoto and Snyder's 1990–91 survey. This survey tapped a somewhat different population of volunteers: 51 percent of their sample were "buddies" for PWAs, and 12 percent helped on telephone hotlines (163). Of their sample, 35 percent had no religious affiliation.

2. I use the term "religious" here rather than "spiritual," given that *religion* evokes the structures of the sacred (however those are defined) that are reproduced in practice. It is important to note that talking about "religion" in this sense makes sense only in conjunction with *practice.* Practice emphasizes both the "intentional" and individually articulated aspects of activity and also those "habituated" structures and ideas that are unwittingly reproduced by those same individuals or groups. To put it a bit more abstractly, *practice* places emphasis on the ways individuals apprehend institutional and communal articulations of religion and use them to forge religious lives within particular structures and settings. Daily practices create and hold up structures we take for granted; likewise, our practices orient how we view and apprehend those structures and institutions. Bourdieu,

Logic of Practice, and Bakhtin, *"Speech Genres" and Other Late Essays,* make this point about practices and genres respectively. Practices are not wholly the product of institutions, nor are practices wholly the product of agents. Both agents and structures are produced, as we can understand them and respond to them, through practice.

3. Interviews were open-ended. I asked people to relate the story of their journey to God's Love We Deliver and to tell me about their experiences of cooking in the kitchen. I asked about volunteers' current religious, political, and other volunteer activities as well. In this context and also in the kitchen, I tried to situate my interest in religion and spirituality within the "context" of other interests and pursuits. On techniques that mitigate the problems associated with interviews' "flagging" topics the researcher wishes to learn more about, see Harry F. Wolcott, *The Art of Fieldwork* (Walnut Creek, Calif.: Alta Mira Press, 1995), 103–4, and Alfred C. Kinsey, Wardell B. Pomeroy, and Clyde E. Martin, *Sexual Behavior in the Human Male* (Philadelphia: W. B. Saunders, 1948), chap. 2.

4. For many reasons, we do not say that individuals construct stories sui generis. They draw on particular narrative structures when telling stories. These structures develop in communities and give legitimacy to their experiences, even as they reshape them to conform to certain ideals and notions about identity and belonging. See Dorothy Holland et al., *Identity and Agency in Cultural Worlds* (Cambridge: Harvard University Press, 1998); Elaine Lawless, "Rescripting Their Lives and Narratives: Spiritual Life Stories of Pentecostal Women Preachers," *Journal of Feminist Studies in Religion* 7 (spring 1991): 53–71; and James Beckford, "Accounting for Conversion," *British Journal of Sociology* 29, 2 (1987): 249–62.

5. Elaine Lawless, *Holy Women, Wholly Women* (Philadelphia: University of Pennsylvania Press, 1993), chap. 2.

6. Mary Douglas, "Standard Social Uses of Food: Introduction," in *Food in the Social Order: Studies of Food and Festivities in Three American Communities,* ed. Mary Douglas (New York: Russell Sage, 1994), 1–39; Sack, *Whitebread Protestants;* Susan Starr Sered, "Food and Holiness: Cooking as a Sacred Act among Middle-Eastern Jewish Women," *Anthropological Quarterly* 63, 1 (1988): 129–39.

7. Wayne Proudfoot, *Religious Experience* (Berkeley: University of California Press, 1985); Rudolph Otto, *The Idea of the Holy* (New York: Oxford University Press, 1958); Mircea Eliade, *The Sacred and the Profane: The Nature of Religion* (San Diego: Harcourt, Brace, Jovanovich, 1987).

8. Catherine Bell's notion of ritualization becomes particularly useful here. She argues that "rather than impose categories of what is or is not ritual, it may be more useful to look at how human activities establish and manipulate their own differentiation and purposes—in the very doing of the act within the context of other ways of acting" (Bell, *Ritual Theory, Ritual Practice,* 74). She suggests that intention, rather than repetition and habit, is at the heart of ritual. "For example," she writes, "the formal activities of gathering for a Catholic mass distinguish this

'meal' from daily eating activities, but the informality of a mass celebrated in a private home with a folk guitar and kitchen utensils is meant to set up another contrast . . . which the informal service expects to dominate" (92).

9. Ammerman, "Golden Rule Christians," 205. Nina Eliasoph makes a similar argument about "political apathy" among volunteers, suggesting that "by publicly acknowledging only a small, gerrymandered circle of concern, citizens can preserve a sense that democracy is possible, that participation in civil society is meaningful. Keeping this faith alive . . . entails hiding the public spirit" (Eliasoph, " 'Close to Home': Turning Americans' Extravagant Expression of Apathy Inside-Out," manuscript, Department of Sociology, University of Wisconsin, Madison, 1996). Yet spiritual action, as Emily describes it, hints at a metaphysical connection between things happening elsewhere that she is concerned about and her volunteer work at God's Love We Deliver.

10. Wade Clark Roof notes that "more than half of Protestants feel that the churches have lost the spiritual part of religion" (Roof, *Generation of Seekers,* 237).

11. The conceptual division and its various critical counterpoints have been noted by many, including popular religious commentators Richard Cimino and Don Lattin, who call it a "divorce" (*Shopping for Faith: American Religion in the New Millennium* [San Francisco: Jossey-Bass, 1998]), and historian Robert C. Fuller, who demonstrates that "unchurched religious traditions" have a robust place in American religious history (*Spiritual but Not Religious: Understanding Unchurched Americans* [New York: Oxford University Press, 2001]).

12. Roof, *Spiritual Marketplace,* 44–45, 149, 159–61; Ammerman, "Golden Rule Christians"; R. Stephen Warner, "Toward a New Paradigm for the Sociological Study of Religion in the United States," *American Journal of Sociology* 98 (March 1993): 1044–93.

13. Surveying current usage of "spirituality," one can only deduce that it has something to do with the sacred (some say transcendent) that is different from "religion." Robert Wuthnow, for example, terms spirituality "all of the beliefs and activities by which *individuals* attempt to relate their lives to God or to a divine being or some other conception of a transcendent reality." Spirituality is "shaped by larger social circumstances" and tied to beliefs and values found in not only the church or synagogue "but also the wider culture" (Wuthnow, *After Heaven,* viii). Roof is much more reluctant to provide a definition but ends up saying that it "encompasses . . . a source of values for and meaning beyond oneself, a way of understanding, inner awareness, and personal integration" (*Spiritual Marketplace,* 35).

Compared with other attempts, these definitions are paragons of precision. Some commentators define spirituality as more than religion or the core of religion; others suggest that religious traditions can provide the scripts and narratives for spiritual life; and still others say spirituality has nothing to do with traditions of any kind. To give one unexceptional example, spirituality is defined as non-institutionalized forms of religious practice that approximate "lived experience" and alternative ways of looking at the world (Susan M. Schneiders, "Spirituality in the Academy," in *Modern Christian Spirituality: Methodological and Historical Essays,* ed. Bradley Hanson, American Academy of Religion Studies in Religion 62 [Atlanta: Scholars Press, 1990], 25–38). The lack of clarity in definitions in the end gives scholars little analytical leverage.

14. Laurence R. Iannaccone, "Why Strict Churches Are Strong," *American Journal of Sociology* 99 (March 1994): 1180–1211.

15. The argument that religion in its corporate, "democratic" forms helps American society work begins with Alexis de Tocqueville's *Democracy in America,* vol. 1 (1835; New York: Vintage, 1945). Tocqueville postulated a direct link between religious and democratic participation. Current interlocutors similarly view religion as the first among Americans' political institutions, understood as a place where groups gather to make more claims and transform society for the better. The civil rights movement and the Central American sanctuary movement, among others, are lauded as stellar examples of the value of religious organizations, ideologies, and resources for creating a more just society.

That religion has not always been a progressive force for democracy is a point made far less frequently. Those who have noted the nonprogressive aspects of religion often arrive at (or begin with) the question whether religion's historically demonstrated role in social transformation is an adequate benchmark for measuring religious life. For an excellent discussion of moral and ethical positions embedded in the field of religious studies, see Robert Orsi, "Snakes Alive: Resituating the Moral in the Study of Religion," in *In Face of the Facts: Moral Inquiry in American Scholarship,* ed. Robb Westbrook and Richard Wightman (Cambridge: Cambridge University Press, 1997).

16. Put succinctly, individuals with privately articulated religions are "unable to mediate among self, society, the natural world, and ultimate reality" (Bellah et al., *Habits of the Heart,* 237).

17. Bellah et al., *Habits of the Heart,* 235.

18. Jeffrey Stout provides a concise critique of the Bellah team's interview technique in *Ethics after Babel* (Boston: Beacon Press, 1988).

19. Ammerman, "Golden Rule Christians," 208.

20. Roof, *Spiritual Marketplace,* 41–42; Putnam, *Bowling Alone.*

21. Lichterman, *Search for Political Community,* 239.

22. Ann Swidler's simple but apt phrase for this is that we "know more culture than we use" (Swidler, "Culture in Action," 273–86; see also Swidler, *Talk of Love* [Chicago: University of Chicago Press, 2001]).

23. Paul Heelas, *The New Age Movement* (Oxford: Blackwell, 1996).

24. While it is absolutely necessary to take those who call themselves spiritual

(or religious) at their word, relying on a conceptual notion of "religious practice" gives us the tools to analyze how such terms also play a role in structuring those experiences. For instance, when Emily tells us she is spiritual, we nevertheless also see her connections to a bona fide, anchoring religious tradition. Anita's spiritual narrative is less easy to engage on these terms. Individuals who call themselves their own spiritual guides use narrative forms that actively distance them from institutional connections. Such connections, and attendant constraints, may nevertheless be apparent if we employ a notion of "religious practice" to ferret out connections, communities, and accrued religious habits and language.

25. "Praying is not simply a narrative practices, but a narrative practice addressed to someone. . . . Prayer is always a relational imaginative activity" (Orsi, *Thank You, St. Jude*, 203). See also Bakhtin's discussion of the "superaddressee," the third party in a dialogue "whose absolutely just responsive understanding is presumed, either in some metaphysical distance or in distant historical time. In various ages, this superaddressee and his ideally true responsive understanding assume various ideological expressions," including God (Bakhtin, *"Speech Genres" and Other Late Essays*, 126).

26. William James, *The Varieties of Religious Experience* (New York: Macmillan, 1961), 63–64.

27. Renato Rosaldo notes that grief is experienced both through rituals and through "less circumscribed" practices. He argues that while grief is not contained within particular rites or rituals, they are important in defining what we know as grief and how we talk about it (Rosaldo, *Culture and Truth: The Remaking of Social Analysis* [Boston: Beacon Press, 1993], 20).

28. Wayne Proudfoot, *Religious Experience* (Berkeley: University of California Press, 1985), 228.

29. Barbara Myerhoff writes that many of the elderly Jews she met in California faced the issues of aging, and the very real problems of surviving, by drawing on irony, stoicism, and humor (*Number Our Days* [New York: E. F. Dutton, 1978], 223, 250).

30. This was another joke. Libby was referring to Alice B. Toklas's "hashish fudge" recipe in *The Cookbook of Alice B. Toklas*.

31. Laughter connotes a reversal, whether a reversal of power between (for instance) a fascist state and those under its tyranny or a reversal of the meaning of death and life. Death, in such a frame, is "an ambivalent image" (Bakhtin, *Dialogic Imagination*, 407–9).

32. Miriam Therese Winter, Adair Lummis, and Allison Stokes note that many Protestant women remain committed to their churches even if they find the organization "oppressive" and "alienating," either because the church offers resources and opportunities that individuals cannot generate on their own or because they doubt that a nonreligious organization would be any better (Winter, Lummis, and

Stokes, *Defecting in Place: Women Claiming Responsibility for their Own Spiritual Lives* [New York: Crossroads Press, 1994]).

33. Of course, this is what Max Weber himself argues about religious groups moving from charismatic to bureaucratic authority (Weber, *The Sociology of Religion* [Boston: Beacon Press, 1990]). The wide popular acceptance of Weber's model of organizational change has made this shift a socially constructed fact, however, with little thought given to alternatives to this model.

CHAPTER FIVE

1. Stephen L. Carter, *The Culture of Disbelief: How American Law and Politics Trivialize Religious Devotion* (New York: Basic Books 1993); cf. Phillip Hammond, *With Liberty for All: Freedom of Religion in the United States* (Louisville, Ky.: Westminster John Knox, 1998).

2. Eliasoph, *Avoiding Politics,* 21. Eliasoph continues, "investigating footing means asking what members assume 'being a member' requires; what kinds of talk and silence members consider appropriate for that context; whether talk is considered important at all or whether there is another, more non-verbal way of establishing a sense of companionship."

3. Of course, there is nothing really new about studying conversation this way. Anthropologists and others have made a number of advances in the study of speech communication and culture over the past thirty years, ranging from William Hanks's technical analysis of Mayan speech (*Referential Practice: Language and Lived Space among the Maya* [Chicago: University of Chicago Press, 1990]) to Michele Rosaldo's stunning analysis of Ilongot headhunters' changing practices (*Knowledge and Passion: Ilongot Notions of Self and Social Life* [Cambridge: Cambridge University Press, 1980]) and Tamar Katriel's study of modern Israeli daily verbal symbols and "speech modes" (*Communal Webs: Communication and Culture in Contemporary Israel* [Albany; State University of New York Press, 1991]). Each develops a clear portrait of the ways people in very different life situations occupy the world through speech, emotion, and action and, at the same moment, also create those worlds. They ask us to take seriously that the self and its "horizon of schematic knowledge . . . is also produced in practice, through incipient habituation, the regularities of language structure, and the predisposition of actors to schematize their experiences in the very practice of living them" (Hanks, *Referential Practice,* 515).

4. Bakhtin, *"Speech Genres" and Other Late Essays,* 60.

5. Speech genres, in Bakhtin's understanding, are socially and historically constructed categories and are "relatively stable types of utterances." However, they also help to "suggest the social relations between the speakers and their relation to outsiders; to indicate a set of values; to offer a set of perceptions; to outline a field of possible, likely, or desirable actions; to convey a vague or specific sense of time and space; to suggest an appropriate tone; to rule in or rule out various

styles and languages of heteroglossia; and to negotiate a set of purposes" (Morson and Emerson, *Mikhail Bakhtin,*293).

6. The purpose or potential of parodies and other performances to bring the high to a low position and otherwise subvert the normal arrangement of power has been studied in many forms. Bakhtin's work on parody and social change, *Rabelais and His World,* discusses the particular uses of laughter in bringing the high low and being potentially regenerative. Corporate and anarchic laughter was the only possible release and freedom in Rabelais's own social world (see Morson and Emerson, *Mikhail Bakhtin,*443–45). However, in Bakhtin's analysis, parody is effective when everyone laughs, and when everyone laughs both at their own selves and at others. This stands in contrast to the negative forms of satire and parody he notes later, which attempt to do violence, which are not a "laughing laugh" (*"Speech Genres" and Other Late Essays,* 135).

7. This is perhaps a result of the current popular interest in pre-Baroque sacred music, the medieval period, and mystics.

8. Bakhtin, *Problems of Dostoevsky's Poetics,* 72–74, 299.

9. Bakhtin, *"Speech Genres" and Other Late Essays,* 80: "The majority of . . . genres are subject to free creative reformulation; . . . genres must be fully mastered in order to be manipulated freely. . . . Here it is not a matter of impoverished vocabulary or of style, taken abstractly: this is entirely a matter of the inability to command a repertoire of genres of social conversation."

10. Mikhail Bakhtin, *Dialogic Imagination,* 181–83.

11. Bakhtin, *Dialogic Imagination,* 195.

12. For instance, Robert Wuthnow notes that evangelicals use a kind of double-directed language in certain circumstances. In such discourse nothing "signal[s] to the outsider that an evangelical is speaking. And yet, to an insider, the phrasing . . . would seem familiar" (Wuthnow, *Acts of Compassion,* 138–41). See also Wendy Griswold's description of literary metaphors' ability to "carry multiple messages" ("The Fabrication of Meaning: Literary Interpretation in the United States, Great Britain, and the West Indies," *American Journal of Sociology* 92 [March 1987]: 1077–1117, esp. 1079).

13. See Scott, *Weapons of the Weak;* Roy, *Some Trouble with Cows;* and a large range of literature on liberation theology and on subaltern voices and languages, including Ruth Behar and Deborah A. Gordon, eds., *Women Writing Culture* (Berkeley: University of California Press, 1995).

14. Bakhtin, "Discourse in the Novel," in *Dialogic Imagination,* 358–61.

CHAPTER SIX

1. Elizabeth Kübler-Ross's landmark *On Death and Dying* (New York: Collier, 1969) both "exposes" the conspiracy of silence and launches a critique of its effects, which have entered into the practices of bereavement in American culture.

Her argument states that "so long as carers do not engage in conspiracies of silence, so long as they let the patient be and express feelings, then death is not to be feared—patients will naturally progress to the final peaceful stages of acceptance" (Tony Walter, *The Revival of Death* [New York: Routledge, 1994], 71).

2. Neil Small, "Dying in a Public Place," in *The Sociology of Death*, ed. David Clark (Oxford: Blackwell, 1993), and Walter, *Revival of Death*, 194–96.

3. Cindy Patton writes that in the 1980s "no gay person needed to have explained the meaning of this stark black poster with an inverted pink triangle and white lettering" (Patton, *Inventing AIDS* [New York: Routledge, 1990]), 126.

4. On the social construction of sickness and the way patient and victim roles limit active agency, see Mary Douglas, "The Construction of the Physician," in *The Healing Bond: The Patient–Practitioner Relationship and Therapeutic Responsibility*, ed. Susan Budd and Ursula Sharma (London: Routledge, 1994), 23–41, and Patton, *Inventing AIDS*. Both suggest that being sick lessens or strips individuals' agency. Nevertheless, the silence imposed by the closet and the silence that comes with death were not, and are not, equivalent. As Joshua Gamson chronicles in his analysis of the discourse of gay identity politics and people with AIDS movements, the overlap of dissimilar identities and political groups sometimes caused rifts within the groups he studied (Gamson, "Silence, Death, and the Invisible Enemy"). For more on how these roles were disrupted as people with AIDS became activists, see, for instance, Curtis Winkle, "Inequity and Power in the Nonprofit Sector: A Comparative Analysis of AIDS-Related Services for Gay Men and Intravenous Drug Users in Chicago," *Nonprofit and Voluntary Sector Quarterly* 20 (fall 1991): 313–28, and Stephen Epstein, *Impure Science: AIDS, Activism, and the Politics of Knowledge* (Berkeley: University of California Press, 1996).

5. Kayal, "Gay AIDS Voluntarism as Political Activity."

6. Here the words of M. A. K. Halliday resonate again: "Within any pluralistic community, the different social groups have different habits of meaning: different 'sociolinguistic coding orientations.' . . . [W]hat one group interprets as an occasion for a public declaration of private faith may be seen by the second group as an exchange of observations about the objective world, and by a third group as something else again—as a game, for example" (Halliday, *Language as Social Semiotic*, 161).

7. GLWD also played a role in distancing the volunteers from open talk about AIDS in the kitchen. For instance, the term "clients" (instead of "PWAs" or "patients") does not identify them as people with AIDS, even though that definition certainly remains accessible. Similarly, in the kitchen clients were talked about as a group; client confidentiality and the disclosure of clients' identities only on a "need to know" basis meant that kitchen volunteers hardly ever heard the names of clients. Even when the volunteer department posted a thank you letter, it crossed

out or clipped off the client's name and signature. These and other practices limited the space of AIDS.

8. For instance, a bereavement handbook states, "The goal of the mourning process is to integrate the loss that is known to be true in outward reality in order to have it become an emotional reality. This can happen only if you are able to express the anger, pain, despair, and all the other emotions that assail you. Your feelings must be talked about; words and tears must be shared. . . . Feelings need to be released rather than blocked. If freedom of expression is denied, pushed away, or ignored, then the mourning process is inhibited. As with any natural process that is inhibited, halting the mourning process can cause problems" (Savine Weizman and Phyllis Kamm, *About Mourning: Support and Guidance for the Bereaved* [New York: Human Sciences Press, 1985]).

9. Neil Small and Jenny Hockey critically assess the way the bereavement industry compounds the "loss associated with bereavement" by further subordinating the individual within the "discursive practices of [bereavement] experts." They state further that "while there is an extensive history to the notion that the individual who embraces the pain of loss can ultimately be strengthened, contemporary theories and practices associated with bereavement give little space to [an account] of grief as 'an idiom of resistance' where loss can stimulate 'affective enclaves and healing'" (Small and Hockey, "Discourse into Practice: The Production of Bereavement Care," in *Grief, Mourning, and Death Ritual*, ed. Jenny Hockey, Jeanne Katz, and Neil Small [Philadelphia: Open University Press, 2001], 97–124, quotation on 119). See also C. N. Seremetakis, *The Last Word: Women, Death, and Divination in Inner Mani* (Chicago: University of Chicago Press, 1991).

10. Aside from interviews, my main source of information about which volunteers had experienced the death of someone close to them was Christopher, a staff member who like many others had lost his partner to AIDS.

11. Kamala Visweswaran, *Fictions of Feminist Ethnography* (Minneapolis: University of Minnesota Press, 1994), 51. Visweswaran argues for a perspective on agency that includes a "refusal to speak," that is, an active decision to be silent. This kind of "resistance" can be seen in relation to other forms of silence that arise with less active work on the part of agents, that is, "what goes without saying" and "what cannot be said" (Bourdieu, *Outline of a Theory of Practice*, 170). At God's Love We Deliver, the "refusal to speak" and "what goes without saying" worked together to complicate "what cannot be said."

12. Nina Eliasoph argues, as a point of contrast, that silences in voluntary organizations and the like edit out commentary that might be construed as combative. This limits individuals' abilities to make moral claims in public spaces (Eliasoph, *Avoiding Politics*).

13. Jody Shapiro Davie, *Women in the Presence: Constructing Community and Seeking*

Spirituality in Mainline Protestantism (Philadelphia: University of Pennsylvania Press, 1995).

14. As Anthony Cohen writes, the "triumph of community is to contain this variety [of meanings] so that its inherent discordance does not subvert the apparent coherence which is expressed in its boundaries" (Cohen, *The Symbolic Construction of Community* [New York: Tavistock, 1985]).

15. Holland et al., *Identity and Agency in Cultural Worlds;* Berger and Luckmann, *Social Construction of Reality,* 172–73.

CONCLUSION

1. In interviews, volunteers signaled the locations of some of the other social settings where habits and practices were learned (home, synagogue, other voluntary organizations).

2. T. S. Eliot, "The Dry Salvages," in *Four Quartets* (1943; reprint, San Diego: Harcourt Brace Jovanovich, 1971).

3. Cox, *Secular City;* Dietrich Bonhoeffer, *Letters and Papers from Prison* (New York: Macmillan, 1962); Peter Berger, *The Sacred Canopy: Elements of a Sociological Theory of Religion* (Garden City, N.Y.: Doubleday, 1967); Robert Bellah, "Religious Evolution," *American Sociological Review* 29 (1964): 358–74.

4. Swidler, "Culture in Action."

5. Paul Lichterman notes in the appendix to *The Search for Political Community* that it is "best to see how [activists] present themselves in everyday movements settings, and not rely on interviews alone. The personalist tradition, for instance, provides an everyday basis for commitment even if it does not always show itself in the ways activists talk in interviews" (239). Some social facts are accessible only in participant observation of everyday events where people do different kinds of meaning-making work.

6. Some contexts are more heteroglossic than others, but even the most constrained allow for the possibility that other languages will leak, or break through, into social interaction. Robin Wagner-Pacifici provides examples of the overlapping of domestic languages within the language of the state in *Discourse and Destruction: The City of Philadelphia versus MOVE* (Chicago: University of Chicago Press, 1994).

7. This position is well developed in the classical interactionism of George Herbert Mead, where in everyday events, individuals' actions are oriented toward a "generalized other" (rather than specific others we interact with) that represents the rules of the game or the given rules of society. Through testing the rules of childhood games, people learn how to respond to abstract rules that govern behavior. These behavioral patterns are articulated in general terms so that individuals can participate in the shared meaning of community or society by taking on any role in the game, becoming in essence, anyone (Mead, *Mind, Self and Society,* 152–64). This definition allows ethnographers to extrapolate from particular events

to patterned approaches to interaction. See Bender, "Bakhtinian Perspectives on Everyday Life Sociology."

8. Clifford Geertz, *The Interpretation of Cultures* (New York: Basic Books, 1973). Geertz's emphasis on religion as a cultural system brought a new focus on things we could see (signs, symbols, myths, and texts), yet it reasserted that these symbols corresponded to what respondents thought and how they oriented their lives. See the discussion of the drawbacks (and benefits) of the reintroduction of subjectivity in Robert Wuthnow, *Rediscovering the Sacred: Perspectives on Religion in Contemporary America* (Grand Rapids, Mich.: Eerdmans, 1992).

9. Lichterman, *Search For Political Community*; Faye D. Ginsburg, *Contested Lives: The Abortion Debate in an American Community* (Berkeley: University of California Press, 1989).

10. Bakhtin, "From Notes Made 1970–71," 154.

APPENDIX

1. This process is explained similarly by Nicholas Dodier: "The sociologist would start by talking to the inspector [at a factory, for instance] and listing the means he used to make his judgement. Then she could tape record his visit to see how people 'populate the pertinent world.' And she could go on to consider how he formed and gave his judgement. . . . She might not understand all the terms or references to past events though she might extrapolate from some of these to further similar events. But unlike the sociologist described above she would not use these prior conditions to define a preliminary portrait of the inspector within a system of relations between agents" (Dodier, "Action as a Combination of 'Common Worlds,'" *Sociological Review* 41 (August 1993): 556–71, quotation on 562.

2. James Clifford, "Introduction: Partial Truths," in *Writing Culture: The Poetics and Politics of Ethnography*, ed. James Clifford and George Marcus (Berkeley: University of California Press, 1986), 14–15.

3. Using Geertz's case of the Balinese cockfight as a paradigm, Vincent Crapanzano argues that by explaining to his audience what the cockfight "meant" to the Balinese, Geertz "assert[s] Balinese subjectivity." Geertz analyzes how cockfights articulate everyday experience in metaphoric ways, but Crapanzano asks, "For whom does the cockfight" act as a metaphor? "Cockfights are surely cockfights for the Balinese—and not images, fictions, and metaphors. They are not marked as such, though they may be read as such by a foreigner for whom 'images, fictions, models, and metaphors' have interpretive value" (Vincent Crapanzano, "Hermes' Dilemma: The Masking of Subversion in Ethnographic Description," in *Writing Culture: The Poetics and Politics of Ethnography*, ed. James Clifford and George Marcus (Berkeley: University of California Press, 1986), 72–73.

4. See Robert Shields, "Meeting or Mismeeting: The Dialogical Challenge to *Verstehen*," *British Journal of Sociology* 47, 2 (1996): 275–94. Shields's Bakhtinian analy-

sis of dialogue stands in contrast to some of the better-known examples. See Martin Buber, *I and Thou* (New York: Scribner's, 1970), and Habermas, *Theory of Communicative Action*; cf. Dorothy Smith, "Exploring the Social Relations of Discourse: Sociological Theory and the Dialogic of Sociology," in *Writing the Social* (Toronto: University of Toronto Press, 1999).

5. To return to the paradigmatic Balinese cockfight, Michael Burawoy argues that Geertz's description of a cockfight as a "paradigmatic event" makes it look like an unchanging and uniform ritual case. Burawoy argues that such a cultural event needs to be studied as "it varies from place to place, how it has changed over time—as a vehicle for comprehending the forces shaping Balinese society" (Michael Burawoy, "The Extended Case Method," in *Ethnography Unbound: Power and Resistance in the Modern Metropolis*, ed. Michael Burawoy et al. [Berkeley: University of California Press, 1991], 278.

6. David Haberman, *Journey through the Twelve Forests* (New York: Oxford University Press, 1994).

BIBLIOGRAPHY

Alexander, Jeffrey, and Phillip Smith. "The Discourse of American Civil Society: A New Proposal for Cultural Studies." *Theory and Society* 22 (1993): 151–207.

Ammerman, Nancy. *Bible Believers*. New Brunswick, N.J.: Rutgers University Press, 1987.

———. "Golden Rule Christians." In *Lived Religion in America*, ed. David Hall, 196–216. Princeton: Princeton University Press, 1997.

Bakhtin, Mikhail. *The Dialogic Imagination: Four Essays*. Trans. Caryl Emerson and Michael Holquist. Austin: University of Texas Press, 1981.

———. *Problems of Dostoevsky's Poetics*. Ed. and trans. Caryl Emerson. Minneapolis: University of Minnesota Press, 1984.

———. *Rabelais and His World*. Bloomington: Indiana University Press, 1984.

———. *"Speech Genres" and Other Late Essays*. Austin: University of Texas Press, 1986.

———. *Toward a Philosophy of the Act*. Austin: University of Texas Press, 1993.

Beckford, James. "Accounting for Conversion." *British Journal of Sociology* 29, 2 (1987): 249–62.

Behar, Ruth, and Deborah A. Gordon, eds. *Women Writing Culture*. Berkeley: University of California Press, 1995.

Bell, Catherine. *Ritual Theory, Ritual Practice*. New York: Oxford University Press, 1992.

Bell, Daniel. *The Cultural Contradictions of Capitalism*. New York: Basic Books, 1976.

Bell, Michael. *Childerley: Nature and Morality in a Country Village*. Chicago: University of Chicago Press, 1994.

Bellah, Robert. "Religious Evolution." *American Sociological Review* 29 (1964): 358–74.

Bellah, Robert, Richard Madsen, William Sullivan, Ann Swidler, and Steve

Tipton. *Habits of the Heart: Individualism and Commitment in American Life.* Berkeley: University of California Press, 1985.

Bender, Courtney. "Bakhtinian Perspectives on Everyday Life Sociology." In *Bakhtin and the Human Sciences: No Last Words,* ed. Michael Gardiner and Michael Bell, 181–95. Thousand Oaks, Calif.: Sage, 1998.

———. "The Meals Are the Message: The Growth and Congestion of an AIDS Service Organization's Mission in Multiple Organizational Fields." Working Paper 221, Program on Non-Profit Organizations, Yale University, 1995.

———. "You Meet So Many Different People Here: Deciphering Volunteers' Appraisal of Diversity and Its Consequences." Working Paper 259, Program on Non-Profit Organizations, Yale University, 2000.

Berger, Peter. "Reflections on the Sociology of Religion Today." *Sociology of Religion* 62 (winter 2001): 443–54.

———. *The Sacred Canopy: Elements of a Sociological Theory of Religion.* Garden City, N.Y.: Doubleday, 1967.

Berger, Peter, and Thomas Luckmann. *The Social Construction of Reality.* Garden City, N.Y.: Doubleday, 1966.

Boden, Deirdre. *The Business of Talk: Organizations in Action.* Cambridge, Mass.: Polity Press, 1994.

Bonhoeffer, Dietrich. *Letters and Papers from Prison.* New York: Macmillan, 1962.

Bourdieu, Pierre. *The Logic of Practice.* Trans. Richard Nice. Stanford: Stanford University Press, 1990.

———. *Outline of a Theory of Practice.* Trans. Richard Nice. Cambridge: Cambridge University Press, 1977.

Bourdieu, Pierre, and Löic Wacquant. *An Invitation to Reflexive Sociology.* Chicago: University of Chicago, 1992.

Buber, Martin. *I and Thou.* New York: Scribner's, 1970.

Burawoy, Michael, et al. *Ethnography Unbound: Power and Resistance in the Modern Metropolis.* Berkeley: University of California Press, 1991.

Butler, Judith. *Bodies That Matter: On the Discursive Limits of Sex.* London: Routledge, 1993.

Cain, Roy. "Managing Impressions of an AIDS Service Organization: Into the Mainstream or out of the Closet?" *Qualitative Sociology* 17, 1 (1994): 43–61.

Camic, Charles. "The Matter of Habit." *American Journal of Sociology* 91 (March 1986): 1039–87.

Carpenter, Teresa. "A Certifiable Saint." *Harper's Bazaar,* no. 3382 (September 1993): 418–21.

Carter, Stephen L. *The Culture of Disbelief: How American Law and Politics Trivialize Religious Devotion.* New York: Basic Books, 1993.

Casanova, José. *Public Religions in the Modern World.* Chicago: University of Chicago Press, 1994.

Certeau, Michel de. *The Practice of Everyday Life*. Berkeley: University of California Press, 1984.

Chambré, Susan M. "Being Needful: Family, Love, and Prayer among AIDS Volunteers." *Research in the Sociology of Health Care* 12 (1995): 113–39.

———. "Creating New Nonprofit Organizations as Responses to Social Change: HIV/AIDS Organizations in New York City." *Policy Studies Review* 14 (spring–summer 1995): 117–26.

———. "The Secularization of Faith-Based Organizations: Case Studies of Four New York City Organizations." Paper presented at the Association for Research on Nonprofit Organizations and Voluntary Action, November 2000.

———. "Uncertainty, Diversity, and Change: The AIDS Community in New York City." *Research in Community Sociology* 6 (1996): 149–90.

———. "Voluntarism in the HIV Epidemic: Raising Resources for Community-Based Organizations in New York City and Sullivan County." Nonprofit Sector Research Fund of the Aspen Institute, Washington D.C., 1994.

———. "Volunteers as Witnesses: The Mobilization of AIDS Volunteers in New York City, 1981–1988." *Social Service Review* 65 (December 1991): 533–47.

Cimino, Richard, and Don Lattin. *Shopping for Faith: American Religion in the New Millennium*. San Francisco: Jossey-Bass, 1998.

Clifford, James, ed. *The Predicament of Culture*. Cambridge: Harvard University Press, 1988.

Clifford, James, and George E. Marcus, eds. *Writing Culture: The Poetics and Politics of Ethnography*. Berkeley: University of California Press, 1986.

Cohen, Anthony. *The Symbolic Construction of Community*. New York: Tavistock, 1985.

Cox, Harvey. *The Secular City*. New York: Macmillan, 1967.

Crapanzano, Vincent. "Hermes' Dilemma: The Masking of Subversion in Ethnographic Description." In *Writing Culture: The Poetics and Politics of Ethnography*, ed. James Clifford and George Marcus, 51–76. Berkeley: University of California Press, 1986.

Crimp, Douglas, ed. *AIDS: Cultural Analysis/Cultural Criticism*. Cambridge: MIT Press, 1987.

Davidman, Lynn. *Tradition in a Rootless World: Women Turn to Orthodox Judaism*. Berkeley: University of California Press, 1991.

Davie, Jody Shapiro. *Women in the Presence: Constructing Community and Seeking Spirituality in Mainline Protestantism*. Philadelphia: University of Pennsylvania Press, 1995.

DiMaggio, Paul. "Culture and Cognition: An Interdisciplinary Review." *Annual Review of Sociology* 23 (1997): 263–87.

DiMaggio, Paul J., and Walter W. Powell. "The Iron Cage Revisited: Institutional Isomorphism and Collective Rationality in Organizational Fields." *American Sociological Review* 48 (1983): 147–60.

Dodier, Nicholas. "Action as a Combination of 'Common Worlds.'" *Sociological Review* 41 (August 1993): 556–71.

Douglas, Mary. "The Construction of the Physician." In *The Healing Bond: The Patient-Practitioner Relationship and Therapeutic Responsibility*, ed. Susan Budd and Ursula Sharma, 23–41. London: Routledge, 1994.

———. *Purity and Danger: An Analysis of the Concepts of Pollution and Taboo*. 1966. Reprint, New York: Routledge, 1991.

———, ed. *Food in the Social Order: Studies of Food and Festivities in Three American Communities*. New York: Russell Sage, 1994.

Eiesland, Nancy L. *A Particular Place*. New Brunswick, N.J.: Rutgers University Press, 1999.

Eire, Carlos M. "Major Problems in the Definition of Spirituality as an Academic Discipline." In *Modern Christian Spirituality: Methodological and Historical Essays*, ed. Bradley Hanson, 53–64. American Academy of Religion Studies in Religion 62. Atlanta: Scholars Press, 1990.

Eliade, Mircea. *The Sacred and the Profane: The Nature of Religion*. San Diego: Harcourt, Brace, Jovanovich, 1987.

Elias, Norbert. *The Norbert Elias Reader*. Ed. John Goudsblom and Stephen Mennell. Oxford: Basil Blackwell, 1998.

Eliasoph, Nina. *Avoiding Politics: How Americans Produce Apathy in Everyday Life*. Cambridge: Cambridge University Press, 1998.

———. "'Close to Home': Turning Americans' Extravagant Expression of Apathy Inside-Out." Manuscript, Department of Sociology, University of Wisconsin, Madison, 1996.

———. "Making a Fragile Public: A Talk-Centered Study of Citizenship and Power." *Sociological Theory* 14 (1996): 262–90.

Eliasoph, Nina, and Paul Lichterman. "The Practice of Meaning in Civil Society." Paper presented at the American Sociological Association annual meetings, New York, August 1996.

Eliot, T. S. "The Dry Salvages." In *Four Quartets*. 1943. Reprint, San Diego: Harcourt Brace Jovanovich, 1971.

Emerson, Caryl. "Bakhtin at One Hundred: Looking Back at the Very Early Years." Review article. *Russian Review* 54 (1995): 107–14.

Epstein, Stephen. *Impure Science: AIDS, Activism, and the Politics of Knowledge*. Berkeley: University of California Press, 1996.

Evans, John. *Playing God: Human Genetic Engineering and the Rationalization of Bioethics*. Chicago: University of Chicago Press, 2001.

Fine, Gary Alan. *Kitchens: The Culture of Restaurant Work*. Berkeley: University of California Press, 1996.

Foucault, Michel. *The History of Sexuality*. Vol. 1, *An Introduction*. New York: Vintage Books, 1980.

Fraser, Nancy. "Rethinking the Public Sphere: A Contribution to the Critique of Actually Existing Democracy." *Social Text* 25–26 (1990): 56–80.

Friedland, Roger, and Robert Alford. "Bringing Society Back In: Symbols, Practices, and Institutional Contradictions." In *The New Institutionalism in Organizational Analysis,* ed. Walter W. Powell and Paul DiMaggio, 232–63. Chicago: University of Chicago Press, 1991.

Fuller, Robert C. *Spiritual but Not Religious: Understanding Unchurched Americans.* New York: Oxford University Press, 2001.

Gamson, Joshua. "Silence, Death, and the Invisible Enemy: AIDS Activism and Social Movement 'Newness.' " In *Ethnography Unbound: Power and Resistance in the Modern Metropolis,* ed. Michael Burawoy et al., 33–57. Berkeley: University of California Press, 1991.

Garfinkel, Harold. *Studies in Ethnomethodology.* Englewood Cliffs, N.J.: Prentice-Hall, 1967.

Geertz, Clifford. *The Interpretation of Cultures.* New York: Basic Books, 1973.

Giddens, Anthony. *New Rules of Sociological Method.* 2d ed. Stanford: Stanford University Press, 1993.

Ginsburg, Faye D. *Contested Lives: The Abortion Debate in an American Community.* Berkeley: University of California Press, 1989.

Glasser, Irene. *More Than Bread: An Ethnography of a Soup Kitchen.* Tuscaloosa: University of Alabama Press, 1988.

God's Love We Deliver. Promotional information flier, ca. 1988.

———. Promotional information flier, ca. 1993.

———. Report to the New York State Department of Health, Homeless and Destitute Program Bureau of Nutrition, 1990.

———. Strategic Plan, August 1994.

"God's Love We Deliver." *New Yorker,* February 25, 1991, 28–29.

"God's Love We Deliver: A Lifeline for AIDS Victims." *New York Times,* November 14, 1993. Advertising insert by Charge against Hunger/American Express.

Goffman, Erving. *The Presentation of Self in Everyday Life.* New York: Doubleday, 1959.

Goldner, Fred H., R. Richard Ritti, and Thomas P. Ference. "The Production of Cynical Knowledge in Organizations." *American Sociological Review* 42 (1977): 539–51.

The Good News Letter. Vols. 1–5. God's Love We Deliver, New York, 1988–94.

Griffith, R. Marie. *God's Daughters: Evangelical Women and the Power of Submission.* Berkeley: University of California Press, 1997.

Griswold, Wendy. "The Fabrication of Meaning: Literary Interpretation in the United States, Great Britain, and the West Indies. *American Journal of Sociology* 92 (March 1987): 1077–1117.

Haberman, David. *Journey through the Twelve Forests.* New York: Oxford University Press, 1994.

Habermas, Jürgen. *The Theory of Communicative Action.* Vol. 1. Boston: Beacon Press, 1984.

Hall, David, ed. *Lived Religion in America.* Princeton: Princeton University Press, 1997.

Hall, Peter Dobkin. *Inventing the Nonprofit Sector and Other Essays on Philanthropy, Voluntarism, and Nonprofit Organizations.* Baltimore: Johns Hopkins University Press, 1992.

Halliday, M. A. K. *Language as Social Semiotic: The Social Interpretation of Language and Meaning.* London: Edward Arnold, 1978.

Hammond, Phillip. *With Liberty for All: Freedom of Religion in the United States.* Louisville, Ky.: Westminster John Knox, 1998.

Hanks, William F. *Referential Practice: Language and Lived Space among the Maya.* Chicago: University of Chicago Press, 1990.

Hebdige, Dick. *Subculture: The Meaning of Style.* London: Methuen, 1979.

Heelas, Paul. *The New Age Movement.* Oxford: Blackwell, 1996.

Holland, Dorothy, Debra Skinner, William Lachicotte Jr., and Carole Cain. *Identity and Agency in Cultural Worlds.* Cambridge: Harvard University Press, 1998.

Iannaccone, Laurence R. "Why Strict Churches Are Strong." *American Journal of Sociology* 99 (March 1994): 1180–1211.

James, William. *The Varieties of Religious Experience.* New York: Macmillan, 1961.

Jeavons, Thomas. "Identifying Characteristics of 'Religious' Organizations: An Exploratory Proposal." In *Sacred Companies: Organizational Aspects of Religion and Religious Aspects of Organizations,* ed. N. J. Demerath, 79–96. New York: Oxford University Press, 1998.

Kantor, Rosabeth Moss, and David Summers. "Doing Well While Doing Good: Dilemmas of Performance Measurement in Nonprofit Organizations and the Need for a Multiple-Constituency Approach." in *The Nonprofit Sector: Research Handbook,* ed. Walter W. Powell, 154–66. New Haven: Yale University Press, 1987.

Katriel, Tamar. *Communal Webs: Communication and Culture in Contemporary Israel.* Albany: State University of New York Press, 1991.

Kayal, Philip M. *Bearing Witness: Gay Men's Health Crisis and the Politics of AIDS.* Boulder, Colo.: Westview Press, 1993.

———. "Gay AIDS Voluntarism as Political Activity." *Nonprofit and Voluntary Sector Quarterly* 20 (fall 1991): 289–312.

Kinsey, Alfred C., Wardell B. Pomeroy, and Clyde E. Martin. *Sexual Behavior in the Human Male.* Philadelphia: W. B. Saunders, 1948.

Kosmin, Barry A., and Seymour P. Lachman. *One Nation under God.* New York: Harmony Books, 1993.

Kotarba, Joseph A., and Darlene Hurt. "An Ethnography of an AIDS Hospice: Toward a Theory of Organizational Pastiche." *Symbolic Interaction* 18, 4 (1995): 413–38.

Kübler-Ross, Elizabeth. *On Death and Dying.* New York: Collier, 1969.

Lawless, Elaine. *Holy Women, Wholly Women.* Philadelphia: University of Pennsylvania Press, 1993.

——. "Rescripting Their Lives and Narratives: Spiritual Life Stories of Pentecostal Women Preachers." *Journal of Feminist Studies in Religion* 7 (spring 1991): 53–71.

Lichterman, Paul. *The Search for Political Community: American Activists Reinventing Commitment.* Cambridge: Cambridge University Press, 1996.

Martin, Emily. *Flexible Bodies.* Boston: Beacon Press, 1994.

McNally, Michael. *Ojibwa Singers.* New York: Oxford University Press, 2000.

Mead, George Herbert. *Mind, Self and Society.* Ed. C. W. Morris. Chicago: University of Chicago Press, 1962.

Meyer, John, and Brian Rowan. "Institutionalized Organizations: Formal Structure as Myth and Ceremony." *American Sociological Review* 83 (1977): 340–63.

Morson, Gary Saul, and Caryl Emerson. *Mikhail Bakhtin: Creation of a Prosaics.* Stanford: Stanford University Press, 1990.

Myerhoff, Barbara. *Number Our Days.* New York: E. F. Dutton, 1978.

Olick, Jeffrey. "Genre Memories and Memory Genres: A Dialogical Analysis of May 8 1945 Commemorations in the Federal Republic of Germany." *American Sociological Review* 64 (1999): 381–402.

Omoto, Allen M., and Mark Snyder. "AIDS Volunteers and Their Motivations: Theoretical Issues and Practical Concerns." *Nonprofit Management and Leadership* 4 (winter 1993): 157–76.

Orsi, Robert. "Crossing the City Line." In *Gods of the City,* ed. Robert Orsi, 1–78. Bloomington: Indiana University Press, 1999.

——. "Snakes Alive: Resituating the Moral in the Study of Religion." In *In Face of the Facts: Moral Inquiry in American Scholarship,* ed. Robb Westbrook and Richard Wightman, 201–26. Cambridge: Cambridge University Press, 1997.

——. *Thank You, Saint Jude: Women's Devotion to the Patron Saint of Hopeless Causes.* New Haven: Yale University Press, 1996.

Ortner, Sherry. "Theory in Anthropology since the Sixties." *Comparative Studies in Society and History* 26, 1 (1988): 126–66.

Otto, Rudolph. *The Idea of the Holy.* New York: Oxford University Press, 1958.

Patton, Cindy. *Inventing AIDS.* New York: Routledge, 1990.

Perrow, Charles. *Complex Organizations: A Critical Essay.* 3d ed. New York: Random House, 1986.

Perrow, Charles, and Mauro F. Guillén. *The AIDS Disaster: The Failure of Organizations in New York and the Nation.* New Haven: Yale University Press, 1990.

Powell, Walter W., ed. *The Nonprofit Sector: A Research Handbook.* New Haven: Yale University Press, 1987.

Powell, Walter W., and Paul J. DiMaggio, eds. *The New Institutionalism in Organizational Analysis.* Chicago: University of Chicago Press, 1991.

Proudfoot, Wayne. *Religious Experience.* Berkeley: University of California Press, 1985.

Putnam, Robert D. *Bowling Alone: The Collapse and Revival of American Community.* New York: Simon and Schuster, 2000.

Raz, Joseph. "Multiculturalism: A Liberal Perspective." *Dissent* 41 (winter 1994): 67–79.

Rieff, Phillip. *The Triumph of the Therapeutic.* London: Chatto and Windus, 1966.

Romeyn, Mary. *Nutrition and HIV: A New Model for Treatment.* San Francisco: Jossey-Bass, 1995.

Roof, Wade Clark. *A Generation of Seekers: The Spiritual Journeys of the Baby Boom Generation.* New York: HarperSanFrancisco, 1993.

———. *Spiritual Marketplace.* Princeton: Princeton University Press, 1999.

Rosaldo, Michele. *Knowledge and Passion: Ilongot Notions of Self and Social Life.* Cambridge: Cambridge University Press, 1980.

Rosaldo, Renato. *Culture and Truth: The Remaking of Social Analysis.* Boston: Beacon Press, 1993.

Roth, John K. *Private Needs, Public Selves.* Urbana: University of Illinois Press, 1997.

Roy, Beth. *Some Trouble with Cows: Making Sense of Social Conflict.* Berkeley: University of California Press, 1994.

Sack, Daniel. *Whitebread Protestants: Food and Religion in American Culture.* New York: St. Martin's Press, 2000.

Schmidt, Leigh Eric. *Consumer Rites: The Buying and Selling of American Holidays.* Princeton: Princeton University Press, 1995.

———. *Holy Fairs: Scottish Communions and American Revivals in the Early Modern Period.* Princeton: Princeton University Press, 1989.

Schneiders, Sandra M. "Spirituality in the Academy." In *Modern Christian Spirituality: Methodological and Historical Essays,* ed. Bradley Hanson, 25–38. American Academy of Religion Studies in Religion 62. Atlanta: Scholars Press, 1990.

Schutz, Alfred, and Thomas Luckmann. *The Structures of the Life-World.* Trans. R. Zaner and H. T. Englehardt. Evanston, Ill.: Northwestern University Press, 1973.

Schwartzberg, Steven. *A Crisis of Meaning: How Gay Men Are Making Sense of AIDS.* New York: Oxford, 1996.

Scott, James C. *Weapons of the Weak: Everyday Forms of Peasant Resistance.* New Haven: Yale University Press, 1985.

Sedgwick, Eve Kosofsky. *Epistemology of the Closet.* Berkeley: University of California Press, 1990.

Seltzer, Michael, and Katherine M. Galvin. "Organized Philanthropy's Response to AIDS." *Nonprofit and Voluntary Sector Quarterly* 20, 3 (1991): 249–66.

Sered, Susan Starr. "Food and Holiness: Cooking as a Sacred Act among Middle-Eastern Jewish Women." *Anthropological Quarterly* 63, 1 (1988): 129–39.

Seremetakis, C. N. *The Last Word: Women, Death, and Divination in Inner Mani.* Chicago: University of Chicago Press, 1991.

Sewell, William H., Jr. "A Theory of Structure: Duality, Agency, and Transformation. *American Journal of Sociology* 98 (July 1992): 1–29.

Shields, Robert. "Meeting or Mismeeting: The Dialogical Challenge to *Verstehen.*" *British Journal of Sociology* 47, 2 (1996): 275–94.

Shilts, Randy. *And the Band Played On: Politics, People and the AIDS Epidemic.* New York: Penguin, 1988.

Skocpol, Theda, Marshall Ganz, and Ziad Munson. "A Nation of Organizers: The Institutional Origins of Civic Voluntarism in the United States." *American Political Science Review* 94 (September 2000): 527–46.

Small, Neil. "Dying in a Public Place: AIDS Deaths." In *The Sociology of Death,* ed. David Clark, 87–111. Oxford: Blackwell, 1993.

Small, Neil, and Jenny Hockey. "Discourse into Practice: The Production of Bereavement Care." In *Grief, Mourning, and Death Ritual,* ed. Jenny Hockey, Jeanne Katz, and Neil Small, 97–124. Philadelphia: Open University Press, 2001.

Smith, Christian, and Michael Emerson. *American Evangelicalism: Embattled and Thriving.* Chicago: University of Chicago Press, 1998.

Smith, Dorothy. *Writing the Social.* Toronto: University of Toronto Press, 1999.

Stacey, Judith. *Brave New Families.* New York: Basic Books, 1993.

Stark, David. "Work, Worth and Justice in a Socialist Mixed Economy." Working Paper 5. Harvard University Center for Eastern European Studies, 1988.

Stark, Rodney. "Secularization R.I.P." *Sociology of Religion* 60 (fall 1999): 249–73.

Steinberg, Marc. "Dialogic Analysis of Repertoires of Discourse among Nineteenth-Century English Cotton Spinners." *American Journal of Sociology* 105 (November 1999): 736–80.

Stout, Jeffrey. *Ethics after Babel.* Boston: Beacon Press, 1988.

Swidler Ann. "Culture in Action: Symbols and Strategies." *American Sociological Review* 51 (1986): 273–86.

———. *Talk of Love.* Chicago: University of Chicago Press. 2001.

Tipton, Steven. *Getting Saved from the Sixties: Moral Meaning in Conversion and Cultural Change.* Berkeley: University of California Press, 1982.

Tocqueville, Alexis de. *Democracy in America.* Vol. 1. 1835. New York: Vintage, 1945.

Tuchman, Gaye, and Harry Levine. "New York Jews and Chinese Food: The Social Construction of an Ethnic Pattern." *Journal of Contemporary Ethnography* 22 (1993): 382–407.

Visweswaran, Kamala. *Fictions of Feminist Ethnography.* Minneapolis: University of Minnesota Press, 1994.

Wagner-Pacifici, Robin. *Discourse and Destruction: The City of Philadelphia versus MOVE.* Chicago: University of Chicago Press, 1994.

Walter, Tony. *The Revival of Death.* New York: Routledge, 1994.

Warner, R. Stephen. *New Wine in Old Wineskins: Evangelicals and Liberals in a Small-Town Church.* Berkeley: University of California Press, 1988.

———. "Toward a New Paradigm for the Sociological Study of Religion in the United States." *American Journal of Sociology* 98 (March 1993): 1044–93.

Weber, Max. *The Sociology of Religion.* Boston: Beacon Press, 1990.

Weizman, Savine, and Phyllis Kamm. *About Mourning: Support and Guidance for the Bereaved.* New York: Human Sciences Press, 1985.

Williams, Rhys. "Constructing the Public Good: Social Movements and Cultural Resources." *Social Problems* 42, 1 (1995): 124–44.

Williams, Rhys, and Jeffrey Blackburn. "Many Are Called but Few Obey: Ideological Commitment and Activism in Operation Rescue." In *Disruptive Religion,* ed. Christian Smith, 167–88. New York: Routledge, 1996.

Winkle, Curtis. "Inequity and Power in the Nonprofit Sector: A Comparative Analysis of AIDS-Related Services for Gay Men and Intravenous Drug Users in Chicago." *Nonprofit and Voluntary Sector Quarterly* 20 (fall 1991): 313–28.

Winter, Miriam Therese, Adair Lummis, and Allison Stokes. *Defecting in Place: Women Claiming Responsibility for Their Own Spiritual Lives.* New York: Crossroads Press, 1994.

Wolcott, Harry F. *The Art of Fieldwork.* Walnut Creek, Calif.: Alta Mira Press, 1995.

Wolfe, Alan. *One Nation after All.* New York: Viking, 1998.

Wuthnow, Robert. *Acts of Compassion: Caring for Others and Helping Ourselves.* Princeton: Princeton University Press, 1991.

———. *After Heaven: Spirituality in America since the 1960s.* Berkeley: University of California Press, 1998.

———. *Meaning and Moral Order: Explorations in Cultural Analysis.* Berkeley: University of California Press, 1987.

———. *Producing the Sacred.* Urbana: University of Illinois Press, 1994.

———. *Rediscovering the Sacred: Perspectives on Religion in Contemporary America.* Grand Rapids, Mich.: Eerdmans, 1992.

———. *The Restructuring of American Religion.* Princeton: Princeton University Press, 1988.

———. *Sharing the Journey: Support Groups and America's New Quest for Community.* New York: Free Press, 1994.

Zukin, Sharon. *The Cultures of Cities.* Cambridge, Mass.: Blackwell, 1995.

INDEX

AIDS: and confidentiality, 9–10; and death, 118, 174n4; in public discourse, 13–15; role in kitchen, 117–18, 132–33; and silence, 14, 121–26. *See also* clients; silence

AIDS Memorial Quilt, 31

AIDS service organizations, 32–35, 162n24, 163n26

Bakhtin, Mikhail, 92–93, 108–9, 140–41

blood, symbolism, 50

Buddhism, 95

Catholicism, 90, 104–5; public figures, 103–4

chefs: credentials, 34; perceptions of kitchen work, 49, 54; relations with volunteers, 52–53, 84

Child, Julia, 51

Christians, conservative, 105; "Golden Rule," 68–70

church: discourse in, 88; and speech genres, 93–98; volunteers'

participation, 75, 87, 93–94, 112–13

civility, and public discourse, 127–28

clients: demographics, 11, 36–38; homebound status, 35, 163n31; perceptions of, 9–11, 14–16, 44–46, 120–21, 175n7. *See also* people with AIDS; volunteers

coincidence, in spiritual narratives, 71–73

contamination, 166n9; and boundaries, 48–51, 58; and pollution, 165n3. *See also* food safety

cooking: aesthetics, 60; expertise, 52–53, 55; as practice, 49–52, 60–61; and religion, 65–66, 76; as response to AIDS, 14–5; standards, 55–56. *See also* home cooking

cultural repertoires, 25; development of, 26; and institutions, 160n1; in organizations, 25–26, 39; strategic uses, 45–46, 58–60, 78, 81, 132–33; volunteers' views of, 39–41